BEYOND THE LETTER OF THE LAW

Essays on Diversity in the Halakhah

in honor of

Moshe Zemer

STUDIES IN PROGRESSIVE HALAKHAH

General Editor: Walter Jacob, published in association with the Solomon B. Freehof Institute of Progressive Halakhah

Walter Jacob and Moshe Zemer (eds.) DYNAMIC JEWISH LAW, Progressive Halakhah - Essence and Application

Walter Jacob and Moshe Zemer (eds.) RABBINIC - LAY RELATIONS IN JEWISH LAW

Walter Jacob and Moshe Zemer (eds.) CONVERSION TO JUDAISM IN JEWISH LAW - Essays and Responsa

Walter Jacob and Moshe Zemer (eds.) DEATH AND EUTHANASIA IN JEWISH LAW - Essays and Responsa

Walter Jacob and Moshe Zemer (eds.) THE FETUS AND FERTILITY IN JEWISH LAW - Essays and Responsa

Walter Jacob and Moshe Zemer (eds.) ISRAEL AND THE DIASPORA IN JEWISH LAW - Essays and Responsa

Walter Jacob and Moshe Zemer (eds.) AGING AND THE AGED IN JEWISH LAW - Essays and Responsa

Walter Jacob and Moshe Zemer (eds.) MARRIAGE AND ITS OBSTACLES IN JEWISH LAW - Essays and Responsa

Walter Jacob and Moshe Zemer (eds.) CRIME AND PUNISHMENT IN JEWISH LAW - Essays and Responsa

Walter Jacob and Moshe Zemer (eds.) RE-EXAMINING PROGRESSIVE HALAKHAH

Walter Jacob and Moshe Zemer (eds.) THE ENVIRONMENT IN JEWISH LAW - Essays and Responsa

Walter Jacob (ed.) BEYOND THE LETTER OF THE LAW - Essays on Diversity in the Halakhah

BEYOND THE LETTER OF THE LAW

Essays on Diversity in the Halakhah

in honor of

Moshe Zemer

Edited by

Walter Jacob

Rodef Shalom Press
Pittsburgh, Pennsylvania

Published by the Rodef Shalom Press
4905 Fifth Avenue
Pittsburgh, Pennsylvania
U.S.A.

Copyright © 2004 Solomon B. Freehof Institute of Progressive Halakhah

Library of Congress Cataloing-in-publication Data

Jacob, Walter 1930 -

ISBN 0-929699-16-5

CONTENTS

Acknowledgments vii

Introduction ix

Moshe Zemer: An Appreciation
    Walter Jacob 1

German Romanticism and the Jews: The Intellectual Basis for Halakhic Reform
    Peter Haas 4

Against Method: Liberal *Halakhah* Between Theory and Practice
    Mark Washofsky 17

"It is Time to Act for the Lord:" Toward a Hermeneutics for Progressive *Halakhah*
    Peter Knobel 78

Halakhah and the Modern Temper
    Jack Cohen 92

Writing Responsa: A Personal Journey
    Walter Jacob 103

Ethics Versus Ritual
    John D. Rayner 119

On the Standard of Holiness in Jewish Law
    Jonathan Cohen 142

Tzedakah: Aspiring to a Higher Ethic
    Daniel Schiff 156

Rabbi Eliyahu Guttmacher on Conversion
 David Ellenson 178

The Responsa of Rabbi Solomon B. Freehof: A Reappraisal
 David Golinkin 190

The Rabbinic Riddle
 Louis Jacobs 202

Contributors 227

ACKNOWLEDGMENTS

The Freehof Institute of Progressive Halakhah continues to be most grateful to the Rodef Shalom Congregation for its support and assistance in technical matters connected with this volume. My thanks as well to Barbara Bailey for her efforts with portions of the typescript along with her help and that of Hanna Gruen with proof reading. Thanks also to our copy-editor for her careful reading and suggestions.

INTRODUCTION

This volume takes a serious look at some basic elements of Liberal *halakhah* along with a few other subjects. We do so a little more than a decade after the founding of the Solomon B. Freehof Institute of Progressive *Halakhah*. In the intervening years a host of authors, mainly, but not exclusively from North America, have provided insights into some of the issues which face us. We have looked at many areas and provided different perspectives through essays and selected responsa.

This volume is primarily concerned with providing different ways of approaching Reform *halakhah*. We are not seeking a consensus, but rather wish to demonstrate the various methods and paths which can be used. A few of the essays deal with entirely different topics and have only an indirect bearing on our primary theme.

In future volumes we will continue the pattern of looking at specific issues with two goals in mind: (1) We wish to give the Jewish community broad halakhic grounding for the decisions which need to be made. Philosophy, *aggadah*, sociology, and many other areas will have a voice in these decisions, but *halakhah* with its deep roots in the past, traditional and Reform, needs always to be consulted and to have a major, and often decisive voice. (2) We want to encourage a generation of individuals – Jewish scholars as well as interested members of the community to study the sources along with their modern interpretations and thus broaden the basis for sound decision making.

As Liberal Judaism is strongest in North America, the views presented are principally American, but not entirely. We welcome perspectives from other nations where Reform Judaism has continued to grow to present their views and concerns. Judaism has always been multi-faceted and we wish to encourage that. Pluralism has been a hallmark of the *halakhah* as is visible from the talmudic period to our own day. This needs little encouragement as strong divergent opinions are expressed among all Jewish groups, be they Reform, Orthodox, or Conservative.

Occasional it is appropriate to take a broader and more general look at the modern, Liberal study of the *halakhah*. This volume fulfills that role and its is good to do so in honor of Moshe Zemer.

Walter Jacob
Erev Purim 5764

Chapter 1

❖ ❖ ❖

MOSHE ZEMER – AN APPRECIATION

Walter Jacob

We congratulate Moshe Zemer on his seventieth birthday through this volume. These essays by friends and colleagues recognize his work in Israel and our joint effort for the Freehof Institute. They deal with halakhic decision making and its ethical implications, as well as the broader realm of rabbinic studies.

Moshe has been one of the pioneer Reform rabbis in Israel in the second generation which sought to actually establish a movement rather than just individual institutions and congregations. Moshe, who emigrated to Israel in 1963, has spent virtually his entire rabbinate in Israel. Born in Los Angeles, a graduate of the University of California, with his rabbinic education at the Hebrew Union College in Cincinnati, he very early became interested in helping the growth of Reform Judaism in Israel. He is the founder of three of our congregations, first Emet VeAnavah in Ramat Gan, then HaSharon in Kfar Shmaryahu, and finally Kedem Synagogue-Bet Daniel in Tel Aviv. The establishment of each of these congregations encountered the usual difficulties placed in our way by the religious establishment. Obtaining a site, occupancy and building permits, and everything else was difficult. Moshe never gave up and poured energy and devotion into the growth of these congregations; they have flourished and continue to be important for the growth of Reform Judaism in Israel.

These struggles were interrupted by many happier moments especially after he met Ilana, who would become his wife in 1965. Their three children, Hilla, Moriah, and Barak and their four grandchildren have provided much happiness.

Moshe understood that the Reform movement needed not only congregations and a network of institutions such as kindergartens and schools, but also an intellectual foundation appropriate for Israel. He continues to provide it through his halakhic writings. They are based on a century and a half of such efforts in North America and Europe and have been expanded by Moshe to provide the Israeli movement with a strong foundation. His voice along with a handful of others has demonstrated the historic diversity of the *halakhah*. He has fought for pluralism in the Israeli halakhic realm. Moshe's editorials and short pieces which were published in *Ha-aretz*, *Davar*, and other papers brought Reform *halakhah* to a broader reading public. These pieces stressed the flexibility of the *halakhah* through the centuries from the beginning and showed that the *halakhah* could accommodate major changes in the contemporary world.

During these years, Moshe proceeded with formal halakhic studies as he worked for a doctorate, which he received from the Hebrew Union College in 1991. At the same time he lectured in rabbinics at the Hebrew Union College in Jerusalem. This enabled him to meet with both the Israeli students preparing for the Reform rabbinate in Israel and with the American students who spend their first year of study in Israel, and he gained disciples.

In the late 1980s, Moshe at the same time as I sought to widen the interest in *halakhah* within the Reform movement. He came to Pittsburgh with the idea of some kind of halakhic setting that would meet the needs of Israel and perhaps the United States. We were both very much on the same track because I, after a decade and a half as chair of the Responsa Committee of the Central Conference of American Rabbis, had just proposed a new committee or commission that would provide a halakhic foundation for the practical issues facing us.

We decided that an independent institute would be the proper route as it could move quickly, with a minimum of structure and no bureaucracy. As Solomon B. Freehof, who had done so much for Reform *halakhah* had just died, we sought and received permission to use his name for the institute, founded in 1989 with its initial meeting in London. We have sponsored one or two seminars subsequently each year in North America, Israel, and Europe Our membership, which soon became international, provides the funds for our publications and supports halakhic efforts in Israel. Interest in the Institute among colleagues and lay people continues to grow.

Most of the symposia, regularly held since 1989, have been planned jointly. Twelve volumes, the results of the symposia, have been published by the Institute since its founding – in other words a volume each year. The editorial process, setting up, publishing, and distribution, as well as handling the organizational finances, membership, and the associated inquiries proved cumbersome at a distance, even with e-mail, so I have done all of this. Nancy Berkowitz, who copy–edited many volumes, and Barbara Bailey have been helpful. The *HalakhaH*, which appears three times each year, is also handled by me in Pittsburgh.

Moshe spent considerable effort through the years on his book, *Halakhah Shefuyah*, which is a fine introduction to Reform *halakhah* and has received good reviews. Published in Israel in 1993, it was soon translated into German and English (1999). This volume has helped the understanding of Reform *halakhah* and we are indebted to Moshe for this significant effort. Moshe has published almost a hundred essays on halakhic topics in Israel and North America and has contributed to most of the volumes of the Freehof Institute.

Moshe continues to be active not only with the Institute but also with frequent lectures on halakhic topics for leading institutes in Israel. These presentations published in journals and the Israeli press have helped to establish an intellectual foundation for Reform Judaism in Israel. As we celebrate Moshe Zemer, we hope for his continued involvement in Reform Judaism in Israel and in the Solomon B. Freehof Institute of Progressive *Halakhah*. May the years ahead be good and productive and be happy for him and his family.

Chapter 2

❖ ❖ ❖

GERMAN ROMANTICISM AND THE JEWS:
The Intellectual Basis for Halakhic Reform

Peter Haas

For the rise of Reform Judaism in Germany, one of the "red letter" events was the appointment of Abraham Geiger in 1838 as associate rabbi and *dayyan* in Breslau. What was so striking about this appointment was that it was made over the resolute and unequivocal opposition of the traditionalist senior rabbi of the community, Salomon Tiktin. Ismar Schorsch has used this incident to symbolize the emergence of the modern rabbi, that is, the replacement of the traditional Ashkenazi talmudic scholar with a university-trained preacher and pastor. What Geiger's appointment also demonstrates is that even an authority with the stature of Tiktin could at best delay, but not prevent, the course of Jewish religious development in mid–eighteenth century Germany.[1]

The massive change in the notion of the rabbinate that was spreading across Central Europe during this period was, of course, part of a much broader shift in how German Jews were coming to understand their Judaism. Part of this metamorphosis was, naturally enough, a reevaluation of the content, structure, and even validity of *halakhah*. The connection with a reevaluation of the office of the rabbi was clear and direct. We know from numerous sources that the role of the rabbi in the Jewish communities of pre-Enlightenment Germany was almost entirely judicial. Consider, for example, the description of the job as penned by Hirschel Levin, the last *Oberlandesrabbiner* of Berlin. In about 1798, complaining about the demands of his position he wrote to Friedrich Wilhelm III, King of Prussia, that his post

> requires, in addition to the most exacting execution of all religious prescriptions, an ever watchful eye for maintaining the purity of the faith

among the nation settled here, resolution of all related questions and doubts, responsibility for the continuation of talmudic learning, and finally the most extensive jurisdiction over a large number of juridical cases arising among the nation such as inheritance, divorce, etc.[2]

The shift in perception of the rabbi, at least in the lay community, is impressively illustrated by a comment made barely a generation later, in 1820, by a leading lay member of the Berlin Jewish community, Ruben Gumpertz. Asked by the government of Saxony for input as to what the appropriate functions of a rabbi in Prussia should be, Gumpertz responded that "quite properly and fittingly, therefore, one could call the rabbis... *kosher* supervisors, since as indicated above, their functions relate primarily to decisions regarding permitted and forbidden foods, the *kashrut* of foods and drinks and what pertains to them.[3] Clearly the role and stature of the rabbis were undergoing a revolutionary shift. As university-educated elites rose to positions of leadership within the Jewish community, as Geiger had in Wiesbaden and then Breslau, these men had to define themselves and their positions within this new context. Were they even rabbis at all, and if so, in what sense? If they took on the title of rabbi, then how did the content of the term need to change to accommodate them? These are the issues that stand constantly behind the debates of the 1840s.

When we think about these kinds of questions and changes with German Judaism of the nineteenth century, we tend to think of them in terms of developments internal to Judaism. But as I shall argue below, the reality was more complex. As university-trained intellectuals gradually took over leadership positions in the German Jewish community, the debate over these issues moved out beyond the limits of the traditional talmudic literature. My claim is that these deliberations among the new university trained rabbis were in fact conducted more or less as extensions of controversies that were just then also animating the German academic world. In short, philosophical discussions of the nature of nation, law, and ethics in general were being applied by these men to Judaism in particular.

The transfer of these discussions to the case of Judaism was in fact quite straightforward. As I have just noted, the issue of the new rabbis' relation to the old legal tradition, the *halakhah*, was of central concern. But theories about the origin and nature of law had special urgency at this time in the German-speaking lands of central Europe because of the area's struggle to define itself as a nation-state with its own distinctive cultural, religious and social norms. In other words, as the diverse peoples of German-speaking Central Europe were coming gradually to a common idea of nationality, they found themselves contending with the diversity of their political and economic cultures. The various German legal patrimonies would have to coalesce into a coherent system. While it was clear to nearly everybody that the old medieval legal structure would simply have to go, it was hardly obvious what would replace it. But it was apparent that whatever did replace it would have to be authentic to the nation, or *Volk*. So it turns out that the reformers of Judaism were facing very much the same obstacle as the creators of modern Germany were in theirs. That is, just as people of German nationality were trying to define themselves and their nationality, so were Jews within that population. In fact, the debates in both the general German and the Jewish communities reached a sort of peak in the 1840s, signaled by the revolutions of 1848 on the one hand and the Reform "synods" on the other. My point is that not only did Jews define themselves in the larger context of nationalistic self-definition in central Europe, the terms of semantics and syntax of the debates crossed social and national lines.

In significant part, the development of the philosophy of law (*Rechtsphilosophie*) in the German-speaking lands was provoked by Napoleon's attempt to remake France, and then the rest of Europe, in line with Enlightenment rationality and liberal political principles. One major legal development was, of course, the dissolution in 1806 of the Holy Roman Empire. In the wake of this collapse, the German lands were reorganized as a series of more or less independent kingdoms (Bavaria, Würtemberg, Hanover, Saxony) or Grand Duchies (Baden,

Mecklenburg, Saxony-Weimar). Thus began a series of consolidations that would reach completion only under the premiership of Otto von Bismarck. But along with these political unifications came legal reforms as well, as different economies, social classes, tax structures and the like had to be reconciled and merged. In some cases, German legal reformers looked to the Napoleonic Code as a model. Now, the point of the French codifiers was to exclude from the legal process what they saw as the arbitrary use of power by the elites of the *Ancien Règime*. Instead they proposed to establish a system by which the judges operated as sort of rational computers, applying a complete, stable, and seamless system of rules.[4] For some German philosophers of law, this was just what Germany needed. In fact, Anton Thibaut, a German professor of law at Heidelberg University, publicly proclaimed the need for such a code of law in Germany. But with the fall of Napoleon in 1815 and the rise of German nationalism and anti–French sentiment, reaction against his social and legal reforms set in. It thus turned out that Thibaut's essay "On the Necessity for a General Civil Code for Germany" rather than leading to the adoption of a Napoleonic–type code provoked the exact opposite reaction, and is generally credited with sparking the emergence of a romantic notion of law that came to be called the historical school, to which I shall return in a moment.

The logic of its argument was roughly as follows. One alternative to the Napoleonic code was, of course, to go back to the laws of the pre-Napoleonic period. While calls to do so may have attracted some sympathy from the conservative-minded established estates, this was clearly not a workable solution. First of all, the political landscape had changed dramatically, as we just noted. Second, as the pace of change in Europe quickened and belief in modern science and progress spread, European thinkers came more and more to see the classical period not as one to which a fallen humanity had to return, but one that modern people should overcome, transcend, and move beyond. Certainly the experience of both the

American Revolution and the French Revolution, in which the classical legal systems inherited by medieval Europe were destroyed to make way for new legal structures devised in the light of reason, encouraged the idea that law was a product of the human mind and that different ages produced legal cultures according to the level of their insight into the truths of nature and human society.[5] This conviction came to be reflected in a new historical critical approach to the Roman legal heritage, an approach that was sensitive to the cultural matrix out of which Roman law emerged. The harbinger of this view was a study by Christian F. Glueck entitled *Ausführliche Erläuterung der Pandecten nach Hellfeld*, the second edition of which was published in 1797.[6] Unlike earlier medieval studies, this was not a mere scholastic rearrangement or systematization of Roman law but an attempt to adduce the original meaning and intent of Roman law by paying attention to its cultural and linguistic background.

This view of law led directly to what came to be known as "positivism," which is generally traced back to Gustav Hugo and his *Lehrbuch des Naturrechts als einer Philosophie des positiven Rechts*, published a year later, in 1798. In this study, Hugo set out to prove that what had been claimed by legal scholars of the past to be part of, or derived from, natural law were in fact historically bounded legal enactments. That is, what Hugo adduced from the Roman case was that all legal enactments are "positive" in the sense that they are the results of human institutions that had the power to enact, or posit, laws. There was not a givenness to law to which individual pieces of legislation had to conform, but law is part of the historical development of a people. This notion of law was of course tremendously powerful, and empowering, in the climate of early-nineteenth-century Germany. It gave tremendous intellectual weight to the idea that the legal traditions of the various German states and principalities were legitimately open to change at the hands of a new generation of leaders. But there were two different interpretations as to exactly what mandate this positive character of law gave to the current political leadership. It could be taken to mean that law could simply be made up anew on the basis of scientific reason, much as Napoleon's lawyers presumably had done. German law could thus be rethought and fashioned on the basis of modern science and rationality. One cannot help but think here of the position of some of the more radical religious reformers concerning the positive nature of Jewish law.

But there was a strong reaction against this, which brings me back to what has come to be called the historical school, the acknowledged intellectual light of which was Friederich Karl Savigny. In his 1814 pamphlet, penned in answer to Anton Thibaut, *Vom Berufe unserer Zeit für Gesetzgebung und Rechtswissenschaft*, von Savigny set forth the groundwork for a different view of law. Here he claimed that sudden and arbitrary legislative enactments by politically motivated legislative bodies could never produce true law for the people.[7] Rather, all authentic law had to conform with what he called the *Volkseele* (national soul), which is the source of inspiration of all national characteristics. In other words, law always in the end had to unfold along lines laid down and maintained by the inherent genius of the culture as it underwent historical development. Thus, while new German law could of course be posited willy-nilly, it would be authentic German law only if it grew out of a continuity with the historical law and traditions of the German people. What Savigny called for was a thorough examination of the legal heritage of Germany from Roman times forward as the intellectual basis for any future revision of basic German law. One cannot help but think here of Zacharias Frankel's call for historical positivism in Jewish law. In all events, Savigny went on to make his own contributions to this massive project, publishing studies of both medieval and present-day Roman law.[8] The historical study of the origin and development of folk law that he launched continued to occupy legal scholars in German universities for the greater part of the nineteenth century.

The civil code of law for the German Empire (the so-called *bürgerliches Gesetzbuch*), which was based on this historical study, finally went into effect only in 1900.

The relevance of these nationalistic and philosophical deliberations in the university for the reform of German Jewry hardly needs spelling out. While the first generation of reformers saw reform largely in terms of ad hoc changes in the liturgy and relaxation of halakhic requirements in public, the university-trained rabbis who had taken over leadership by mid-century clearly saw the need for a thorough, systematic, and philosophically rigorous revision of the whole halakhic system. To be sure, there were a few early attempts to tinker with the halakhic system, attempts that included the publication of a number of early reform responsa justifying various specific halakhic reforms. But it soon became clear that not only would this approach not change the mind of anyone not already convinced, but it also missed the real question. The problem was not with this or that particular norm, practice, or *minhag*, but with the system as a whole. Change could not be incremental but would have to be systemic. The contemporary legal experience of Europe, I am arguing, served as an instructive model here. The French revolution was not able to bring France into the forefront of the modern world by tinkering with the statutes of the *Ancien Régime*. Rather, the entire medieval legal legacy had to be thrown out and a whole new system of law set forth. Germany itself was now undergoing this same process, albeit in slower motion. Reform Judaism now came to see itself in precisely the same situation. It should hardly come as a surprise, then, that the debates within the Reform Jewish synods of the 1840s should have echoed the disputes raging at exactly the same moment in the halls of the universities.

There is another aspect of all this that bears mentioning because there is a connection with religion here, as well. This period also saw the beginning of what has come to be called "High Biblical Criticism." This in turn was linked to a significant extent to the need on the part of the German *Volk* to define itself. Northern Germans saw themselves as comprising a Christian, specifically Protestant, nation. In the task of state–building, they had to define themselves against their Catholic counterparts in France, Austria, and Poland, not to mention the Orthodox Christians in Russia. In other words, part of the search for the soul of Germany was the search to recover in its pure form the *religious* heritage that defined the nation or, more precisely, was one of the expressions of the *Volkseele*. One element of this effort took the form of a reexamination of the legal and moral teachings of the Bible. The interest here was threefold. First, Protestant theologians wanted to know what the Bible "really" was saying as opposed to what the Catholic Church was claiming it to be saying. Second, Protestant teachers wanted to uncover the principles behind biblical law so as to be able to sort out the enduring core of biblical morality which was the duty of all Christians to fulfill, from the historically determined legislation that God needed to enact in order to rule the recalcitrant Israelites. And third, of course, Protestants wanted to be able to show why Judaism, as a continuation of the biblical legal tradition, was at best only a continuation in the flesh and not a continuation in spirit. For all three interests, biblical law stood at the center of attention and so, German Judaism also found itself situated at the intersection of three highly charged intellectual concerns. Thus Judaism inevitably became a subject of academic reflection, directly or indirectly, in scholarly circles. The emerging university–trained Jewish leadership was not only trained in these disciplines but also found they had to react to them. To restate my thesis, Jewish intellectuals shaping Reform Judaism in the middle of the century were actually caught up in a much larger discourse about law.

At this point I would like to use one brief example to point out the interconnectedness between the development of German legal studies on the one hand and scientific or critical studies of biblical, and by implication Jewish, law on the other. I refer you back for a moment to Karl von Savigny. Savigny, you will recall, argued that law was not the result of a transhistorical rationality but was rather embedded in the folk. It was to be seen as an expression of the deep genius of a culture, on a plane with other products of the creative imagination such as art and literature. "Law," says Savigny, "has its existence in the common consciousness of the people." W. M. L. de Wette (1780-1849) carried these convictions over to the study of biblical law. He set out, like Savigny, to show that even the so-called Mosaic law was not really a product of a great classical "Golden Age" but actually reflects a later historical stage in the political development of the Israelite people.[9] Basing his argument especially on the presumed lateness of Chronicles, and on the concurrent assumption of the relative priority of the books of Samuel and Kings, de Wette claimed to be able to isolate an early stage of Israel's legal and religious heritage in Samuel–Kings, and a later stage given expression in Chronicles.[10] On the basis of this and other data, he concluded that the Israelite religion became progressively more complex and developed over time such that the more sophisticated laws ascribed to Moses must in fact be quite late. Conversely, the older material such as that found in the Pentateuch is largely mythical, and so must go back to such an ancient time that it is impossible to derive any reliable conclusions from it.[11]

The point for our purposes is that for de Wette biblical law is no longer treated as divine revelation but as a human creation firmly embedded in the historical reality of its community, just as legal scholars were now claiming for Roman law. One could see a development in law — whether Roman or biblical — a development that reflects the ongoing religious, spiritual, and intellectual life of the folk from which it emerges. This was not taken to mean, at least among the theology faculty, that all law is equally good. De Wette makes sure to point out that, in his view, in fact the later articulations of Hebrew law fail again and again to reach the spiritual heights of the Mosaic legislation. But not all scholars of biblical law saw only decline. A good example is Johann Karl Wilhelm Vatke. Vatke, apparently influenced by Hegel, argued that biblical law actually moved in the expected Hegelian fashion from primitive to more developed. That is, for him, Judaism is not seen as a falling away from a more developed type, as de Wette supposed, but as a stage in the growth of the biblical heritage to a more mature state. In posing matters in this way, Vatke provided a useful model for Jewish scholars. He saw the evolution of law as a rational and thoughtful process in reaction to the concrete, indeterminate history of the community. In particular, he situates the development in Israel's religious life in the context of the community's on-going struggle against Canaanite worship. But in all events, the evolution of ancient Jewish religion and law, then, can be portrayed as a progressive struggle on the part of the people to overcome the limitations of their environment in order to enact more perfectly their cultural and religious heritage.

It is in light of these developments that we can make sense of the debates going on within the reforming community of Jewish intellectuals. Consider for a moment the following comments by Abraham Geiger:

> Not everything that has been handed down to us from ages past stems from hoary antiquity or from the very beginning of time. Later periods have grafted many a twig onto the ancient trunk, and have added many a new link to the chain of tradition. Only a dull and simple mind can believe that things have always been as they are now ... The mind which lives on in the present sees the structure only as it is now, apparently complete and grown together not a homogeneous whole, and views it as composed entirely of essentials, so that anyone who would dare touch the sanctuary thereby violates it.[12]

There are, as it were, two subtexts to this paragraph. To Jewish ears, Geiger is clearly addressing the Orthodox, that is, those who claim that the current state of *halakhah* is a "homogeneous whole" that is "composed of essentials" and was given to Moses from "ages past" in "hoary antiquity." In short, he is paraphrasing the notion that the *halakhah* is a timeless and unchanging construct given at Sinai. Using this view, any change must be a turn away from perfection and truth, a view that leads directly to Moses Sofer's dictum that *"Kol hadash asur min hatorah."* But to the ear of a German legal academic, Geiger's statement sounds like the restatement of current progressive academic presuppositions as regards the study of law in general. What Geiger has done is to position Jewish legal reform within the larger context of German legal philosophy, showing at the same time that the Reform movement was in line with the latest academic insights. The rewriting of *halakhah* was not just an internal squabble within Judaism but a movement to rearticulate Jewish law in step with the rearticulation of European law in the modern age.

Within this conceptualization, of course, emerges the debate as to the extent to which a legislative body is free to construct modern law. For those more oriented around positivism, the legislators, or synods, had pretty much a free hand to enact what changes they saw as necessary in light of reason and current needs. The historicist movement was meant to counter this by requiring that the historical voice of the *Volk* be given a hearing. That is, modern legislators have to be constrained by what Savigny called "the common consciousness of the people."

This stance should sound familiar to anyone who has read the debates in the Reform synods of the mid-nineteenth century. Let me just cite one example, this one from Zacharias Frankel from his "On Changes in Judaism" (1845):

> True Judaism demands religious activity, but the people is not altogether mere clay to be molded by the will of the theologians and scholars. In religious activities, as in those of ordinary life, it decides for itself. This right was conceded by Judaism to the people. At such times as an earlier religious ordinance was not accepted by the entire community of Israel, it was given up. Consequently, when a new ordinance was about to be enacted it was necessary to see whether it would find acceptance by the people. When the people allows certain practices to fall into disuse, then the practices cease to exist.[13]

What I hope I have made clear is that the shaping of the German Jewish attitude toward *halakhah* and changes in *halakhah* is deeply embedded in German legal science of the nineteenth century. The leaders of German Jewish reform were not operating in a vacuum but were extending intellectual debates from their university training directly into their Jewish communities. A fuller understanding of the forming forces of German Reform a century and a half ago depends on our looking not only at the Jewish thinkers themselves but also at the intellectual culture in which they were formed.

Notes

1. Ismar Schorsch, *"The Emergence of the Modern Rabbinate"* in Werner Mosse, Arnold Paucker and Reinhard Rürup (eds.), *Revolution and Evolution: 1848 in German-Jewish History* (Tübingen: J.C.B.Mohr, Paul Siebeck, 1981), pp. 205-7.

2. *Ibid.*, p. 207.

3. *Ibid.*, p. 229.

4. J. M. Kelly, *A Short History of Western Legal Theory* (Oxford: Clarendon, 1994), p. 312.

5. See for example, Stig Strömholm's discussion in his *A Short History of Legal Thinking in the West* (Stockholm and Littleton, Conn: Norstedts, 1985), pp. 266f.

6. *Ibid.*, 208.

7. *Ibid.*, 266.

8. *Geschichte des römischen Rechts in Mittelalter*, 7 volumes, 1815-1831 and *System des heutigen römischen Rechts*, 8 volumes, 1840-1849. See Strömholm, *Short History.* p. 266.

9. My analysis here revolves primarily around de Wette's *Einleitung in das Alte Testament* (Halle,:1806-7).

10. George Christie (ed.), *Jurisprudence: Text and Readings in the Philosophy of Law* (St. Paul: West, 1973) pp. 605-6.

11. A major influence on de Wette's theory of religion as described here was J. F. Fries, a professor of de Wette's at Jena and subsequently a life–long friend.

12. *"Present–Day Judaism and Its Intellectual Trends"* in *Wissenschaftliche Zeitschrift für Jüdische Theologie*, cited in Max Weiner (ed.), *Abraham Geiger and Liberal Judaism: The Challenge of the Nineteenth Century* (Philadelphia: Jewish Publication Society, 1962), p. 266.

13. Cited from Paul Mendes and Jehuda Reinharz (eds.), *The Jew in the Modern World*, 2nd ed. (New York: Oxford University Press, 1995), p. 196.

Chapter 3

❖ ❖ ❖

AGAINST METHOD:
Liberal *Halakhah* Between Theory and Practice*

Mark Washofsky

I find the topic of this volume both fascinating and frustrating. It is fascinating because, well, this is what we liberal halakhists *do*. Much of our work, perhaps even its essence, centers upon the effort to go "beyond the letter of the law," to work toward a more exalted understanding of the halakhic tradition, a vision of *halakhah* that is more lenient, flexible, affirmative of contemporary values, and morally uplifting than that promulgated in the halakhic writings of nonliberals. It is our guiding conviction that the stringent *pesak* or *pesikah* (halakhic decision making) of today's Orthodox rabbinate, a trend that we associate with the "letter" of the law, represents neither the only nor the best available interpretation of Jewish legal thought on a host of important questions. To borrow a word or two from our teacher Moshe Zemer, to whom we pay tribute in these pages, we liberals believe in an "evolving" and "sane" *halakhah*,[1] one that is fully capable of yielding answers and guidance that cohere with our highest conceptions of religious truth.

Our topic is frustrating because we can't get anyone to listen to us. We liberal halakhists occupy a middle ground between two groups of Jews who respond to our work with a mixture of apathy and disdain. To our left stand those Jews who dismiss traditional Jewish law as at best irrelevant and at worst positively injurious to our most deeply cherished liberal values. Jewish law, they claim, supports doctrines and teachings that inevitably contradict our intellectual and ethical commitments on issues such as human freedom and autonomy, social justice, gender equality, and the relations between Jews and the non-Jewish world. No approach to Jewish law, however "liberal" it might be, can successfully alter its parochial and backward-looking nature; Jewish religious liberals thus have little use for halakhic thinking and should not waste their time trying to reform, reread, or otherwise, "*kasher,*" the recalcitrant texts of the Jewish legal tradition. To our right are those in the Orthodox camp who, deeply devoted to the halakhic process, reject our liberal halakhic conclusions as uninformed, misguided, or just plain wrong. As they see it, our "evolving" or "sane" *halakhah* is not *halakhah* at all but a pastiche of liberal political and cultural values masquerading as *halakhah*. The decisions we render in its name violate the correct interpretation of the sources and texts of Jewish law. And since no authentic Jewish practice exists outside the framework of *halakhah*, it follows that our practice is not and cannot be considered as authentically Jewish.

Oddly enough, for all that separates the religious outlook of these two groups, they are at one in their definition of Jewish law. Both see *halakhah* as a body of objectively correct legal decisions. That is, there exists something that one can identify as "the" *halakhah*, a collected mass of rulings, interpretations, and behaviors that comprise the authoritative core and content of Jewish legal teaching. This core and content, it turns out, are identical with the understanding of Jewish law presented in contemporary Orthodox *pesikah* so that, according to both groups, "the" *halakhah* is whatever today's Orthodox rabbinate says it is. From this, it follows that any ruling, interpretation, or behavior that differs from contemporary Orthodox *pesak* deviates from the true *halakhah*. Our critics to both our left and our right therefore consider the term "liberal *halakhah*" an oxymoron: any suggestion that we might arrive at a conception of an "evolving" or "sane" *halakhah* through the study and application of the sources of Jewish law is but a snare and a delusion. There is no *halakhah* other than the currently existing body of substantive rulings, interpretations, and behaviors that bear the name.[2] Our choice is simply to accept or reject this body of rules in toto. On that point, the two groups diverge; they are united, however, in denying any intellectual justification to our efforts to derive a liberal *halakhah*.

This criticism, which goes to the heart of our enterprise, rests upon the assumption that it is possible to determine the objectively correct answers to all or most questions of Jewish law, so that answers that differ are by definition incorrect or deviant. And if it is possible to determine objectively correct answers to questions of Jewish law, there must be a proper *method* by which to make that determination. After all, halakhic decisions are based upon the interpretation of the literary texts and sources of Jewish law, the Talmud and the vast corpus of commentaries, codes, and responsa devoted to the Talmud's elucidation. Since legal sources are famously open to differing readings and understandings, there must be some procedure by which to weed out those interpretations that are incorrect. That procedure is the "halakhic method" of Orthodox *pesak*, a set of rigorous techniques of textual interpretation that, when applied to the literary sources of Jewish law, distinguish objectively "right" understandings from "wrong" ones.[3] The belief in the existence of such a method and its identification with Orthodox *pesak* allows our critics on both the left and the right to identify that *pesak* as "the" *halakhah* and our own interpretations, which deviate from it, as incorrect, as wrong, as non-*halakhah*.

I want to offer a challenge to this assumption. I argue that there is no such thing as the one objectively correct answer to a question of *halakhah*. I argue this because I do not believe in the existence of some procedure or set of techniques called the "halakhic method" that works as a formula to produce the right interpretations of Jewish legal texts. The appeal to such a method allows for the claim that *halakhah* is like mathematics or the hard sciences, a discipline governed by fixed and rationally discoverable rules of procedure that, if properly applied, do yield objectively correct answers. The resort to "method" as a way of explaining the halakhic process resembles nothing so much as the doctrine of legal formalism,[4] once the reigning theory of law the "orthodoxy" of jurisprudence–in the United States.[5] By now, however, generations of scholars have dismantled that doctrine, and other accounts of legal reasoning and judicial decision have replaced it.[6] I contend that, just as legal "method" is no longer viewed as a mechanism that produces objectively right answers in law, so we ought to abandon the notion of a method that distinguishes between objectively right and wrong interpretations of the *halakhah*.

As the title of this essay proclaims, therefore, I am "against method" as a description of the process of halakhic decision making.[7] This does *not* mean that I define the halakhic process as a kind of anarchy, in which the halakhist derives whatever lessons he (or she) wishes to derive from the texts without having to pay attention to rules, principles, procedures, and the like. I readily concede that rules, principles, and procedures are an integral aspect of the practice of *halakhah*; indeed, *halakhah* could hardly be a "practice" – that is, an organized intellectual discipline – without such things. How I understand the term "practice" and how I apply it to *halakhah* are questions I will address in the latter part of this article. At the outset, though, it is enough to say that I do not believe that "method" is a proper or accurate description of that practice. To put this differently, while rules, principles, and procedures figure prominently in what the halakhist does, they do not determine the conclusions that the halakhist draws.

In order to develop this argument, I want to look at a particular example of halakhic practice – a body of halakhic interpretations and rulings that were actually put forward by Jewish legal authorities over a significant period of time – that displays two important characteristics. First, it is a "different" *halakhah*. These teachings and rulings, that is, deviate substantially from the previously existing trends in mainstream Orthodox *pesikah* to the extent that, as I shall argue, they warrant the descriptive labels "innovative" and "progressive." Second, the practitioners of this innovative *halakhah* were all "orthodox" rabbis whose halakhic bona fides could not be questioned. Their work, in other words, cannot be summarily dismissed as the product of Reform or Conservative rabbis who are declared by rabbinical fiat to be *apikorsim*, heretics who by definition exclude themselves from the halakhic circle.[8] What we have, therefore, is a case study in halakhic pluralism: two widely divergent, contradictory approaches to *pesak* that coexist within a common intellectual structure, so that the advocates of both approaches claim that theirs is "correct" *halakhah*, a valid form of halakhic practice. This claim, we shall see, is not based upon any appeal to a halakhic "method" that, when properly followed, yields indisputably right answers. I argue, rather, that the existence of these two schools of halakhic thought demonstrates that no such method exists. The fact of halakhic pluralism and the claim of both sides that their view is the "correct" understanding of Jewish law suggests that we need another, more accurate explanation of the halakhic process.

A "Zionist *Halakhah*"

The decades of the early to mid-twentieth century witnessed a remarkable burst of halakhic creativity, a flood of books, essays, articles, and responsa that addressed issues surrounding the emerging Jewish state. I call this body of writing "Zionist *halakhah*,"[9] because it was largely produced by rabbis associated with the "national religious" or "Mizrachi" Zionist movement. The slogan of the Mizrachi movement – "the land of Israel for the people of Israel according to the Torah of Israel" – expressed the Orthodox Zionist credo that the establishment of a sovereign Jewish state prior to the coming of the Messiah was fully consistent with Torah and *halakhah*. This, in turn, implied that the Jewish state should function in accordance with Jewish law and that the *halakhah* was fully capable of serving as the legal foundation of such a state. Yet to put this belief into practice was a daunting challenge. It was not at all obvious that the *halakhah*, as it was formulated at the dawn of the Jewish national movement, was up to the task that the Orthodox Zionists set for it.[10] In neither the realm of private law (torts, contracts, property) nor that of public administrative law and constitutional theory had the *halakhah* attained the necessary sophistication to address the exigencies of a modern society. Although classical halakhic literature does deal with these subjects,[11] the loss of national sovereignty in 70 C. E. and the disappearance of Jewish juridical autonomy with the advent of Emancipation had removed these areas of private and public law from the practical jurisdiction of the rabbinical courts.[12] The result was that, as Orthodox Zionists fully recognized,[13] the *halakhah* of statehood (*hilkhot medinah*) was terribly outdated and simply did not speak to the requirements of contemporary national political life. Accordingly, a group of Orthodox Zionist scholars took upon themselves the mission of reexamining and restating the existing corpus of Jewish law so that it might speak effectively to the requirements of the modern state.

The work of these rabbis can be seen as the religious counterpart to the *mishpat ivri* movement among secular jurists and legal academicians who sought to establish Jewish law as the legal structure of the new state. Unlike the latter, about which much has been written,[14] we find comparatively little in the way of description or analysis of the literary product of the Zionist rabbis. Fortunately, a large-scale study is presently in progress;[15] in the meantime, we can at least note the scope of their achievement. Among the authors were some of the leading figures of the rabbinical community in Palestine/Israel: Yitzchak Halevy Herzog, the chief Ashkenazic rabbbi of Palestine/Israel from 1937 to 1959, who devoted the most sustained and systematic thought to these matters;[16] Ben Zion Meir Chai Ouziel, chief Sephardic rabbi of Palestine/Israel from 1939 to 1953,[17] regarded by many within the Mizrachi community as the Zionist *posek* par excellence;[18] Shaul Yisraeli, "who committed the bulk of his public life to halakhic study and legal rulings on questions of Torah and statehood";[19] and Eliezer Yehudah Waldenberg, one of the most outstanding contemporary authors of responsa.[20] Their studies and comments appeared in newspapers, collections of responsa, rabbinical court rulings, and halakhic journals. The most outstanding of the latter was *Hatorah Vehamedinah* (*HTM*), appearing annually or biannually from 1949 to 1962, edited by R. Shaul Yisraeli under the sponsorship of various Orthodox Zionist institutions.[21] The authors who published in *HTM* were, in the main, younger scholars who saw their task not to issue decisions but to study the legal sources on public and political questions in the hope that their findings might be helpful to the Chief Rabbinate, an institution that did possess the authority to render actual *pesak*.[22] A glance at the article titles in these volumes reveals the range of their concerns: the halakhic constitutional theory of a sovereign, pre-Messianic Jewish state; rules governing the conduct of a Jewish army; the criminal and penal code of the state; the structure of government institutions and the qualifications of public officeholders; the political status of women; the status of non-Jews under a Jewish government; the halakhic validity of secular legislation (i.e., of the Knesset and other administrative bodies); taxation; marriage law, inheritance, and child custody; urban planning; how the police and other vital services may function on Shabbat; national service for women and for yeshiva students; the Sabbatical year; the observance of Yom Ha`atzma'ut and other "secular" Jewish holidays; and more.

At the beginning of this section, I used the words "halakhic creativity" to describe the work of these Zionist rabbis. I should stress that this "creativity" did not take the form of invention. The authors of the articles that appear in *HTM* do not call for *takanah* (legislation), the creation of new *halakhot* or new legal institutions. Some Orthodox observers, to be sure, advocated such remedies. Convinced that the existing halakhic process was too limited and cumbersome to respond adequately to the challenges posed by political sovereignty, they called for more radical measures, including far-reaching rabbinical legislation[23] and even the revival of the ancient Sanhedrin.[24] Most of the Zionist rabbis, however, regarded these suggestions as excessive and, at worst, as transgressions against the *halakhah* itself.[25] An outside observer might note that there is nothing essentially anti-halakhic about legislative enactments; legislation, after all, is one of the primary "legal sources of Jewish law."[26] Still, even modern Orthodox scholars hesitated to push for the introduction of fundamental changes in the structure of the *halakhah*.[27] The Zionist rabbis preferred the time-honored "judicial" method of interpretation and analogical reasoning (*dimu'i milta lemilta*), which, though more piecemeal and gradual than legislation, is for that reason less threatening to the integrity of traditional *halakhah*. Even though Talmudic reasoning can be quite "creative" (halakhists refer to the ideas developed through the interpretive method as *chidushei halakhot*, "new legal ideas"), it is generally not perceived as the creation of new law (i.e., legislation) but rather as the unfolding of the implied meaning of the existing law, the logical extension of the content of the legal sources.

The essays on constitutional theory that appear in the first two volumes of *HTM* provide a good example of this "judicial" method at work.[28] Perhaps the most basic halakhic problem that the Zionist rabbis had to solve was that of the very legitimacy of a modern sovereign state: does Jewish law permit the establishment of a commonwealth in the land of Israel prior to the age of the Messiah? Many scholars answer this question in the negative, basing themselves upon a Talmudic tradition that recounts that when the Temple was destroyed, God adjured Israel never again to rebel against the nations or to attempt to seize Jerusalem by force.[29] Mizrachi theorists had to argue that this prohibition no longer applies or, if it does, that it does not forbid the sort of political activity involved with the formation of the state.[30] Beyond the legitimacy of the idea of statehood, moreover, lay the problem of sovereign power: even if the *halakhah* permits the founding of a state, it is far from certain that it permits the government of the state to exercise the kinds of authority normally associated with sovereignty. While the Talmud and the classical codes (particularly Rambam's *Mishneh Torah*) do speak to the issue of governmental authority, these sources presume the existence of a Jewish commonwealth in all its Toraitic accouterments: a king, prophets, priests, Sanhedrin, and ordained judges (*shoftim*). One might well conclude from these sources that the corpus of Jewish law has nothing to say to the political reality of contemporary statehood. The articles in *HTM* therefore seek to locate a sufficient source of sovereign power within existing halakhic theories of governance. Some of the authors based their constitutional theories upon the institution of *takanot hakahal* (community ordinances), the recognized power of local communities to act through representative bodies to adopt regulations and to levy taxes. They reasoned that this theory, which lay at the foundation of Jewish self-government throughout the Middle Ages, could be applied as well to a national commonwealth. Others sought the roots of sovereign power in the doctrine of *dina demalkhuta*, "the law of the kingdom," the notion that the government legitimately exercises a range of powers necessary to its existence and proper function. The question here is whether the concept of *dina demalkhuta*, cited in the Talmudic sources to justify halakhic recognition of certain acts of a gentile government, might apply as well to a Jewish regime in the land of Israel; several authors in *HTM* argued that the answer is "yes." Finally, Rabbi Shaul Yisraeli contended that the foundation of sovereign Jewish power lay in the legal tradition of *malkhei yisrael*, the powers and prerogatives that the Torah grants to a Jewish king in the land of Israel. This theory faced an obvious difficulty: we do not have a Jewish "king" of Davidic lineage, nor do we have the institutions (a prophet and a Sanhedrin) required to invest him in office. Yisraeli responded to these objections by adopting a *chidush* (a new halakhic idea) offered by Rabbi Avraham Yitzchak Hakohen Kook,[31] namely that in the absence of a Davidic monarch the powers of kingship (*malkhut*) do not disappear but rather revert to the people; the people, in turn, may bestow these powers upon any person or governmental institution they choose.[32]

Each of these articles displays that mixture of innovation and conservatism that marks the "judicial" approach to the *halakhah* at its creative best. Grounding themselves firmly in precedent and halakhic consensus, the authors endeavor to extend old texts and settled principles of Jewish law to a new and unprecedented political situation. The innovative, groundbreaking nature of their work is readily apparent. The Zionist rabbis have without question created new law, for the classical halakhic doctrines of government never envisioned the rise of a pre-Messianic sovereign state. At the same time, however, no rabbinical activity is more "traditional," more conservative, more respectful of established ways of legal thinking than the discovery of implicit, inherent meanings in canonical halakhic sources. Such, after all, is what rabbis do and have always done. In this way, the Zionist rabbis demonstrated their faith in the creative possibilities inherent in the traditional halakhic process, their confidence that the *halakhah* as it presently exists offers the flexibility and the dynamism needed to arrive at the sought-for solutions.

One of the leading Zionist rabbis, Ben Zion Meir Chai Ouziel, formulated what is perhaps the most comprehensive statement of this faith. In the introduction to the first volume of his collected responsa, Ouziel notes that his efforts to derive halakhic answers to contemporary problems are criticized by two distinct groups within the Jewish community. The first group of critics, "the lovers of reform in our generation," claim that he is wasting his time; in their view, the traditional *halakhah* is insufficiently flexible to respond to today's needs. The other group, while firmly devoted to *halakhah* and Jewish observance, reject the premise of his work on the grounds that today's *posek* is forbidden to depart from the decisions of his predecessors. In response to the "reformers," the critics on his left, Ouziel declares his conviction that *halakhah*, properly interpreted, can yield fitting and sufficient solutions to the challenges posed by modern life. And while reassuring the critics on his right that he is free of any and all reformist tendencies "I am creating no new law (*ein ani mechadesh kelum*), nor are we entitled to do so"– he offers them the following outlook on the

nature of halakhic decision:
> The judge or the *posek* must not say to himself, or to those who seek his guidance on any question, "bring the book, let us look up the law, let me decide the *halakhah* automatically, in accordance with the written word." Such is not the path that halakhic authorities should tread. It is their duty rather to study carefully the sources of the law and to subject them to thorough analysis, to test them in the crucible of their training, knowledge, and reason, and to arrive thereby at the correct determination of the law. Whoever decides the *halakhah* simply by citing the written sources without such a process of analysis and without an effort to truly understand the law is one to whom our Sages refer as "a destroyer of the world."[33]

Those who understand *halakhah* as the rote, mechanical application of black-letter rules are in serious error. For Ouziel, traditional halakhic argument (*masa umatan*) is a flexible and dynamic intellectual activity, capable of meeting new challenges and accommodating changing insights. This process, which in a midrashic metaphor he likens to the dew that refreshes and reinvigorates the grass,[34] demands independence of legal thought. The halakhist must be prepared to slip the stifling bonds of precedent. He may not defer to the authority of codes and compilations. Instead, he must claim for himself the freedom of judgment that belongs to all knowledgeable students of Jewish law, the freedom to arrive at one's own conclusions based upon one's own reading of the sources, no matter how innovative, even if those conclusions disagree with the conclusions of other rabbis.[35] It is vital that the contemporary *posek* proceed in this way, because circumstances of life, transformations in culture, scientific and technological developments in each and every generation create halakhic problems that demand resolution. We are not entitled to ignore these questions by invoking the slogan *hadash asur min hatorah*, i.e., anything that our predecessors have not already permitted must by that light be forbidden. . . . It is rather our duty to [find answers] through the time-honored path of legal analogy (*lilmod satum min hameforash*).

Hadash asur min hatorah literally, "everything new is forbidden by the Torah" – was, of course, the polemical watchword of Rabbi

Moshe Sofer (the Chatam Sofer) in his campaign against the innovations introduced by the Reform movement during the early nineteenth century.[36] Rabbi Ouziel here emphatically renounces Sofer's rejectionism in favor of a different vision of *halakhah*, one that supports an open and positive relationship to the "new," to the challenges posed by the experience of modernity.

Ouziel's attempt to justify his halakhic activity against the attacks of critics to both his left and his right closely resembles my own depiction, at the outset of this article, of the situation faced by today's liberal halakhist. Indeed, I think liberal halakhists share much in common with Ouziel's vision of himself as occupying a middle ground between more extremist positions. Yet for all his talk of a dynamic and flexible *halakhah*, a rhetoric that is quite congenial to our own, let us not forget that Ben Zion Ouziel was *not* a liberal rabbi. He was an Orthodox halakhist, *kasher lemehadrin*, a chief rabbi of the state of Israel. Like all Orthodox halakhists, he denies that he is an innovator, and he opposes the conscious introduction of change that is, "reform" into the corpus of Jewish law. He describes his approach as nothing more or less than the traditional process of *masa umatan* that has been the hallmark of halakhic thought for centuries. Similarly, we should not forget that the entire Zionist halakhic endeavor was an Orthodox product, promoted by Orthodox rabbis faithful to the halakhic system in its accepted Orthodox version. Rejecting calls for reform and innovation, the Zionist rabbis speak of their work as *berur* ("study," "examination," "clarification"), a term that comprehends traditional halakhic *masa umatan*.[37] Their traditionalist stance does much to explain their astonishment at the profoundly negative response by other Orthodox halakhists to the Zionist halakhic program. Despite all the effort invested by the Zionist rabbis to derive a Jewish legal basis for the new state of Israel, their opponents, a group that included the preponderant majority of the *gedolei hador* (the recognized halakhic authorities), greeted their writings with indifference, silence, and outright hostility.[38] We hear the echoes of this reaction in the introductory words penned by Rabbi Shaul Yisraeli to the first two volumes of *HTM*. In volume 1,[39] Yisraeli emphasizes the urgency of the intellectual task that the Zionist rabbis have set for themselves. He writes:

> Had we but foreseen the sudden rise of a sovereign Jewish state, we would long ago have set up a council of scholars who would have devoted the requisite effort to develop a halakhic constitution and legal code for the new Jewish polity. Yet even now – the spring of 1949 – it is not too late: the laws of the state, which still rest largely upon the legal foundation laid during the period of the British mandate, will be replaced, and it is our urgent mission to see to it that they are replaced by a truly *Jewish* legal system.

Yisraeli realizes that the nonobservant segment of the population, particularly those enamored of all things gentile and who regard Jewish tradition as inferior and outdated, will have no use for this effort. Yet he is more concerned about opposition from "Torah scholars who fear a public study of contemporary halakhic issues, who hesitate to issue rulings on these matters lest the wider community make improper use of their words. They urge caution, abstention, and inactivity."[40] Yisraeli rejects these fears. Those who wish to make "improper use" of the words of Torah will do so in any event, no matter what we rabbis do. Our task is to study and publish our findings for the benefit of those who sincerely wish to know what the Torah has to teach us. He adds the following:

> This would appear to be one of the chief reasons for the failure of observant Judaism, that out of fear and hesitation we tend to ignore contemporary problems. But it is in the nature of things that problems do not disappear simply because they are ignored. And if the leading Torah sages do not search for solutions, other hands are ready to find other, and unhappy, solutions.

By the following year,[41] Yisraeli's criticism of his Orthodox opposition had grown angrier and more despondent. He noted that "there are those who cast a suspicious eye upon our work, as they do upon all the activities of the Rabbinical Council of Hapo`el Hamizrachi. Halakhic rulings, they contend, should be the exclusive province of veteran rabbinical scholars." Yisraeli concedes that such ought to be the case. Were the great sages of our day to take on the duty of readying the *halakhah* for the immense challenges posed to it by statehood, his Rabbinical Council might assume the more humble task of studying and disseminating the writings of those scholars. Unfortunately, the great sages have refused the challenge.

> To our sorrow, things have worked out differently. Some of our greatest authorities regard the state as a plague visited upon us (*gezerah min hashamayim*), to which they respond in the spirit of the Talmudic dictum: a plague will end some day.[42] They wall themselves off in splendid isolation, declaring everything that happens outside their little world to be of no import. We will not debate with them, both out of our respect for their honor and out of the knowledge that nothing we say can change their opinion in the least. For our part, we regard it as a divine punishment (*onesh min hashamayim*) upon our generation that we have not merited to see our great teachers march before us to show us the way. It is a punishment just as surely as the failure of our rabbis to bring our people to the land of Israel (in advance of the Holocaust) was a divine punishment.

The Insufficiency of Method

This emotional reference to the passivity of the *gedolei hador*, the great rabbinical sages of Europe, in the face of the impending Nazi destruction neatly expresses R. Shaul Yisraeli's bitter disappointment in the *gedolei hador* of his own time. He speaks of another tragically missed opportunity, of a loss of rabbinical nerve at another moment that required bold rabbinical leadership. His tone of frustration suggests that he knew then what we know now: namely, that the Zionist halakhic project was doomed. By this, I do not mean that the Mizrachi rabbis had accomplished nothing of value. Far from it: they succeeded in producing an impressive cache of writings that can be said to enrich the halakhic discussion to this day.[43] Rather, the Zionist halakhic project was a failure in its most fundamentally practical aim: it did not persuade the bulk of the recognized *poskim* to join in or even to pay much attention to the work of deriving a *halakhah* of Jewish statehood. By 1962, its energy spent, the Rabbinical Council of Hapo'el Hamizrachi ceased the publication of *Hatorah-Vehamedinah*, having given up hope that the leading rabbinical sages would participate in its enterprise.[44]

Observers suggest various reasons for this failure.[45] Some attribute the silence of the *poskim* to *yir'at hora'ah*, which we might translate as "judicial humility," the traditional reluctance of rabbinical authorities to issue rulings on substantive, controversial legal questions. Some Orthodox authorities also feared that the nonobservant public acting, for example, through the secular legislature – might misinterpret and misapply far-reaching and creative halakhic decisions, thereby distorting the "true" *halakhah*.[46] First and foremost, though, this failure was the inevitable outcome of a long-standing clash of ideologies within the Orthodox community. Many, particularly among the *charedim* ("ultra-Orthodox"), opposed Zionism, even of the religious variety, on theological and halakhic grounds. They denied that the Jewish people was entitled to establish a sovereign state prior to the coming of the Messiah and the rebuilding of the Temple. That state would be governed by a Davidic monarch and *not* by some political institution exercising the powers of *malkhut* in the absence of a legitimate king. In their view, the creation of the secular state of Israel was a violation of the divine order of Jewish history, a trespass upon the limits that God had set at the time of the destruction of the Second Temple.[47] Those who held this opinion, who (to use Yisraeli's language) saw the creation of the state as a *gezeirah min hashamayim*, would hardly interpret contemporary Jewish history in the same light as those who regarded Zionism as a sign of God's deliverance.

The argument over Zionist *halakhah*, in other words, could not be settled by the application of halakhic "method." The technical rules and procedures that comprise traditional halakhic analysis did not - nor could they - produce demonstrably correct answers to questions of Jewish law as they related to issues of government and society in the sovereign Jewish state. This failure was not for lack of trying, for the Zionist rabbis were nothing if not "methodological." They described their work, remember, as *berur* or *masa umatan*, terms that denote the thoroughly traditional approach to halakhic reasoning and *pesak*. They insisted that they were doing nothing "new." Safely and surely "Orthodox," they denied any revolutionary tendencies in their legal thinking and conclusions.[48] The whole point of their enterprise was to demonstrate that Jewish law in its accepted, existing (i.e., "Orthodox") manifestation could accommodate the establishment of a sovereign state and support the institutions necessary to its survival and function. Yet for all their faithfulness to traditional halakhic "method," the Zionist rabbis did not succeed in persuading other Jewish legal authorities, who were surely no less "Orthodox" than they, that their conclusions were correct readings of the *halakhah*. Each of the Orthodox camps, one Zionist and the other anti-Zionist, observing the requirements of the halakhic process in all its appropriate stringency, arrived at a set of decisions and understandings that differed radically from those of the other.

The same holds, I contend, across the board, for *all* questions of Jewish law, regardless of subject. Halakhic method does not produce *the* correct *pesak* because, to repeat, there is no such thing as the one objectively correct answer to a question of *halakhah*. An "objectively correct" answer is correct in a formal and systemic way, an answer the correctness of which cannot be doubted by any serious practitioner of the *halakhah*. Objective correctness is not established through argument and persuasion; it is a matter of definition rather than debate. Much like a mathematical equation, the objectively correct answer to a halakhic question would be dictated by the inherent logic of the system and its decision-making rules. To doubt the correctness of such a conclusion is to violate the system's integrity, to damage and diminish the system as a whole. Such formal correctness does not obtain in halakhic reasoning, and no "method," however diligently followed, can achieve it.

Between *Halakhah* and Meta-*Halakhah*

One might at this point object that the evidence I have presented does not support the broad, "across-the-board" statement I make in the preceding paragraph. One might say that the dispute between the Zionist halakhists and their opponents is so totally attributable to clashing ideologies as to render the *machloket* an exceptional case that teaches us little or nothing about halakhic thought and practice in general. Professor Marc B. Shapiro makes precisely this observation:

> Zionist rabbis author responsa showing how one must live in Israel, serve in the army, say Hallel on Yom Ha-Atsma'ut. Non- and anti-Zionist rabbis write halakhic treatises proving the exact opposite. Often, both sides claim to be approaching the sources with objectivity, but it is clear to the outside observer that this is not the case. . . . These *poskim* are building a halakhic decision in large point upon ideology and not *vice versa*. . . . [With regard to more extreme examples of this sort of writing] many would assert what we are dealing with is simply propaganda masquerading as halakhic discourse.[49]

To Shapiro, "what we are dealing with" is a dispute so fundamentally ideological that it cannot truly be regarded as a matter of *halakhah* at all. Although each side expresses its ideology in traditional halakhic language, hoping thereby to win the hearts and minds of the observant community, they are divided not so much over the meaning of legal texts as over irreconcilable issues of *weltanschauung*. If the Zionist rabbis fail to prove the halakhic correctness of their positions, that is because their positions are not in fact based upon *halakhah* but upon theological and ideological assumptions that their opponents simply do not share. It is for this reason that there is no one obviously correct answer to the question, "Can Jewish law accommodate the creation of a sovereign state in our time?" Such indeterminacy presumably would not obtain when the question under discussion is a properly halakhic one, when the conflicting points of view can be tested and judged by the accepted procedures of Jewish law. A halakhic controversy that *is* halakhic, a question that fits comfortably within the standard framework of Jewish legal discourse without touching upon divisive ideological commitments, can be solved, convincingly and correctly, through the diligent application of halakhic method. This is, on the surface, an eminently reasonable distinction. Surely, Professor Shapiro suggests, when we read halakhic responsa we can tell the difference between arguments that are halakhic and arguments that are more properly ideological or "meta-halakhic" in nature.[50] By "halakhic" factors he means the hard, textual, and formal–legal elements cited in a ruling, while "meta-halakhic" describes all those considerations, arguments, and reasons given by the *posek* that "are not subject to proof or disproof on the basis of textual sources, but depend upon an overall view of which ruling will best serve the community a view which other authorities need not share."[51] From this it follows that a rabbinical decision that rests significantly upon meta-halakhic factors is more a matter of ideology than of law, even if that decision is conveyed in a halakhic responsum and is expressed in traditional Jewish legal language. It also follows that a ruling *not* based upon meta-halakhic factors could well be determined by the operation of the objective, ideologically neutral legal method that, in the Orthodox account of things, serves to distinguish the "right" from the "wrong" halakhic answers. Yet though it be reasonable I do not accept this distinction, and I want at this point to suggest why I think that Professor Shapiro is wrong.

Professor Shapiro is wrong because his distinction between *halakhah* and meta-*halakhah* is based upon the common but erroneous identification of legal (and halakhic) discourse as a matter of rules, "definite, detailed provisions for definite, detailed states of fact,"[52] abstract or general statements of what the law permits or requires of classes of persons or things in classes of circumstances.[53] Rules tend to be statements of black-letter law that we look up in codes and apply in a formal, mechanical, and quasi-mathematical fashion[54] to a specific set of facts: if the facts the rule stipulates are given, and if the rule itself is valid, then there is no recourse but to accept the answer it supplies.[55] Examples of rules in the *halakhah* include: that the flesh of a pig is forbidden for consumption; that two witnesses are required to establish proof in a Jewish court;[56] and that one who inadvertently breaks a pitcher that was left lying in the public thoroughfare is exempt from liability.[57] It is quite easy to tell the difference between a legal rule and some other, less definitive statement in a legal text. Were law to consist entirely of rules, as some scholars indeed suggest,[58] then it would be relatively easy to distinguish between "legal" and "nonlegal" elements of judicial decision making: any statement by a judge that does not conform to or apply a legal rule would by definition be a statement of nonlaw, "meta-law," or at least something other than "law."[59]

Yet law cannot be reduced to rules and their logical application. Rules must be applied to cases or questions, specific instances of reality for which a legal response is sought. It is the job of the judge or decision maker to determine the legal rule that best fits the circumstances of the case or question. This, however, is no simple task. Even when it is clear to legal observers that a particular rule disposes of a case, it may be far from obvious just how the rule is to be applied. To take a famous example:[60] suppose there is a law that forbids a person from taking a vehicle into a public park. This prohibition would seem clearly to forbid the entrance of automobiles into the park. Does it apply as well to bicycles, roller skates, or toy automobiles? What about a military truck placed on a pedestal as a memorial to the soldiers who fought in the last war? The rule does not simply and obviously answer any of these questions. The judge called upon to decide this case will have to interpret the rule to make it yield an answer.[61] Consider a well-known rule of Jewish law: the Torah disqualifies the "wicked" person (*rasha*) from serving as a witness, and those who habitually violate the Torah's commandments are customarily defined as "wicked."[62] Question: in the opinion of Orthodox jurists, does the exclusion enunciated in this rule apply to Jews in our day who for a variety of reasons do not adhere to an Orthodox standard of religious observance? Many Orthodox authorities disqualify non-Orthodox Jews from serving as witnesses at weddings on precisely these grounds. On the other hand, a 1946 ruling by the Supreme Rabbinical Court of *Eretz Yisrael* accepts the testimony of nonobservant Jews and therefore recognizes the halakhic validity of weddings at which they served as witnesses.[63] The judges reason that the prohibition is rooted in the concern that one who violates any of the Torah's commandments is likely to bear false witness before the court; this concern, they say, does not apply in an age of widespread nonobservance of Jewish ritual law. In this nonreligious age we can easily conceive of the possibility that a Jew might violate the laws of Shabbat or *kashrut* and yet be an honest person who would tell the truth as a matter of ethical behavior. A nonobservant Jew is therefore not necessarily "wicked" in the Torah's definition; thus, courts may decide on a case-by-case basis whether he is sufficiently trustworthy to accept his testimony. Our purpose here is not to consider the extent to which this decision, which departs from the conventional approach to the question among most Orthodox *poskim*, might influence the actual course of development of Jewish law.[64] It suffices to point out that although a clear rule of Jewish law prohibits a "wicked" person from serving as a witness, the two trends of *pesak* - to accept or reject the testimony of a ritually nonobservant Jew - divide sharply over the very meaning of the word *rasha*, over the application of that legal category to the circumstances of contemporary Jewish life. That application requires a judgment about the nature and purpose of the rule, a judgment that, although necessary to decide the law, is not itself dictated by the law. To put this differently, no rule or text can control its own interpretation; "the language of a rule does not itself determine whether many particular cases come within the class of cases designated by the rule."[65] The judge has no recourse but to choose an interpretation from among the available alternatives, and that choice, because it is absolutely essential to the process of legal decision, is as much a part of the law as is the rule the judge must interpret.

A second reason why law is not exclusively a function of rules is that even when the definition and circumference of a particular rule are tolerably clear, it may not be certain whether *that* rule or an alternative rule is the one that fits the facts of the case. In such an instance, because the competing rules do not by themselves determine their application,[66] the judge must choose between them. An example of this phenomenon in Orthodox jurisprudence is the question of the halakhic validity of marriages between Jews solemnized in the civil courts or in a Reform synagogue. One approach denies any validity whatsoever to these wedding ceremonies, on the grounds that they do not conform to the rules that define the contracting of Jewish marriage (*kiddushin*).[67] A conflicting approach recognizes these ceremonies as halakhically valid, not because the *halakhah* approves of civil marriage or Reform Judaism per se, but because the rule of common–knowledge testimony (*anan sahadei*, "we are witnesses") establishes the evident desire of the Jewish couple to live together legally as husband and wife, and that desire is sufficient evidence to the intent to form a valid Jewish marriage.[68] The Orthodox halakhist may utilize either of these two sets of rules to define the marital status of the couple. Each set is thoroughly steeped in halakhic doctrine; neither is more obviously "right" than the other. The *posek* must choose between them. It is a fateful choice indeed, for it will determine whether either spouse requires a *get* prior to remarriage. But it *is* a choice, a decision that the rules themselves do not dictate in advance.

A third reason why law cannot be understood simply as a system of rules is that judicial decision rests upon other sources of law much less precise and objective than rules. Among these other sources are legal *principles*, "general premises for judicial and juristic reasoning."[69] A principle is "a standard to be observed, not because it will advance or secure an economic, political, or social situation deemed desirable, but because it is a requirement of justice or fairness or some other dimension of morality."[70] A principle differs from a rule in that it offers a reason for a decision but does not necessitate that decision. Principles do not *require* that judges decide cases in a particular way, because there may be other principles in the law that would support a different outcome. The judge in each case must first determine whether a principle applies and then weigh the relative importance of that principle against other principles that would argue for a different outcome. Take, for example, the well-known American case *Riggs v. Palmer*,[71] in which the court ruled that a man named as the heir in his grandfather's will could not inherit under that will because he had murdered his grandfather in order to do so. The court defended its ruling on the basis of the principle that "no one shall be permitted to take advantage of his own wrong." While this was certainly a good reason on which to found the decision, it did not obligate the court to reach that finding. Other principles, such as the need to establish a clear title, or to enforce the stated will of the testator, or to refrain from inflicting punishments beyond those stipulated by the legislature, argued in favor of the opposite decision. An example of conflicting principles in Jewish law can be discerned in halakhic practice with respect to the *agunah*, the woman unable to remarry due to her husband's disappearance or his inability or refusal to grant her a divorce. On the one hand, the sources enunciate the principle that it is a *mitzvah* to search for every possible leniency in the law in order to release the unfortunate *agunah* from her plight. On the other hand, the serious consequences that would result if a legally married woman were permitted to remarry she would be committing adultery, and her children by her subsequent husband would be *mamzerim* induce many authorities to invoke a competing principle, namely that a *posek* must assume a posture of conservatism and caution in matters of marital status and not support a leniency unless he is absolutely sure it is warranted by settled *halakhah*.[72] Here, too, valid principles can be invoked by the legal authority to support two very different rulings on the case in question. The judge will have to choose between them, and this choice may depend as much if not more upon "background" factors the judge's ethical and social values, perhaps as upon more technically legal ones.

The final reason why law cannot be reduced to the application of rules is that judicial decisions inevitably depend upon and cannot be made in isolation from the very sorts of "metalegal" factors that Professor Shapiro wishes to distinguish from the more purely legal aspects of *pesak*. My point is that, in practice, "meta-*halakhah*" simply cannot be distinguished from "*halakhah*." This is not to say that some of the source materials that judges and rabbis cite in their rulings are less formally "lawlike" than others. It is to say simply that *all* of these sources are essential to the making of what is ultimately a *legal* ruling, a *halakhic* decision. During the past century and more, legal scholarship has fairly well demolished the ideal of *elegantia juris*, the notion that law is best characterized as a system displaying formal logical integrity,[73] in favor of a conception that includes political, social, and moral commitments within the disciplinary confines of law. The "legal realism" movement that flourished in American jurisprudence during the first half of the twentieth century taught that the true motivations of law's development lay not in its formal, inner logic but in its social, economic, and political context. A judicial decision, in other words, owes as much if not more to the judge's *Weltanschauung* as it does to the more purely technical, "objective" (*wertfrei*) legal factors mentioned in the opinion.[74] Prominent jurists began to recognize that social values play a vital and inevitable role in the judicial function. Benjamin Cardozo gave this idea its classic literary formulation in his description of how a judge actually decides cases:[75]

> The final cause of law is the welfare of society. The rule that misses its aim cannot permanently justify its existence. . . . Logic and history and custom have their place. We will shape the law to conform to them when we may; but only within bounds. The end which the law serves will dominate them all. There is an old legend that on one occasion God prayed, and his prayer was "Be it my will that my justice be ruled by my mercy."[76] That is a prayer which we all need to utter at times when the demon of formalism tempts the intellect with the lure of scientific order. I do not mean, of course, that judges

> are commissioned to set aside existing rules at pleasure in favor of any other set of rules which they may hold to be expedient or wise. I mean that when they are called upon to say how far existing rules are to be extended or restricted, they must let the welfare of society fix the path, its direction and its distance.

The conception of the welfare of society - what Shapiro calls "an overall view of which ruling will best serve the community" - is therefore not an extralegal factor at all. It serves along with such "legal" elements as logic, history, and custom as one of "the directive forces of our law."[77] Indeed, it is the most decisive of these forces, for "when the social needs demand one settlement rather than another, there are times when we must bend symmetry, ignore history and sacrifice custom in the pursuit of other and larger ends."[78] As Justice Haim Cohn summarizes Cardozo's view:

> Culture, ethics, sociology, and economics are not to be defined as "poor cousins standing at the threshold" of "law." Rules and statutes are nothing other than the mirror in which law finds its reflection; its substance and essence are hidden from view. All these disciplines enter law's domain and are absorbed by it, to a greater or lesser extent. They are not distant relatives; they are the flesh of our flesh.[79]

We find much the same contention, though applied to a much broader canvas of human experience, in Robert Cover's famous declaration that law can never be understood in isolation from its normative context and setting:[80]

> We inhabit a *nomos* – a normative universe. We constantly create and maintain a world of right and wrong, of lawful and unlawful, of valid and void. The student of law may come to identify the normative world with the professional paraphernalia of social control. The rules and principles of justice, the formal institutions of the law, and the conventions of a social order are, indeed, important to that world; they are, however, but a small part of the normative universe that ought to claim our attention. No set of legal institutions or prescriptions exists apart from the narratives that locate it and give it meaning. For every constitution there is an epic, for every decalogue a scripture. Once understood in the context of the narratives that give it meaning, law becomes not merely a system of rules to be observed, but a world in which we live. In this normative world, law and narrative are inseparably related. Every prescription is insistent in its demand to be

> located in discourse – to be supplied with history and destiny, explanation and purpose. . . . (P)rescription, even when embodied in a legal text, [cannot] escape its origin and its end in experience, in the narratives that are the trajectories plotted upon material reality by our imaginations.

Our normative commitments determine how we interpret and apply law's "rules and formal institutions"; the narratives that supply law's purpose tell us what the law is. In this sense, it is futile to draw firm methodical boundaries between law and meta-law. These insights speak just as directly to the Jewish legal process. All the elements cited in a rabbinical responsum, the "nonlegal" as well as the "legal," are "halakhic" in that they function to support and justify the halakhic conclusion. Both are integral and essential to the process of *pesak*, because *pesak* does not and cannot take place without them. A judgment of "which view will better serve the community" may in fact be a subject of controversy, but take away that meta-halakhic judgment and you knock the legs out from under the legal decision itself.

This point is as crucial as it is banal: halakhic decision does not take place in an ideological vacuum. The point is crucial in that, as I have argued, one cannot account for the halakhic decision of a *posek* without taking into account the fundamental value commitments that constitute his religious, intellectual, and cultural worldview. The point is banal in that it has been made by many others, many times.[81] With respect to our own subject, at any rate, Mizrachi activists[82] clearly and openly recognized that the halakhic differences between them and their opponents resulted from the ideological divide that separated the two camps. The "correct" halakhic decision on matters of *hilkhot medinah* depends in large part upon the rabbi's normative commitments and their supporting "narrative," his sympathy for Zionism or his rejection of it. The Zionist halakhists and their opponents read the same Talmudic and halakhic sources that speak to issues of politics, government, and national economy, but they approach these legal texts on the basis of very different narrative structures that each group applies to the facts of contemporary Jewish history. One group sees in the progress of the Zionist movement the beginning of the fulfillment of God's promise of redemption to the Jewish people.[83] The other group tells a very different story about the work of the Zionist activists and settlers, a story that stigmatizes their efforts as an arrogant forcing of God's hand, an unwarranted hastening of the divine timetable of salvation.[84] These narratives do differ in form from the formal halakhic citations – the rules, principles, and precedents – that fill the writings of these rabbis. "Narrative" is the translation we often give to the term *aggadah*, which we tend to distinguish from *halakhah*. Yet the halakhic conclusions that these writings advance would be incoherent (if they could be formulated at all) in the absence of the normative commitments that the agadic narratives express. Call those normative commitments by any other name: ideology, theology, politics; they are necessarily and inescapably *halakhic* all the same.[85]

Responsa are for that reason *halakhic*, not "ideological" documents, even when the motivating factor behind the rabbinical decision seems to be something other than law in the pure and narrow sense. As against Shapiro, I would view rabbinical legal discourse as an integrated experience of language and argument, a way of thinking and of talking that comprises any and all intellectual elements that rabbis utilize in their journey toward *pesak*. Since the ruling ultimately rests upon all these elements, the meta-halakhic as well as the halakhic, no essential distinction can be drawn between them. True, Shapiro's "outside observer" might perceive such a distinction. To such a reader, rabbinical disputes over governmental and political issues might better be classified as examples of *da'at torah*, expressions of the rabbis' social and political ideology, rather than as instances of *pesak halakhah*.[86] Yet responsa are written not by outside observers but by scholars who stand *within* the conceptual world of *halakhah*. And in our case, those insiders, those practitioners of rabbinical legal discourse, present their work as *berur halakhah*, Jewish legal analysis; they do *not* refer to what they are doing as ideology, *weltanschauung*, or *da'at torah*. These rabbis could, of course, be wrong, but I do not know why we should regard the outsider's definition of their activity as more convincing than their own.

Halakhah as a Social Practice

To summarize thus far: I have argued against the contention that liberal *halakhah* is an incorrect and invalid understanding of the tradition of Jewish law. This is so because in order to sustain that judgment, those who make it must demonstrate the existence of a set of formulaic criteria – some sort of method – by which to measure the objective correctness or incorrectness of any particular interpretation of the *halakhah*. The controversy over the Zionist halakhic tradition shows that such a method does not exist: neither side in that dispute could convince the other of the correctness of its legal viewpoint through the application of the formal procedures of halakhic analysis. The irreconcilability of that disagreement is no unique or exceptional case, because law and legal decision in general cannot be reduced to the application of a system of hard and fast rules. Before they can reach their answers, judges must define the terms of the rules; they must decide which of several alternative rules covers the case; and they will frequently resort to other legal sources such as principles that are much less specific than rules. All of these moves involve acts of judicial choice that cannot be determined by the formal rules of law. Rather, they are determined by the so-called metalegal factors that function as the inevitable and necessary context for all legal decision making. For these reasons, "method" cannot define or establish the correctness of any statement of law or *halakhah*. And for *that* reason, Orthodox halakhists cannot summarily reject our work as an incorrect or invalid understanding of Jewish law.

At this point, the reader might well sniff an aroma of relativism wafting from my argument. If halakhic decision making is inevitably grounded in an act of rabbinical choice among alternative outcomes, and if that choice is not determined by a value-neutral halakhic method, then *halakhah* is nothing more than the will of the *posek* (his "will" in the sense that the choice depends upon his own moral and cultural proclivities, his subjective sense of "which view will better serve the community"). Yet we tend to think of *halakhah*, as of law in general, as something other than the judge's will, as something other than politics or ethics or economics; in short, the law "is claimed to be its own thing and not entirely reducible to anything else."[87] Law, precisely because it "wishes to have a formal existence," demands its own rules and procedures by which it can speak in its own unique language and arrive at its conclusions in its own autonomous fashion.[88] This is the sense in which legal method understands itself as "value-neutral": "the law is an order, and therefore all legal problems must be set and solved as order problems. In this way legal theory becomes an exact structural analysis of positive law, free of all ethical - political value judgments."[89] This is not to imply that legal decision is a purely mechanical affair in which the judge, in oracular fashion,[90] pronounces the ruling that is dictated by the controlling forces of law's immanent logic. Law is not mathematics or a "hard" science.. As with any activity that demands interpretation, the determination of legal meaning cannot aspire to the clear-cut correctness that is the outcome of a syllogism or an equation. The formality of law *does* mean, however, that the act of interpretation is constrained by means of the "disciplining rules" of legal analysis that, by directing the judge's inquiry along the proper path, insure that his decision is objectively correct.[91] Such a formal approach safeguards the rule of law, which holds that decision makers should wield power in a community not in accordance with personal whim or even with deeply held personal conviction but with previously agreed upon rules and standards.[92] Law is law, and nothing other than law. To say otherwise, to deny law its status as a self-authenticating process, is to herald "the death of the law" by assimilating it into some other discipline or disciplines.[93] And if this is so, then we have entered the universe of

legal relativism, a situation in which, as a matte[r ...]
the activity of judging, or of *pesak*, is not co[...]
and is nothing more than the ad hoc, unprinci[pled ...]
judge's subjective value commitments, be t[hey ...]
emotion, or "gut reasoning."[94] For all these reasons, the reader might conclude, it would be inaccurate (not to say disastrous) to reject the concept of method as definitive of the legal process.

I agree with almost everything stated in the preceding paragraph. To me, no less than to the reader to whom I impute these sentiments, "law" makes no sense if we cannot understand it as an autonomous discipline that, no matter how much it draws upon or shares in common with other bodies of thought, operates by its own procedures. Judicial decision accordingly must be constrained by the boundaries that law – and no other discipline – sets. A judge is a "judge" by virtue of the fact that her ruling is not simply her own opinion as to what ought to be but rather a *judgment*, an interpretation of legal doctrine made by a legal professional and its application to the case at hand. Judges, as far as I am aware, do not regard themselves as free to render whatever decisions they wish but as bound by their duty to rule in accordance with the law. *Poskim* similarly express a clear sense of the limits under which they work: the Torah and the *halakhah* constrain them to rule correctly, even when they would wish for a different outcome.[95] All this is an essentially persuasive account of legal and halakhic process. Yet from the fact that law constrains (or ought to constrain) the freedom of the decision maker, it does not necessarily follow that there exists a method that imposes this constraint in an objective way, serving as a barometer of legal correctness, as the formula by which the judge or *posek* can arrive at the "one right answer" to a question of law or *halakhah*. Legal decision, as I have indicated above, does not take place in a value-free zone or outside of an ideological context. The key fact here is judicial *choice*: judges and *poskim* are constantly confronted with plausible alternative interpretations and applications of legal rules and principles. They must choose the better or best of the available alternatives, and there is no "method" that can determine for them the right choice in a non controversial way.

This argument, which I have framed in language specific to legal theory and *halakhah*, stands firmly within a much more general "critique of methodology," a term that comprehends the contemporary intellectual "attack on the claims of objectivity that have been advanced by a broad range of academic disciplines."[96] I cannot, within the confines of this essay, begin to do justice to this broad and deep trend in academic and professional thought and to the many thinkers who have contributed to it.[97] I would only say that the critique is a reaction against the "Enlightenment project," the effort undertaken by thinkers during the past three centuries to locate rational bases for human inquiry.[98] According to that conception, objective knowledge – that is, knowledge based upon reason alone, untainted by appeals to authority, prejudice, or tradition – is attainable by the human mind. The goal of philosophy, and by extension all intellectual disciplines, is to discover the proper method by which to attain it, by which to distinguish real and objective knowledge from mere opinion. This method presupposes the existence of *foundations*, of matrices, contexts, or categorical schemes that function as the basis of all knowledge. These foundations are the permanent, ahistorical, culturally neutral, and value-free grounding for all claims of knowledge and truth. All thought, evidence, or argument proceeds from these foundations, appeals to them, and is judged by them. A method is therefore a set of techniques that discovers information and tests it against the foundations that, within a particular form of inquiry, serve as the indices of truth and objective knowledge.[99] Such foundations underlie a variety of approaches in modern legal theory, from the conceptualist "orthodoxy" of Christopher Columbus Langdell,[100] through the writings of the natural law thinkers,[101] to the analyses of the legal positivists.[102] As divided as these approaches may be on fundamental issues, they are as one in their contention that true and objectively correct legal knowledge can be attained through the application of the proper method of study.

The "critique of methodology" (or "antifoundationalism"[103]) is a pervasive skepticism about the existence of self-evident foundations of knowledge that are not contingent upon human experience.[104] According to this critique, questions of fact, truth, validity, and correctness cannot be answered by any ahistorical, noncontextual, or noncontroversial set of facts or rules. All human knowledge is situated within the social and historical circumstances of particular communities. Our very perception of reality is conditioned by thought processes that we have developed through our participation in human culture and community. It follows that our modes of inquiry, the ways in which we seek out and determine the truth, are themselves products of the same circumstances: "the problems people perceive, the categories they establish, the hypotheses they generate, the methodologies they employ, the arguments they use, and the criteria of validity they accept are all specific choices, made in the midst of history, as part of ongoing intellectual traditions."[105] The implication for all forms of human inquiry is that there exists no "method" based in a value-free rationality that can serve as the index to objective knowledge. Many of the trends and "movements" within legal theory during the past century have proceeded from this sort of critique. For all the differences that separate them, the scholars associated with these schools of thought recognized that legal decision is rendered by judges who are inevitably rooted within the culturally contingent *loci* of particular legal communities. Exemplary of this trend are the legal pragmatists, those theorists who

> reject the notion that there is a universal, rational foundation for legal judgment. Judges do not, in their view, inhabit a lofty perspective that yields an objective vision of the case and its correct disposition. Instead, these scholars understand the role of judging more pragmatically; they recognize that all judges bring their own situated perspectives to the case and do the

best they can under all the circumstances to reach a fair and just disposition.[106]

A glance at the literature reveals that virtually all contemporary legal theorists have abandoned the excesses of the formalist past in favor of a more realistic, pragmatic conception of the process of judicial decision making.[107] The account I have rendered here of the ideologically centered nature of *pesak* and the inevitability of rabbinical-judicial choice between available alternatives fits firmly within this trend.

But if "foundationalism" is dead, what is to protect us from relativism and even nihilism in disciplines such as law? Where are the constraints upon judicial discretion? Is the law in fact whatever the judge or judges say it is? In the absence of objective, nonideological, and noncontextual reference points against which to measure our knowledge, are we not forced to conclude that "anything goes," that our decisions and judgments are based upon nothing more solid than beliefs and opinions that cannot be adjudicated in any rational way? This dichotomy between objectivism and subjectivism, between "knowledge" and "opinion," has of course been raging ever since Socrates battled the Sophists, and the Platonic literary record of that debate leaves us in no doubt that the former prevailed over the latter. Yet it is just possible that the Sophists have gotten a bum rap, that they were not suggesting that statements of truth in the spheres of politics, ethics, and law were based on nothing more than taste and mere opinion. Not a few contemporary observers have concluded that the Sophists in fact offered a middle ground, one that, though located through rhetoric and persuasive discourse rather than through "philosophy" and scientific proof, rescues us from the clutches of that false dichotomy.[108] A similar observation can be made concerning the obsession with method that characterizes much of modern philosophy: perhaps we are dealing here with the "Cartesian anxiety," the fear that "unless we can ground philosophy, knowledge, or language in a rigorous manner we cannot avoid radical skepticism."[109] Again, many theorists locate a middle ground between these two poles in the form of *praxis*, or what we might call situated knowledge. The starting points of our reasoning are contingent, rooted in our cultural traditions, the product of "our heritage from, and our conversation with our fellow-humans."[110] An intellectual discipline, an organized way in which we seek to gain knowledge, is therefore a *communal* (as opposed to an objectively rational) enterprise. It "is not a body of objective information, or a set of techniques for discovering such information, but a practice; a system of socially constituted modes of argument shared by a community of scholars."[111] Inquiry, in this view, is more rhetorical than logical, proceeding and succeeding by way of a conversation carried on among practitioners, a persuasive argument addressed to a particular historically and culturally situated audience. The "critique of methodology," in other words, is much more than the critique of rationality; it is a broad-based effort to identify a different *kind* of rationality, one that is rooted within communities of interpretation and practice, a rationality that tests its propositions through rhetoric and argument rather than through "a Method claiming neutrality and universality."[112] The goal of inquiry is to prove its propositions through "normal discourse,"[113] the attainment of consensus by way of a conversation among practitioners. "Truth" is conceived in "intersubjective" rather than in "objective" terms, and it is measured in the extent to which communities of interpretation and practice gather around and give assent to propositions. Is consensus a sufficient guarantee against radical skepticism? It certainly would not suffice for a Descartes or a Kant or the logical positivists. Yet more and more thinkers are coming to the conclusion that its very rootedness within community is the guarantee that inquiry will not degenerate into pure subjectivism or irrationality. When even the so called "hard" sciences, hardly bastions of irrationality, have now been described as communities of practice in which argument and conversation assume a major role in determining truth,[114] it would seem that we need not fear that we are standing over the abyss of nihilism.

How does this approach to rationality apply to law? It begins by envisioning law as a community of interpretation and practice. As I have noted, legal theorists of widely divergent political views have rejected foundationalism, the notion that legal reasoning is a value free, neutral method that stands apart from the practice of law in order to render an objective critique of the work and writings of legal actors. Legal reasoning is rather embedded *within* the practices and the culture of specific legal communities; it is the name we give to the cluster of techniques, conventions, and traditions that describe what lawyers do and thus comprise the craft of law.[115] This turn in jurisprudential thought draws heavily upon numerous and diverse sources: the writings of the pragmatic philosophers,[116] Ludwig Wittgenstein,[117] and the scholars identified with philosophical hermeneutics[118] and in the contemporary "recovery of rhetoric."[119] It is committed to the proposition that law is a social practice or, to put it differently, a language, a set of texts and of ways of arguing about their meaning that is the vernacular of a particular legal community.[120] To understand law in this way allows one to concede that legal truth is, when tested against the standard of objective, philosophical certainty, radically indeterminate. Good arguments can usually be made for either side of a contested point of law, so that a firm and sure perception of "truth" is well-nigh unattainable.[121] Thus, while jurists might well approach their work on the faith that there does exist "one right answer" to any particular legal question, that answer cannot be identified with anything approaching absolute certainty.[122] Yet the very nature of law as a language or social practice preserves it from the acids of indeterminacy and radical skepticism. Legal decision may well involve choices among alternatives, but lawyers and judges are not free to rule arbitrarily, to impose any choice they wish. The choice may not be determined by the law's rules and principles; it is directed, nonetheless, by the fact that lawyers and judges make that choice *as* lawyers and judges. This means, first and foremost, that they approach the work of interpretation in a communal way, as members of a profession who must account for their views before an audience of fellow practitioners. They are the participants in a tradition of craft and techniques such as practical reasoning[123] that, learned and internalized by lawyers, teach them how to approach the rules and principles in a manner recognizable to their fellow practitioners and guide their understanding of doctrine and of the "leeways" it permits. In this way, "law" does constrain the freedom of decision makers: not through any restrictive power of its rules and principles but through its embodiment as a social practice that guarantees the predictability of legal decision.[124]

Like law in general, *halakhah* is a species of practice, an endeavor that is always *situated* within a particular community of legal interpretation. *Pesak* is therefore not a science but a craft, the conversation of a self-identified community of practitioners, the accumulated set of interpretive techniques and assumptions that allow each practitioner to gain a "situation sense"[125] of what sorts of rulings and claims of meaning will be acceptable or unacceptable in the eyes of his colleagues. It is useless to speak of a halakhic "method" if by that we mean a set of rules or criteria to evaluate in an objective way the correctness of a particular halakhic decision or line of decisions. To perform that function, any such rule would have to exist separate and apart from the practice of *halakhah* itself in a noninterpreted fashion: that is, all practitioners of *halakhah* would have to agree upon its precise meaning, and circumference. Yet as we have seen, rules do not work this way in law and in *halakhah*. Rules are constantly being interpreted by lawyers and judges in the course of their work. Rules do not "mean" anything until they are applied to the facts and circumstances of the particular question, and every act of application reshapes, modifies, and transforms the meaning of the rule; thus, the language of a rule does not define its own application.[126] In short, there is no objective methodological basis on which to judge the work of a practice; any and all standards of judgment are exercised by the practitioners themselves in the course of their work.

If there is no such "method" external to halakhic practice by which to determine the correctness of a halakhic decision, does this mean that there is no such thing as a "wrong" decision? Are there no constraints upon what a *posek* might say in the name of Torah and *halakhah*? Not at all. There *are* constraints, and powerful ones, too, that severely hem in the range of rabbinical discretion. Like the judge (and, for that matter, like the participant in any other intellectual practice), the *posek* is constrained because he speaks and writes from within a particular community of practitioners. He is not free to say whatever he wishes, not because he is constrained by "foundations" or formal criteria of halakhic validity, but because he must address himself and his words to that community in a language that they will understand as the discourse of their practice. His ruling is an argument rehearsed before a particular audience composed of scholars who share his "situation sense" as to what constitutes acceptable halakhic argumentation. His interpretation is "correct" to the extent that it secures the adherence of that audience, that it persuades them to form a community around his words, that it brings them to interpret Torah and *halakhah* in the way that he reads them. It is this situatedness, the fact that the *posek* must speak in a professional discourse that defines a particular community of practice, that places real limits upon his discretion. The proper term to apply to this process is "rhetoric," not "method." If we insist upon using the term "halakhic method," it can only mean the discourse and the rhetoric of the halakhic community. It will and must operate as part of the language and experience of textual analysis and argument. It will always be interpreted and modified as it is applied; thus, it cannot control its own application. Such a "method" is not a formula that declares in some objective, *a priori* way what halakhists ought to do. It is no more and no less than a description of what halakhists do in fact.

If halakhic practice always takes place within a *particular* community of interpretation, we should not be surprised that very different sorts of interpretation and consensus will emerge from different halakhic communities. We have seen that the Zionist halakhists and their Orthodox opponents operate on the basis of fundamentally different sets of assumptions as to how the Jewish legal tradition speaks to the question of sovereignty and statehood. When Rabbi Shaul Yisraeli writes in such evident frustration that "we will not debate with" the anti-Zionists, he is merely affirming that on these issues the two groups comprise separate and distinct interpretive communities, so that further discussion is pointless. Lacking the common definitions and professional discourse that are the *sine qua non* for productive argument, neither side can hope to persuade the other of the rightness of its own view. The two communities cannot resolve their disagreements by appeal to a "metaprinciple," a value neutral halakhic method that adjudicates impartially between their competing interpretations. Again, no such method exists, for any decision-making rule can function only *within* the practice of a particular halakhic community, as part of the shared assumptions and techniques that direct the conversation of its practitioners. As it is, the failure of the two groups to arrive at a common discourse is evidence of the absence of any sort of method for determining objectively correct answers.

For similar reasons, we should not be surprised at the continuing Orthodox rejection (to which I alluded at the beginning of this paper) of the ideas and insights put forward by liberal halakhists. Keep in mind that liberal halakhic writers present their interpretations, which cover such matters as liturgical practice, the role of women in synagogue ritual, Shabbat and festival observance, *kashrut*, marriage and divorce law, and more, in standard halakhic terminology. Well supported by text citation and analysis, these liberal responsa are framed in what looks and sounds like traditional halakhic discourse; in other words, they discuss the same questions and read the same texts as those found in Orthodox responsa on the subjects at hand. Yet none of this seems to matter to Orthodox rabbis, who simply ignore liberal responsa, something they would never do to the responsa of other Orthodox rabbis with whom they disagree. Liberal halakhic opinions are never cited in Orthodox legal discourse, except when the goal of the particular Orthodox writer is to demonstrate the heresy of the liberals and to prevent misguided members of his own community from drawing the conclusion that such ideas *might* be valid *halakhah*.[127] Some liberal halakhists, unwilling to take "no" for an answer, do try to argue their way into Orthodox halakhic conversation. They will contend that their responsa are examples of "kosher" *halakhah* because they meet the formal test of halakhic validity: that is, they are supported by talmudic reasoning and are authored by scholars who are loyal to the halakhic system. Yet Orthodox rabbis still brand these responsa as halakhically illegitimate. The reason for this is that a "formal test for halakhic validity" is a methodological principle, intended to serve as a neutral and objective index of correctness. And as I have argued, such "method" does not exist outside of and apart from the accepted practice of a particular community of interpretation. Although Orthodox halakhists do cite formal rules and methodological principles in their writings, they do so as *Orthodox* rabbis. The rules and principles will always yield an "orthodox" conclusion, because they will and must be applied and determined by practitioners who see themselves as forming a distinctly *Orthodox* community of halakhic interpretation. Orthodox rabbis do not accept liberal *pesak* as a correct interpretation of Jewish law, not because some formal method constrains them to reject it, but because it is rendered by *apikorsim*, outsiders, Jews who by definition dwell outside the boundaries of *halakhah*. They cannot admit us and our ideas into their halakhic conversation and remain a self-consciously Orthodox community. No matter what we say, no matter how well we argue our positions, our words strike Orthodox ears as a foreign language, a conversation other than *halakhah*. Attempts by liberal scholars to convince Orthodox observers of the correctness of our own understandings of Jewish law are therefore doomed to fail.[128]

The Practice of Liberal *Halakhah*

All of the above applies to us, as well. Liberal *halakhah*, like the Orthodox variety, is the intellectual practice of a particular selfdefined community of interpretation. It is *our* practice, and we, its practitioners, need not seek legitimacy or validation in the eyes of another community of interpretation. Our decisions are "correct" when they satisfy *us*. Our responsibility, therefore, is to ourselves and our own practice, the same responsibility shouldered by the participants in any other intellectual discourse: we should seek to conduct our practice according to *our* own best understanding of it. I use the word "best" to imply a sense of aspiration, which is part and parcel of the activity of any intellectual practice.[129] Professionals are not as a rule content to accept any and all examples of their practice as equally valuable. On the contrary: lawyers, philosophers, literary theorists, and others tend to operate on the assumption that there are better and worse ways to practice their craft. Their discussions center upon the critical examination of the work of their colleagues, in order to determine by means of accepted intradisciplinary argument just what counts as a "good" (or "better," or "best," or "not-so-good") example of their community discourse. If liberal *halakhah* is such a discourse, a similar aspiration ought to be at work in our discussions and teaching. I begin with the assumption that we *do* have standards, that those who participate in the liberal halakhic endeavor do not do so with the idea that anything goes or that every interpretation presented in the name of "liberal *halakhah*" is as good (or as bad) as every other one. Each of us who works in the field does so according to a vision of what liberal *halakhah* is and ought to be. Though we need not seek Orthodox approval of our work, we do seek our own; we measure it according to the criteria of value that motivate us. We should at the very least strive to see that it meets our own standards of what constitutes liberal *halakhah* at its very best.

What precisely are those standards? Well, there's the rub. If I am "against method" as an objective index of halakhic correctness, I cannot offer a set of rules or criteria by which to evaluate the objective correctness of any particular piece of liberal halakhic writing. I do have my own ideas as to what constitutes liberal *halakhah* at its best,[130] but I cannot impose these as a formulaic definition of our practice or as a kind of calculus by which to evaluate "right" and "wrong" decisions. The best we can do is to say that our standards must emerge from our practice itself, the day-to-day functioning of liberal halakhic conversation by which we analyze, challenge, and ultimately strengthen each other's work. Standards of excellence or "correctness" in liberal *halakhah*, like the standards of any other rhetorical practice, are therefore fixed not by method or formula but through argument. Again, there is no method that allows us to distinguish in objective fashion between good and bad arguments.[131] The standards we apply are therefore the ones that we have, the ones that we as a community of practice determine to insist upon as the yardsticks by which to evaluate our efforts. Accordingly, a "good" example of liberal halakhic practice is a piece of writing to which we resonate and around which we coalesce as a community. An example of liberal halakhic practice can be a good one even if we do not adopt the proposal it advocates or the solution it offers. After all, *machloket*, principled disagreement, has always been a central feature of halakhic discourse.[132] The point is that a good liberal responsum makes a case that our community must take seriously, presents an argument that we as liberals *could* find convincing. A successful essay in liberal *halakhah* is one that frames and supports its conclusion whether we happen to agree with it or not – in the language of *our* community, that raises the intellectual and moral level of our discourse, and that speaks to us in a voice that we can recognize or wish to recognize as our own.[133] In other words, the standards by which we evaluate the quality of liberal halakhic thought and writing are the same sort of standards by which we evaluate the work of any other intellectual practice: they are *community* standards, the demands that those who write and read liberal halakhic literature the "producers" and "consumers" of liberal *halakhah* place upon the work we do. If we wish to raise the level of those standards, we may do so, but we can do so only through the very same process of intradisciplinary rhetoric by which we have created the standards that currently exist.

Like many other observers of the contemporary scene, I am "against method" as a way of establishing meaning in such discourses as law and *halakhah*. "Method" is a refuge, a simple and ultimately artificial formula for determining correctness that allows practitioners to marginalize their opponents while sparing themselves the hard work of argument and debate. In fact, there *is* no method, no refuge from that hard work. From this, we can derive two important lessons. The first is that the critics of liberal *halakhah*, whether to our right or to our left, have no "objective" basis upon which to declare that our halakhic teachings are incorrect. In the absence of formal halakhic method, they can declare us to be "wrong" only on the basis of argumentation that we, a distinct community of Jewish legal interpretation and practice, find persuasive and convincing. The second lesson is that we need to pay close and careful attention to the way in which we arrive at our decisions. That there is no formal halakhic method for determining objective correctness does not mean that anything goes, that any liberal halakhic idea is as good as any other. Our ideas are "right" to the extent that they pass the test of argument as imposed, understood, and practiced by our own community. Argument, when you get right down to it, is all that liberal halakhists and, for that matter, *any* halakhists – have. Yet that, if we do it right, is quite enough. Our task, like that of halakhists who form communities other than our own, is to facilitate the conduct of our argument, to make sure that it can be carried on honestly, vigorously, and respectfully, and that in pursuing it, we practitioners keep before our eyes the goal of making our practice the best that it can be. These conditions do not ensure that any one of us will win the arguments in which we participate. But they will do much to see to it that what emerges from our debate will be a result that can command our attention, our respect, and our assent.

Notes

* To Moshe Zemer, whose life in *halakhah* and in its instruction is an example for us all.

1. Moshe Zemer, *Evolving Halakhah: A Progressive Approach to Traditional Jewish Law* (Woodstock, VT: Jewish Lights Publishing, 1999). This is the translation of Rabbi Zemer's *Halakhah Shefuyah* (Tel Aviv: Devir, 1993)–i.e., a "sane" *halakhah*. In this way, he teaches us that Jewish law can remain sane or healthy only so long as it is free to respond in a positive way to the changes in outlook, technology, and social reality that occur in every age.

2. Yitzchak Englard takes a similar view of Jewish law from the perspective of academic jurisprudence: there is no "Jewish law" apart from the actual decisions of the rabbis. For discussion and critique of his position, see Bernard S. Jackson, *Modern Research in Jewish Law* (Leiden: Brill, 1980), especially the articles by Englard, Menachem Elon, and Bernard S. Jackson in that volume.

3. I use the term "method" in the sense that Edward L. Rubin uses the term "methodology." See his "The Practice and Discourse of Legal Scholarship," *Michigan Law Review* 86 (1988), 1838, n. 21: "'Methodology' means any independent, systematic set of arguments or criteria which claims to arrive at a true or accurate account of the subject matter under consideration." Rubin's "true" and "accurate" parallel my term "objective": a conclusion is "objectively" correct when its correctness can be satisfactorily determined by the application of criteria that are internal to the particular discipline, such as law or *halakhah*.

4. It is difficult to define "legal formalism" with absolute precision, since it is used in the scholarship to refer to a number of different phenomena. The common denominator that runs through all the descriptions is that legal decision is a matter of decision by rule. Formalists hold that all valid legal decision flows from a complex of authoritative legal rules that are themselves grounded in some authoritative legal principle. These rules and principles comprise a system that is sufficiently comprehensive to answer any and all questions that arise under the law; this system–the "law"--dictates the ruling of a judge in a contested case. The decision of the judge, who must rule in accordance with the "law" rather than with his or her personal predilections, takes the form of a deductive application of the rules and the principles of the relevant legal institutions. The decision is "correct" because it is determined by the workings of an objective set of techniques that constrain the judge's discretion and lead to the one right outcome; it is determined, that is, by legal method. For extensive discussion, see: Steven J. Burton, *An Introduction to Law and Legal Reasoning* (Boston: Little, Brown, 1985), 167-169; Neil Duxbury, *Patterns of American Jurisprudence* (Oxford: Clarendon Press, 1995), 10; Gary

Minda, *Postmodern Legal Movements* (New York: New York University Press, 1995), 13-16; and Robert S. Summers, *Instrumentalism and American Legal Theory* (Ithaca NY: Cornell University Press, 1982), 137*ff.*

5. Thomas C. Grey, "Langdell's Orthodoxy," *University of Pittsburgh Law Review* 45 (1983), 1-53.

6. See, in general, the works cited in note 4. The attack on formalism has assumed a number of different names: legal realism, legal skepticism, instrumentalism, legal pragmatism, critical legal theory, and others. In their more radical manifestations, these approaches conceive of "law" as nothing more than politics (or sociology, or ideology, or economics, or ethics) conducted by legal officials, so that "legal decision" as a separate and distinct mode of thought does not exist and that "law" as such does not formally constrain the choice of the decision maker. Not-so-radical versions of these approaches concede that logic and formal reasoning do play a role in law and judicial decision but that they do not dictate the outcome in some deductive or mechanical way.

7. I have lifted the title of this essay from Paul Feyerabend, *Against Method* (Revised edition. London: Verso, 1988). Feyerabend claims that the scientific method, which almost everyone thinks of as the *sine qua non* of true scientific research, in fact stultifies and limits the creativity of researchers. The best results, he argues, have always been obtained by scientific "anarchists" who followed their own lights to important discoveries. Whether Feyerabend is right or wrong about the desirability of renouncing "method" in the hard sciences is a controversial subject into which I am certainly not qualified to intervene. I do think, though, that his insights apply with telling force to inquiry in the social sciences, humanities, law, and–by extension–*halakhah*.

8. On this topic, see J. David Bleich, *Contemporary Halakhic Problems, Volume 3* (New York: Ktav/Yeshiva, 1989), 91, at note 6; Joel Roth, *The Halakhic Process: A Systemic Analysis* (New York: Jewish Theological Seminary, 1986), 71-74; and Mark Washofsky, "Responsa and the Art of Writing," in Peter S. Knobel and Mark N. Staitman, eds., *An American Rabbinate: A Festschrift for Walter Jacob* (Pittsburgh: Rodef Shalom Press, 2000), at 175-177.

9. *Hagufa kashya*: the term "Zionist *halakhah*" may seem to embody an internal contradiction. *Halakhah*, after all, symbolizes the old, established forms of Jewish life and behavior, while Zionism constituted a veritable revolution in Jewish self-definition. (That Zionism is legitimately described as a "revolution" is a commonplace in Zionist thought and historiography. See Arthur Hertzberg, ed., *The Zionist Idea* [New York: Atheneum, 1975], 16; Shelomo Avineri, *Hara`ayon Hatziyoni Legevanav* [Tel Aviv: Am Oved, 1985], 13-24; and David Vital, *Hamahapechah Hatziyonit*, vols. 1-3 [Tel Aviv: Am Oved, 1978-1991]. Yet is should be recalled that "Orthodox Zionism," the movement from which these halakhic writings gushed forth, was also a revolutionary departure from much traditional Jewish religious thought and experience. There is, of course, a wealth of literature on the history and ideology of Orthodox Zionism. See, in general, Yosef Tirosh: *Religious Zionism: An Anthology* (Jerusalem: World

Zionist Organization, 1975); Yosef Tirosh, *Hatziyonut Hadatit VehameDinah: Kovetz Ma'amarim* (Jerusalem: World Zionist Organization, 1978); Dov Schwartz, *Hatziyonut Hadatit Bein Higayon Lemeshichiyut* (Tel Aviv: Am Oved, 1999); and S. Almog, Y. Reinharz, and A. Shapira, eds., *Tziyonut Vedat* (Jerusalem: Mercaz Zalman Shazar, 1994).

10. For an argument that the *halakhah* as fashioned by the Rabbis is "anti-political" at its core and was therefore never intended to serve as the legal or constitutional basis for a Jewish state, see Gershon Weiler, *Teokratiah Yehudit* (Tel Aviv: Am Oved, 1976), especially at 143-160.

11. To take Maimonides' *Mishneh Torah* as tool of measurement, four out of the fourteen books that compose that code are devoted to *dinei mamonot*, that is, to property law, penal law, court procedure, and the structures of government.

12. By the "disappearance of Jewish juridical autonomy," I mean the practice that developed with the rise of the modern nation-state for the citizens of a state, Jews as well as Gentiles, to adjudicate their legal disputes in the state courts. This practice, writes Menachem Elon, brought about serious consequences for Jewish law. "Since Jewish law no longer operated within a functional legal system, its organic development was severely stunted. The harm was compounded by the fact that this historically crucial development in the evolution of Jewish law occurred at the dawn of the nineteenth century, when social, economic, and industrial revolutions were profoundly affecting the law in many fields, especially commercial and public law"; *Jewish Law: History, Sources, Principles* (Philadelphia: Jewish Publication Society, 1994), 1586.

13. See, for example, the plea that "our Rabbis instruct us" (*yelamdenu rabbeinu*), along with a detailed agenda of the halakhic problems awaiting resolution, offered by the Mizrachi theoretician S. Z. Shragai before the Tenth National Conference of Hapo'el Hamizrachi, *Din Vecheshbon* (Jerusalem, 1950), 45-55.

14. *Mishpat ivri* encompasses two broad, related-but-not-identical trends. The more "purely" academic trend applies the scholarly canons of contemporary jurisprudence and legal history (*Rechtswissenschaft* and the various theories that have succeeded it) to the study of Jewish law. The second trend reflects the desire among many, though not all, *mishpat ivri* scholars that the state of Israel adopt Jewish law to the greatest extent possible as the foundation of its legal system. See, in general, Elon, *Jewish Law* (note 12, above), as well as the essays collected in Ya'akov Bazak, *Hamishpat Ha'ivri Umedinat Yisrael* (Jerusalem: Mosad Harav Kook, 1969). For a critical, "postmodernist" reassessment of the *mishpat ivri* movement, see Assaf Likhovski, "The Invention of 'Hebrew Law' in Mandatory Palestine," *American Journal of Comparative Law* 46 (1998), 339-373.

15. Professor Zvi Zohar has announced plans to produce a monograph entitled *Halakhic Creativity in The State of Israel, 1948-1998*. In the meantime, see Mark Washofsky, "Halakhah and Political Theory: A Study in Jewish Legal Response to Modernity," *Modern Judaism*,

October, 1989, pp. 289-310. Mosheh Una, *Bederakhim Nifradot: Hamiflagot Hadatiot Beyisrael* (Gush Etziyon: Yad Shapira, 1984), 83-105, offers a good journalistic survey of the various and unsuccessful efforts by Orthodox Zionists to prepare Jewish law to serve as the legal foundation of the new state.

16. Most of Herzog's Zionist halakhic writings are collected in the posthumous three-volume collection *Techukah Leyisrael Al Pi Hatorah* (Jerusalem: Mosad Harav Kook, 1989). See also his *Pesakim Ukhetavim*, nine volumes (Jerusalem: Mosad Harav Kook, 1989), particularly volume nine, which deals with issues in *Choshen Mishpat*. Finally, we should mention his *Main Institutions of Jewish Law*, two volumes (London: Soncino, 1936), which attempts a restatement of Jewish civil and monetary law (*dinei mamonot*) and which hints at its author's desire to see the *halakhah* "updated" as part of the movement toward statehood (see v. 1, xv-xvi). Herzog's career as a halakhist is explored in B.S. Jackson, ed., *Jewish Law Association Studies V: The Halakhic Thought of R. Isaac Herzog* (Atlanta: Scholars Press, 1991) and by Itamar Warhaftig, "Rabbi Herzog's Approach to Modernity," in Moshe Sokol. Ed., *Engaging Modernity: Rabbinic Leaders and the Challenge of the Twentieth Century* (Northvale, NJ: Jason Aronson, 1997), 275-319.

17. R. Ouziel's responsa are collected in his *Mishpetei Ouziel* (Tel Aviv: 1935-1947). A selection of these responsa that speak to "contemporary issues are published as *Piskei Ouziel Beshe'elot Hazeman* (Jerusalem: Mosad Harav Kook, 1977). On R. Ouziel see: Shabbetai Don-Yechya, *Harav Benzion Meir Chai Ouziel: Chayav Umishnato* (Jerusalem: Histadrut Hatziyonit, 1955); the entry by Geulah Bat-Yehudah in *Encyclopaedia Shel Hatziyonut Hadatit* (Jerusalem: Mosad Harav Kook, 1971), 4:173-184; Chaim David Halevy, "Pesikat Hahalakhah Ve`ahavat Yisrael bemishnat R. B. Z. Ouziel," *Niv hamidrashyah* 20-21 (1978-1979), 55-69; Mark Washofsky, "Responsa and Rhetoric," in John C. Reeves and John Kampen, weds., *Pursuing the Text: Studies in Honor of Ben Zion Wacholder* (Sheffield, UK: Sheffield Academic Press, 1994), 386*ff.*

18. The Mizrachi ideologue S. Z. Shragai, reflecting upon Rabbi Ouziel's readiness to respond too all such inquiries directed to him, calls him "*hameshiv hagadol behilkhot hamedinah le'or hatorah*"; Y. Refael and S. Z. Shragai, eds., *Sefer Hatziyonut Hadatit* (Jerusalem: Mosad Harav Kook, 1977), 1:72.

19. The quotation is from A. Y. Sharir, the editor of *Harabanut Vehamedinah* (Jerusalem: Erez Publishing, 2001), a collection of Yisraeli's articles and essays. Yisraeli's responsa, rabbinical court rulings and other halakhic writings on matters relating to Jewish statehood appear in his books *Amud Hayemini* (Tel Aviv: Moreshet, 1966), *Mishpat Sha'ul* (Jerusalem: Makhon Mishpat Vehalakhah Beyisrael, 1997), and *Havat Binyamin* (Kefar Darom: Makhon Hatorah Veha'aretz, 1992). As we shall see, Yisraeli was also the editor of the Zionist halakhic journal *Hatorah Vehamedinah*.

20. Rabbi Waldenberg, perhaps best known for his multi-volume responsa collection *Tzitz Eliezer*, authored a three-volume work entitled *Hilkhot Medinah* (Jerusalem, 1952-1955). On this subject, see Mark David Strauss-Cohn, *Hilkhot Medinah: Halalkhah and The Modern State of Israel*, Rabbinical Thesis, HUC-JIR, Cincinnati, 1998.

21. At first, the journal was brought out by the Rabbinical Council of Hapo`el Hamizrachi. Eventually, the sponsorship passed to the National Religious Party and the Department for Torah Education and Culture in the Diaspora of the World Zionist Organization, with financial assistance from Mosad Harav Kook.

22. See the introductory remarks of Rabbi K. P. Techorsh in *HTM* 1 (1949), 8.

23. One who called for *takanot* was the noted Orthodox philosopher Professor Yeshayahu Leibowitz, who portrayed the *halakhah* as a Diaspora product. Jewish public law in its current form reflected the situation of a community enjoying legal autonomy while dwelling under the sovereignty of another people. As such, it was essentially silent on the requirements facing a sovereign government, and this lacuna could be filled only by means of active legislation on the part of rabbinical authorities. As his prime example, Leibowitz pointed to difficulties surrounding the observance of Shabbat in the Israeli public realm. See his *"Hashabbat Bamedinah," Beterem* no. 128 (1951), 6-15, reprinted in his *Yahadut, Am Yehudi Umedinat Yisrael* (Jerusalem: Schocken, 1975), 108-120.

24. Most prominent among those who advocated this step was the Mizrachi activist Rabbi Yehudah Leib Hakohen Maimon, author of *Chidush Hasanhedrin Bemedinateinu Hamechudeshet* (Jerusalem: Mosad Harav Kook, 1951). On this work see Lawrence Alan Bach, *"The Renewal of the Sanhedrin in Our Renewed State"*, Rabbinical Thesis, HUC-JIR, Cincinnati, 1998.

25. For example, R. Moshe Tzvi Neryah, a leading rabbinical figure in Hapo`el Hamizrachi and a leader of the Benei Akiva youth movement, rejected Leibowitz's assertion that the founding of a sovereign state posed a "crisis" for Judaism that could be addressed only by means of radical rabbinical legislation. Indeed, Neryah charged, Leibowitz's proposed changes smacked of reformist tendencies. See *"Hilkhot Shabbat Vehalikhot Hamedinah"* in *Beterem*, no. 145 (1952), 22 *ff.*

26. Elon devotes eight chapters of his *Jewish Law* (pp. 477-879) to the subject of *takanah* and suggests that the reinvigoration of this rabbinical power in our day would do much to solve some pressing halakhic problems.

27. A major exception was Rabbi Yitzchak Halevy Herzog, who sought to convince the rabbinical community to institute by way of *takanah* some fundamental changes into the traditional Jewish law of inheritance. Herzog realized that the Toraitic standard, under which daughters are excluded as heirs, could not possibly be adopted by the new state of Israel. He

also, it seems, had some ethical and practical objections of his own to imposing this particular *din torah* upon a modern society. He believed, too, that legislation might be the only effective halakhic means for responding to some of the complex social and economic problems faced by a modern state. In early 1949 Herzog circulated among the Israeli rabbinate a monograph containing his arguments for a *takanah* granting inheritance rights to daughters. Yet this exception also proves the rule I discuss in the text: the rabbinical community showed little interest in altering the established *halakhah* in such a direct fashion. See volume two of Herzog's *Techukah leyisrael*, and especially the introduction by Itimar Warhaftig, the volume's editor (11-37). Warhaftig cites the indifference of government legal authorities as an additional factor that contributed to the failure of Herzog's effort. See also the article by Ben Tzion Greenberger in Jackson, ed., *Jewish Law Association Studies V: The Halakhic Thought of R. Isaac Herzog* (note 16, above).

28. On the following, see Washofsky, note 15, above.

29. See Ket. 110b-111a for the oaths that God administered to Israel. The most detailed halakhic discussion of this tradition, which figures prominently in much Orthodox anti-Zionist polemic, is that of the Satmarer rebbe, R. Yoel Teitelbaum, in *Vayo'el moshe* (Brooklyn, 1959). It is, moreover, a tradition with considerable staying power: R. Ovadyah Yosef uses it to great effect in his ruling permitting the return of the territories occupied by Israel during the Six Day War as part of a lasting peace treaty with the Palestinians. Yosef's point is that the oaths render inoperative the commandment to seize and to possess the land of Israel; that *mitzvah* will resume its obligatory force only upon the cancellation of the oaths, which will come along with the Messiah. For R. Yosef's responsum and a rejoinder by R. Shaul Yisraeli, see *Techumin* 10 (1989), 34-61.

30. See the response of R. Yitzchak Halevy Herzog, printed posthumously in *Techumin* 4 (1983), 13-23, and in his *Techukah Leyisrael*, 1:121-133.

31. The *hidush* is found in Kook's responsum *Mishpat Kohen*, no.144, section 14.

32. Yisraeli builds upon these ideas in his *Amud Hayemini* (note 19, above), chapters 7-9.

33. Ouziel refers to a *baraita* in Sotah 22a, which declares: "*tanaim* are destroyers of the world." The amora Ravina applies this saying to those who specialized in the memorization of Tanaitic literature so that they might "recite" it for the benefit of the scholars in the Babylonian *yeshivot* (hence the title *tanaim*, which means, literally, "those who recite from memory"). Why are these *tanaim* called "destroyers?" Because, says Ravina, "they issue halakhic rulings directly from their *mishnah*," by rote citation of the sources they have memorized. In so doing, they "err, because they do not know the reason behind that *mishnah*" or that the later tradition has interpreted it in a particular way; see Rashi, *Sotah* 22a, *s.v. shemorin halakhah mitokh mishnatan*.

34. *Sifrei Devarim*, ch. 306 to Deut. 32:2.

35. Ouziel cites here the words of R. Asher b. Yechiel (*Hilkhot Harosh, Sanhedrin* 4:6), who affirms the right of the halakhist who knows the law to decide on the basis of that knowledge, "even though some other sage has ruled differently."

36. *Hadash asur min hatorah* is a pun on *M.* Orlah 3:9. For a concise review of the literature on Sofer's life and work, see Jacob Katz, *Halakhah Vekabalah* (Jerusalem: Magnes, 1984), 353*ff*. A translation of Katz's article by David Ellenson is available in Frances Malino and David Sorkin, eds., *East and West* (Cambridge, MA: Basil Blackwell, 1990), 233-266. My own essay, "*Halakhah* in Translation: The Hatam Sofer on Prayer in the Vernacular," will appear in the forthcoming *festschrift* for Rabbi A. Stanley Dreyfus.

37. Thus, "halakhic analysis and clarification" (*habechinah veha'iyun hahilkhati vehaberur ha'inyani*; Techorsh in *HTM* 1 [1949], 8); "fundamental clarification" (*berur yesodi*; Techorsh *loc. cit.* at 9); "the analysis of the laws pertaining to statehood" (*berur hilkhot medinah*; Yisraeli in *HTM* 1 [1949] 11); and "the work of clarification" (*avodat haberur*; Yisraeli, *loc. cit.* at 12).

38. See Techorsh, *HTM* 1 (1949), 9: "It is worthwhile to note that we invited the leading halakhic authorities (*gedolei harabanaim*), those of great rabbinical prestige and knowledge of Torah, to submit articles to this volume. Our hope was that this forum might be enhanced by the opinions of these outstanding sages and by their in-depth halakhic analyses (*berureihem hama'amikim*). For some reason, however, their articles have not yet arrived."

39. *HTM* 1 (1949), 11-13.

40. While Yisraeli does not specify the nature of this "improper use," it is reasonable that he refers to the reality that the findings and conclusions of the Zionist rabbis would ultimately have to be adopted–and therefore debated, amended, and modified–or rejected by the Knesset. Would the rabbis be comfortable at the prospect of a secular legislature having the final word upon these issues of Jewish law, thereby replacing rabbinical authority with that of the Israeli voter? See the article by Yitzchak England in Bazak (note 13), 110-134.

41. *HTM* 2 (1950), 5-7.

42. See Ket. 3b. The word *gezerah* also carries the sense of "persecution," particularly that imposed by a Gentile government upon the Jews.

43. In some ways, the project of *Hatorah Vehamedinah* is carried on today by the journal *Techumin*, an annual collection of articles and responsa on matters of "Torah, society, and state" published by Zomet, an institute based in Elon Shevut. The introduction very first volume of the journal (1980) makes the connection to *HTM* explicit (pp. 9-11). Yet the editors of *Techumin* mention no hope on their part that their studies might influence the *pesikah* of the *gedolei*

hador. That this element, so prominent in *HTM,* is missing from *Techumin* suggests that by 1980 the Zionist halakhists had long since realized that they were speaking exclusively to observant Jews who shared their ideological perspective.

44. See Una, note 15, above, 95.

45. See Una, note 15, above, 102.

46. See Yitzchak Englard (above, note 40).

47. For a collection of such opinions by the leading Orthodox rabbis of recent times see A. Rosenberg, *Mishkenot Haro'im* (New York, 1983).

48. This was not a purely formal necessity. Some Orthodox Zionists, such as Yeshayahu Leibovits (see note 23, above), who perceived more clearly a revolutionary element in the Jewish national movement, called for a "new" *halakhah* or approach to legal thinking that would accommodate itself to the radically new condition of Jewish life portended by the approach of statehood. This was especially true of Rabbi Haim Hirschensohn, a Zionist activist whose book *Malki Bakodesh* (St. Louis: Moinester, 1919-1928, 6 vols.) developed pioneering new approaches to halakhic reasoning precisely because the new world of approaching Jewish statehood demanded such revolutionary innovations. On Hirschensohn, see Eliezer Schweid, *Democracy and Halakhah* (Lanham, MD: University Press of America, 1994). Schweid contrasts Hirschensohn to Rabbi Avraham Yitzchak Hakohen Kook, who though audacious in his theology manifested a much more conservative approach than did Hirschensohn to halakhic interpretation. Schweid, for his part, is exceedingly critical of Kook's halakhic conservativism on matter affecting the settlement of the land of Israel; see his *Hayahadut Vehatarbut haHilonit* (Tel Aviv: Hakibutz Hame'uchad, 1981), 136. The halakhic thought of Rav Kook is a distinct subject of research. For contrasting views as well as bibliography, see M. Z. Nehorai, *"He'arot Ledarko Shel Harav Kook Befesikah," Tarbiz* 59 (1990), 481-505, and Avinoam Rosenak, *"Hahalakhah Hanevu'it Vehametzi'ut Befesikato Shel Harav Kook," Tarbiz* 69 (2000), 591-618).

49. Marc B. Shapiro, "Sociology and Halakhah," *Tradition* 27 (Fall, 1992), 83, n. 7.

50. See, in addition to the article cited in the previous note, Marc B. Shapiro, *Between the Yeshiva World and Modern Orthodoxy: The Life and Works of Rabbi Jehiel Jacob Weinberg, 1884-1966* (London: The Littman Library of Jewish Civilization, 1999). Shapiro makes much of this distinction in his consideration of Weinberg's responsum on the "humane slaughter" issue (117-129) and of his rulings concerning the observance of *bat mitzvah* (206-221). In each case, Shapiro stresses that the dispute between Weinberg and his opponents was in essence "meta-halakhic" rather than "halakhic," so that both positions could claim to be correct as a matter of Jewish law.

51. *Ibid.*, 119.

52. Roscoe Pound, *An Introduction to the Philosophy of Law* (New Haven: Yale U. Press, 1954), 56.

53. This formulation is taken from Burton (note 4, above), at 13. Burton speaks only of "classes of persons" and not "things," but the latter fits well with the classical conception of law as dealing with things (property, obligations, etc.) as well as with persons.

54. See the definition of "black-letter law" in Bryan A. Garner, *A Dictionary of Modern Legal Usage* (New York: Oxford University Press, 1987), 88-89: "legal principles that are fundamental and well-settled or statements of such principles in quasi-mathematical form."

55. Ronald Dworkin, *Taking Rights Seriously* (Cambridge, MA: Harvard University Press, 1978), 24.

56. There are, of course, exceptions to this rule, such as the reliance upon the testimony of a single witness in order to establish a presumption of a state of ritual prohibition (*ed echad ne'eman be'isurin*; Git. 2b-3a; *Yad, Hil. Edut* 11:7). Yet a rule can be formulated so as to account for its exceptions.

57. *M. Bava Kama* 3:1.

58. Chief among these are the legal positivists, the most famous of whom is H. L. A. Hart, *The Concept of Law* (Oxford: Oxford U. Press, 1961). Hart defines law as entirely a system of primary rules (that is, rules establishing norms of behavior) and secondary rules (rules that stipulate how primary rules are established, enacted, or repealed). If a particular case cannot be decided by appeal to a rule–that is, if it falls outside the clear circumference of the established rules–then it is not properly speaking a matter of "law" at all. It is rather a subject for judicial discretion, in which the judge in effect reaches beyond the law in order to legislate a new answer to the question.

59. Something of this idea can be seen in the distinction in the common law tradition between the "holding" or "rule" of the judicial opinion, which is binding upon future judges, and everything else that the judge writes, which is called "dicta" and is not binding. See Rupert Cross, *Precedent in English Law* (Oxford: The Clarendon Press, 1977), 38*ff.*

60. The example is a hypothetical debated by H. L. A. Hart, "Positivism and the Separation of Law and Morals," *Harvard Law Review* 71 (1958), 593-629, and Lon L. Fuller, "Positivism and Fidelity to Law: A Reply to Professor Hart," *Harvard Law Review* 71 (1958), 630-672.

61. While both Hart and Fuller (see previous note) accept the need for interpretation in this case, they differ sharply over its nature. For Hart, the issue is one of the meaning of language. For all linguistic terms, such as "vehicle," there is both a settled core of meaning (a set of instances that clearly fit within the parameters of the term) and a "penumbra" of unsettled meaning. The judge must decide whether the penumbral case does or does not fit within the language of the rule. This decision is an act of legislation, a creative attempt by the judge to make new law in accordance with some conception of public need or social policy. In Fuller's view, the issue here is not linguistic–"what is a 'vehicle'?"-- but rather a matter of applying the purpose of the law–what the rule "is aiming at in general"--to the case at hand. There is a significant difference between these two approaches to legal textual interpretation. For our purposes, though, it is sufficient to say that both regard the written rule as insufficient to decide the case.

62. Ex. 23:1; San. 27a; *Yad, Hil. Edut* 9:1*ff.*

63. Chief Rabbinate of Israel, *Osef Piskei Din* (1950), 337-338. The court refused a petition to annul a marriage on the grounds that the wedding was not conducted according to proper halakhic form.

64. For an analysis of the ruling see Menachem Elon, *Miba'ayot Hahalakhah Vehamishpat bBmedinat Yisrael* (Jerusalem: Hebrew University, Institute for Contemporary Judaism, 1973), 22*ff.* What we can say is that the judges of the court were anything but obscure and insignificant figures in the world of *halakhah*. They included the two chief rabbis of Eretz Yisrael, Yitzchak Halevy Herzog and Benzion Meir Hai Ouziel, along with R. Meshulam Ratta, the well-known author of the responsa collection *Kol Mevaser*.)

65. Burton (note 4, above), 21.

66. *Ibid.*, 41-57; Lief H. Carter, *Reason in Law* (4th edition; New York: HarperCollins, 1994), 17*ff.*

67. On Reform weddings, see R. Moshe Feinstein, *Resp. Igerot Moshe, Even Ha'ezer* 1:76-77.

68. R. Yosef Eliyahu Henkin, *Resp. Teshuvot Ibra*, no. 76.

69. Pound (note 52, above).

70. Dworkin (note 55, above), 22. Dworkin makes a sharp distinction between "principles" and "policies," which he defines as desired social, political, or economic goals and which pertain more appropriately to the sphere of the legislature than to that of the judge. A number of scholars question whether a significant distinction can in fact be made between "principles" and "policies"; see Neil MacCormick, *Legal Reasoning and Legal Theory* (Oxford: Clarendon Press, 1978), 259-264, and Aharon Barak, *Judicial Discretion* (New Haven: Yale U. Press,

1989), 31. Though the difference between these positions is substantive, we need not resolve this *machloket* here. For our purposes, it is enough to say that the concepts "principle" and "policy" can both refer to considerations other than rules that are yet essential to the judge's decision and which therefore determine the law in specific cases.

71. 115 N.Y. 506, 22 N.E. 188 (1889).

72. The two positions are charted by Y. Z. Kahana in his marvelously detailed introduction to *Sefer Ha`agunot* (Jerusalem: Mosad Harav Koook, 1954), 7-76.

73. As Holmes wrote in his critique of the jurisprudence of Christopher Columbus Langdell: "ideal in the law, the end of all his striving, is the *elegantia juris*, or logical integrity of the system as a system. He is, perhaps, the greatest living legal theologian. But as a theologian he is less concerned with his postulates than to show that the conclusions from them hang together. ... so entirely is he interested in the formal connection of things, or logic, as distinguished from the feelings which make the content of logic, and which have actually shaped the substance of law." By contrast, says Holmes, "The life of the law has not been logic; it has been experience. The seed of every new growth within its sphere has been a felt necessity." See Oliver Wendell Holmes, "Review of CC Langdell, *Summary of the Law of Contracts* and WR Anson, *Principles of the Law of Contract*," American Law Review 14 (1880), 233ff, at 234. Cardozo describes *elegantia juris* as "an intellectual passion...for symmetry in form and substance"; Benjamin Cardozo, *The Nature of the Judicial Process* (New Haven: Yale U. Press, 1921), 34.

74. It is a tricky business to summarize "legal realism" in as cursory a fashion as I do in the text, though reasons of space leave me little choice. It should at least be noted that legal realism was not an academic "movement" in any organized sense but rather a *mood*, a particular disposition that took root among American (and some European) legal academics during the first several decades of the twentieth century. Fundamental to this mood was an aversion to the formalist or conceptualist jurisprudence of Langdell (see previous note) that had become predominant in American law schools. Realists emphasized the "real" (*i.e.*, non-doctrinal) causes of legal development and judicial decision, incorporating elements of pragmatist philosophy and social science into their understanding of law. Much has been written about the history of the "movement"; a good recent work that deals incisively with the historiographical controversies is Neil Duxbury, *Patterns of American Jurisprudence* (Oxford: The Clarendon Press, 1995), 65-160.

75. Cardozo (note 73, above), 66-67.

76. That "old legend" is found in Ber. 7a.

77. Cardozo (note 73, above), 64.

78. *Ibid.*, 65.

79. Haim H. Cohn, *Hamishpat*. (Jerusalem: Mosad Bialik, 1991), 79.

80. Robert M. Cover, "Foreword: *Nomos* and Narrative," *Harvard Law Review* 97 (1983), at 4-5.

81. See, for example, the essay by Chaim I. Waxman, "Toward a Sociology of *Pesak*," in Moshe Sokol, ed., *Rabbinic Authority and Personal Autonomy* (Northvale, NJ: Jason Aronson, 1992), 217-237. That the volume is published by "The Orthodox Forum Series, A Project of the Rabbi Isaac Elchanan Theological Seminary," testifies just how mainstream and unobjectionable this idea has become. There are, of course, many works devoted to the relationship between social and ideological factors and the development of Jewish law. Among these, the many studies of the late Professor Jacob Katz deserve special mention. One of his essays that I find particularly helpful in setting *pesak* within its social context is his "Ha'im chidush hasanhedrin hu begeder pitaron?"in Jacob Katz, *Le'umi'ut yehudit: masot umechkarim* (Jerusalem: World Zionist Organization, 1979), 181-190. On Katz's contributions to Jewish studies see Jay M. Harris, ed., *The Pride of Jacob* (Cambridge, MA: Harvard University Press, 2002).

82. See the memorandum on the Chief Rabbinate by S. Z. Shragai, reprinted in his *Sha'ah Venetzach* (Jerusalem: Mosad Harav Koook, 1960), 326-336. Shragai describes the Chief Rabbinate as "the fruit of Orthodox Zionist (*dati-le'umi*) thought, an institution whose authority is based upon its recognition that the establishment of the state reflects the divine will. Its halakhic rulings must therefore reflect this Orthodox Zionist perspective, in much the same way that the pronouncements of the Council of Torah Sages of Agudat Yisrael reflect the anti-Zionist ideology of that movement. Halakhic decision takes place within this ideological framework," for an individual must accept the governing ideology of the rabbi before turning to that rabbi as his personal halakhic authority.

83. Perhaps the most comprehensive treatment of this theme is R. Ben-Zion Meir Chai Ouziel, *Hegyonei Ouziel* (Jerusalem: Hava'ad Lehotza'at Kitvei Harav, 1991).

84. See above, at note 29.

85. I have in mind here Bialik's classic essay *"Halakhah Ne'agadah," Kitvei Ch. N. Bialik* (Tel Aviv: Dvir, 1935), vol. 2, 260-275, which portrays a symbiotic relationship between these two modes of religious expression, albeit in literary rather than in jurisprudential terminology.

86. On the institution of *da'at torah* as a means of expressing Orthodox rabbinical ideology on subjects that do not fit comfortably under the heading of *halakhah*, see Lawrence Kaplan, "Daas Torah: A Modern Conception of Rabbinic Authority," in Moshe Z. Sokol, ed., *Rabbinic Authority and Personal Autonomy* (Northvale, NJ: Jason Aronson, 1992), 1-60.

87. Allan C. Hutchinson, *It's All In The Game: A Nonfoundationalist Account of Law and Adjudication* (Durham, NC: Duke University Press, 2000), 25.

88. "The law wishes to have a formal existence. This means, first of all, that the law does not wish to be absorbed by, or declared subordinate to, some other–nonlegal–structure of concern... and second, the law...desires that the components of its autonomous existence be self-declaring and not be in need of piecing out by some supplementary discourse." Stanley Fish, "The Law Wishes to Have a Formal Existence," in Austin Sarat and Thomas R. Kearns, eds., *The Fate of Law* (Ann Arbor: University of Michigan Press, 1991), 159-208. The quotation is at 159.

89. Hans Kelsen, *The Pure Theory of Law* (Berkeley: University of California Press, 1967), 192.

90. I take this description from G. Edward White, who describes the once-predominant conception of judges as "oracles" who merely find the law and do not make it, "mechanically applying existing rules to new situations" and "who could discover the law's technical mysteries but who could not influence the content of the law itself." See *The American Judicial Tradition* (New York: Oxford University Press, 1976), 7-8. I presume that White derives his description from Sir William Blackstone, *Commentaries on the Laws of England* 1:3 (facsimile first edition, 1765. Chicago: University of Chicago Press, 1979), 69.

91. See Owen Fiss, "Objectivity and Interpretation," *Stanford Law Review* 34 (1982), 739-763.

92. For moral arguments of behalf of the "rule of law" see Lon L. Fuller, *The Morality of Law* (New Haven: Yale University Press, 1969) and Neil MacCormick, "The Ethics of Legalism," *Ratio Juris* 2 (1989), 184-193.

93. See Owen M. Fiss, "The Death of the Law?" *Cornell Law Review* 72 (1986), 1-16, who attacks two legal academic "movements," Law and Economics and Critical Legal Studies, for distorting the purposes of law by denying the integrity of its own discourse.

94. "Gut reasoning," translated literally into Hebrew, *sevarat hakeres*, a concept found in numerous responsa (see, for example *Resp. Terumat Hadeshen* 2:92, near the end). In my experience, *sevarat hakeres* almost always conveys a less-than-positive connotation. It is invoked in support of the view that a *posek* ought to have a better and more formally halakhic reason to justify his conclusion than an argument he feels, as it were, from his *kishkes*.

95. See the regrets of the rabbis forced to rule stringently on the *agunah* question in Kahana (note 72, above).

96. The precise term "critique of methodology" is taken from Edward L. Rubin (note 3, above) at 1838*ff*. The quotation is at 1839.

97. Rubin (note 3, above) provides a helpful bibliography at pp. 1835-1836. See also Stanley Fish, *Doing What Comes Naturally: Change, Rhetoric, and the Practice of Theory in Literary and Legal Studies* (Durham: Duke University P:ress, 1989), 345.

98. On all that follows see Richard J. Bernstein, *Beyond Objectivism and Relativism: Science, Hermeneutics, and Praxis* (Philadelphia: University of Pennsylvania Press, 1983). As Bernstein notes at p. 8, the tension between "objectivist" and "subjectivist" accounts of truth has been around ever since Plato battled the Sophists. The "modern" turn in this conflict comes with the "Enlightenment project," the attempt to locate non-religious and rational foundations for human inquiry. On the "Enlightenment project," see Alisdair MacIntyre, *After Virtue: A Study in Moral Theory* (Notre Dame: University of Notre Dame Press, 1981), 36*ff.* See also H.G. Gadamer, *Truth and Method*, Second, Revised Edition (translation by Joel Weinsheimer and Donald G. Marshall; New York: Continuum, 1993), 277, on "the fundamental presupposition of the Enlightenment, namely that methodologically disciplined use of reason can safeguard us from all error."

99. In the words of Stanley Fish (note 98, above), p. 343: "the successful foundational project will have provided us with a 'method,' a recipe which...will *produce*, all by itself, the correct result.... In literary studies the result would be the assigning of valid interpretation to poems and novels..." (Emphasis in the original).

100. See Thomas C. Grey, "Langdell's Orthodoxy," note 5, above, at p. 5: "Langdell believed that through scientific methods lawyers could derive correct legal judgments from a few fundamental principles and concepts, which it was the task of the scholar-scientist like himself to discover."

101. Although natural law has been around for quite a long time, its post-Enlightenment (*i.e.*, non-openly-religious) manifestation deserves special mention. For a well-known representative, see John Finnis, *Natural Law and Natural Rights* (Oxford: The Clarendon Press, 1980).

102. Chief among these is H. L. A. Hart, *The Concept of Law* (note 58, above). See, in general, Mario Jori, ed., *Legal Positivism* (New York: New York University Press, 1992).

103. See Fish (note 97, above), 342-355.

104. A sharp, brief expression of this critique is that of Richard Rorty, *Consequences of Pragmatism* (Minneapolis: University of Minnesota Press, 1982), xix: Plato's effort to discover the ultimate basis of truth "is the impossible attempt to step outside our skins...and compare ourselves with something absolute."

105. Rubin (note 3, above), 1840.

107. The glance was taken by Richard Rorty, "The Banality of Pragmatism and the Poetry of Justice," in Brint and Weaver (note 107, above), 89-97. He notes that pragmatism is the governing approach even of those theorists who denounce "pragmatism." On the "antifoundational" thrust of much of twentieth-century legal theory, see Minda (note 4, above), especially for the bibliography he provides.

108. For a reconsideration of what the Sophists were really saying, see Anthony T. Kronman, "Rhetoric," *University of Cincinnati Law Review* 67 (1999), 677-709. See as well the description of the Sophistic controversy in Brian Vickers, *In Defense of Rhetoric* (Oxford: The Clarendon Press, 1989). For a response to Socrates' devastating attack upon rhetoric, see James Boyd White, *Heracles' Bow: Essays on the Rhetoric and Poetics of Law* (Madison: University of Wisconsin Press, 1985), 215-237.

109. Richard J. Bernstein (note 99, above), 8. Bernstein's monograph is a comprehensive description of the struggle between the search for foundations and methods (hence the attribution to Descartes) and the attempt to identify new approaches that ground knowledge in something less than objective certainty but something more than pure subjectivism.

110. Rorty, (note 104, above), 166,.

111. Rubin, (note 3, above), 1841.

112. John S. Nelson, Allan Megill, and Donald N. McCloskey, *The Rhetoric of the Human Sciences* (Madison: University of Wisconsin Press, 1987), 6.

113. See Richard Rorty, *Philosophy and The Mirror of Nature* (Princeton: Princeton University Press, 1979), 320: "Normal discourse is that which is conducted within an agreed-upon set of conventions about what counts as a relevant contribution, what counts as answering a question, what counts as having a good argument for that answer or a good criticism of it. Abnormal discourse is what happens when someone joins in the discourse who is ignorant of these conventions or who sets them aside."

114. The proper citation here is Thomas Kuhn, *The Structure of Scientific Revolutions*, Second Edition Enlarged (Chicago: University of Chicago Press, 1970). Fundamental to Kuhn's system is his notion of scientific paradigms: "universally recognized scientific achievements that for a timeprovide model problems and solutions to a *community of practitioners* (viii; emphasis added). See also Richard Rorty, "Science as Solidarity," in Nelson, Megill, and McCloskey (note 112, above), 38-52.

115. Thomas C. Grey, "Holmes and Legal Pragmatism," *Stanford Law Review* 41 (1989), at 798. Among these theorists on the "left" are Stanley Fish (note 98, an argument he repeats throughout the book) and Joseph William Singer, "The Player and the Cards: Nihilism and Legal Theory," *Yale Law Journal* 94 (1984), 1-70. The "right wing" (as these things are

measured in American politics, at any rate) is represented by Richard Posner in many of his writings on legal pragmatism. See, *e.g.*, *The Problems of Jurisprudence* (Cambridge: Harvard University Press, 1990), at 116-117: legal reasoning is "the 'art' of social governance by rules," "a craft," or "a skill such as riding a bicycle or speaking a foreign language."

116. I have no intention of offering a bibliography to this vast subject. I should mention, though, one famous survey of the intellectual history of this movement in the United States, with special reference to its relevance for legal studies: Morton White, *Social Thought in America: The Revolt Against Formalism* (New York: Viking Press, 1949). For the observations of leading pragmatists on law, see John Dewey, "Logical Method and Law," *Cornell Law Quarterly* 10 (1924), 17-27, and Richard Rorty, note 108, above.

117. A Lexis-Nexis search of American law reviews from the years 1992-2002 produces 823 citations of "Wittgenstein." Compare this to citations of thinkers more commonly associated with jurisprudence: "Savigny" (327), and "Salmond" (131). See Dennis Patterson, ed., *Wittgenstein and Legal Theory* (Boulder: Westview Press, 1992), and Thomas Morawetz, "The Epistemology of Judging: Wittgenstein and Deliberative Practices," *Canadian Journal of Law and Jurisprudence* 3 (1990), 35-59.

118. Chief among them Hans-Georg Gadamer (see chiefly *Truth and Method*, note 99, above) and Jürgen Habermas, *The Theory of Communicative Action* (translated by Thomas McCarthy. Boston: Beacon Press, 1984). On the implications the thought of Gadamer and Habermas (and the controversy between them) for law, see David C. Hoy, "Interpreting the Law: Hermeneutical and Poststructuralist Perspectives," *Southern California Law Review* 58 (1985), 135-176.

119. I take the title from R. H. Roberts and J. M. M. Good, eds., *The Recovery of Rhetoric: Persuasive Discourse and Disciplinarity in the Human Sciences* (Charlottesville: University of Virginia Press, 1993). See also Herbert W. Simons, ed., *The Rhetorical Turn: Invention and Persuasion in the Conduct of Inquiry* (Chicago: University of Chicago Press, 1990), as well the volume by Nelson, Megill, and McCloskey (note 113, above). These studies seek to "recover" rhetoric from the anathema pronounced upon it by Plato and, to a lesser extent, by Aristotle, who contrasted it with dialectic as an approach to inquiry. The goal of this "movement" is to remind us that the forms of human inquiry are inescapably rhetorical (as opposed to methodological). Perhaps the most important contemporary work in the theory of rhetoric as a mode and structure of human knowledge is Chaim Perelman and L. Olbrechts-Tyteca, *The New Rhetoric: A Treatise on Argumentation* (J. Wilkinson and P. Weaver, translators. Notre Dame: Notre Dame University Press, 1969). See also Stephen Toulmin, *The Uses of Argument* (Cambridge: Cambridge University Press, 1958), 248: we should demand of arguments "not that they shall measure up against analytic standards but, more realistically, that they shall achieve whatever sort of cogency or well-foundedness can relevantly be asked for in that field."

120. I would cite here almost all the works by James Boyd White. See, in particular, note 109, above, at 77-106. See also his *The Legal Imagination, Abridged Edition* (Chicago: University of Chicago Press, 1985), xiii: "I think that the law is not merely a system of rules (or rules and

principles), or reducible to policy choices and class interests, but that it is rather what I call a language, by which I do not mean just a set of terms and locutions, but habits of mind and expectations–what might also be called a culture... The law makes a world."

121. This is a theme stressed again and again in the literature of the Critical Legal Studies "movement"(CLS): legal doctrine is largely indeterminate because the law, as a discrete, procedural discipline, allows for arguments in more than one direction. The only way to solve these disputes is through a substantive choice in favor of the arguments supporting one particular social vision over those that support another. This sort of choice, though, is political rather than legal. Hence, the title of David Kairys' *The Politics of Law* (New York: Basic Books, 1998), an important collection of essays by a variety of scholars associated with CLS.

122. Many halakhic authorities do believe in the existence of a single, uniquely correct answer to any question of Jewish law; see Shimshon Etinger, *"Machloket Ve'emet: Lemashma'ut She'elat Ha'emet Hahilkhatit," Shenaton Hamishpat Ha'ivri* 21 (1998-2000), 37-69. For other views, see Avi Sagi, *Eilu Ve'eilu: Mashma'uto Shel Hasiach Hahilkhati* (Tel Aviv: Hakibbutz Hame'uchad, 1996). My remarks in this essay, however, go to a more practical level of concern: even if there *is* one right answer to a question of law or *halakhah*, there is no reliable method by which the scholars of the field can identify that answer in any formal way. And this, at the very least, means that the authorities cannot summarily reject any and all divergent points of view from the legal conversation.

123. "Practical reasoning," as distinct from formal logic, is often linked to the Aristotelian term *phronesis*. It is, in the words of Richard Bernstein (note 99, above, at 54) "a form of reasoning that is concerned with choice and involves deliberation... a judgment (in which) there are no determinate technical rules by which a particular can simply be subsumed under than which is general and universal. What is required is an interpretation and specification of universals that are appropriate to this particular situation." In a legal sense, practical reasoning is the idea that judges should decide cases "not by deductive logic, but by a less structured problem-solving process involving common sense, respect for precedent, and an appreciation for society's needs"; Daniel A. Farber, "The Inevitability of Practical Reason: Statutes, Formalism, and the Rule of Law," *Vanderbilt Law Review* 45 (1992), at 536-537. For discussion and bibliography see Thomas F. Cotter, "Legal Pragmatism and the Law and Economics Movement," *Georgetown Law Review* 84 (1996), at 2082-2091.

124. The most important exponent of this point of view is Karl Llewellyn, whose *magnum opus* is *The Common Law Tradition: Deciding Appeals* (Boston: Little, Brown, 1960). See especially the chapter entitled "Major Steadying Factors in Our Appellate Courts," 19-61. The term "leeways" that I use in the text is taken from Llewellyn's treatment of "the leeways of precedent" in this work, pp. 62*ff.* A more accessible version of his approach is *The Case Law System in America* (translated by Michael Ansaldi. Chicago: University of Chicago Press, 1989); see especially at 76-78, along with editor Paul Gewirtz's excellent introductory essay, ix-xxiii. Gewirtz notes the subtle but important difference between Llewellyn's approach and Stanley Fish's notion of practice and "communities of interpretation" (*Doing What Comes*

Naturally, note 97, above, and *Is There A Text In This Class? The Authority of Interpretive Communities* (Cambridge, MA: Harvard University Press, 1980). Where Fish exalts the influence of practice over interpretation and suggests that rules do nothing to constrain it, Llewellyn posits a kind of dialogue between rules and practice, carried on by the professionally-trained practitioner. For an appreciation of Llewellyn's understanding of law, see Anthony T. Kronman, *The Lost Lawyer: Failing Ideals of the Legal Profession* (Cambridge, MA: Belknap/Harvard, 1993), 210-225.

125. A term favored by Karl Llewellyn; see the preceding note.

126. This is a general descriptive statement, of course, and it is only as good as the evidence that can be brought to support it from specific decisions and responsa. Such evidence exists in abundance, scattered throughout numerous studies of halakhic development on particular topics. A common thread uniting all these cases is that the *poskim* arrive at rulings that are unexpected, given the "rules" that presumably ought to have dictated different outcomes. The techniques utilized to support these innovative (deviant?) decisions are varied; the rabbi in question either ignores the limiting rule, or reinterprets it, or finds another rule that "trumps" it. Taken together, though, these individual examples tend to buttress the theoretical approach I offer in this essay: namely, that the "rules" function *within* halakhic discourse but do not judge it. Rabbis use rules as arguments, as tools to construct the rhetoric of justification; the rules do not serve to evaluate in some methodical way the correctness of rabbinical argument. I have addressed this point in a number of venues; see the article cited in note 8, above, as well as Mark Washofsky, "Taking Precedent Seriously: On *Halakhah* As A Rhetorical Practice," in Walter Jacob and Moshe Zemer, eds., *Re-Examining Progressive Halakhah* (New York: Berghan Books, 2002), 1-70.

127. A classic example may be found in the first volume of J. David Bleich's *Contemporary Halakhic Problems* (New York: Ktav/Yeshiva, 1977), 78: "The deliberations and publications of the Rabbinical Assembly [specifically, the Committee on Jewish Law and Standards–MW] do not, in the ordinary course of events, properly come within the purview of a work devoted to *halakhah*. Much is to be said in favor of simply ignoring pronouncements with regard to Jewish law issued by those who have placed themselves outside the pale of normative Judaism. Yet from time to time a particular action is erroneously presented as being predicated upon authoritative precedents, and hence being within the parameters of *halakhah*. Since the unwary and unknowledgeable may very easily be confused and misled by such misrepresentations it becomes necessary to take note of the issues involved."

128. See, for example, Rabbi Joel Roth's efforts to disprove Rabbi Moshe Feinstein's declaration that Conservative Jews are *apikorsim*, or heretics, ineligible to serve on a *beit din*. Roth contests the ruling as a matter of law, but he tragically misses the point. Feinstein is addressing a community of *Orthodox* Jews who define and identify themselves largely on the basis of lines such as the one he draws in that ruling. For sources and discussion, see note 8, above.

129. To this point, I have offered what I think is a descriptive account of halakhic practice, and I do not now want to muddy the waters by switching to normative language, an advocacy of what *ought* to be rather than a discussion of what *is*. (Advocacy has its proper place, but that place is not here.) When I speak of "aspirations," I am saying that a conception of higher standards of practice–the best that the practice can be–is an integral part of the work of any discipline. The members of that community do in fact evaluate each other's work critically against such standards. For example, Ronald Dworkin argues that this sort of aspiration lies at the basis of the activity of literary interpretation; see *A Matter of Principle* (Cambridge, MA: Harvard University Press, 1985), 149*ff* (on the "aesthetic hypothesis," the notion that the activity of literary interpretation aims at showing "which way of reading...the text reveals it as the best work of art). My idea of "aspiration" here is quite similar: halakhists aspire to produce a *halakhah* that is "the best it can be," that meets the highest standards of evaluation that exist within the practice.

130. See Mark Washofsky, *Jewish Practice* (New York: UAHC Press, 2001), xxii-xxv. I do believe that the concepts and values I set forth there (such as our commitments to gender equality, the moral dignity of all human beings, and our openness to innovation and creativity in the forms of religious life) are integral to any decent understanding of the practice of liberal *halakhah*. Yet they are at the same time necessarily vague and general. They are *descriptive* of our practice, in the sense that any ruling or essay in liberal *halakhah* will most likely have to explain itself in accordance with them. But they cannot *prescribe* just what decision a liberal halakhist ought to reach on any particular question. The meaning of any rule or criterion of liberal *halakhah*–like the meaning of rules and criteria in any other discipline--can take shape only in practice, through argument carried on among a community of interpreters.

131. See, for example, Perelman and Toulmin in the works cited in note 120, above. Both of these authors criticize the tendency among prior theorists to evaluate the validity of argumentation on the basis of formal, analytical logic. And if argumentation is, as they suggest, a matter of practical reasoning (contextualized to the audience it addresses or to the field within which it functions), then it is much less likely that we can agree upon any formal standard by which to judge its correctness. See also Dale Hample, "What Is a Good Argument?" in W. L. Benoit, D. Hample, and P. J. Benoit, eds., *Readings in Argumenation* (Berlin: Foris Publications, 1992), 313-336. Hemple examines three foundations upon which rhetorical theorists might establish criteria for evaluating argument: public (that is, the audience to whom the rhetor directs his or her address); logic (that is, the rationality of the argument itself); and "field" (that is, the specific discipline within which the argument takes place. He concludes that no general theory based upon any of these foundations can predict which arguments will be "good" ones in particular cases. This is another way of saying that there is no "method" by which to judge the correctness of an argument.

132. See Hanina Ben-Menahem, Natan Hecht, and Shai Wasner eds., *Hamachloket Bahalakhah*, 2 vols. (Jerusalem: Hamakhon Letikhnun Mediniut Be-Yachasei Yisrael Vehatefutzot, *1991)*.

133. I am relying here upon the insights emerging from the field of "ethical criticism," best exemplified by such writers as Wayne C. Booth, *The Company We Keep: An Ethics of Fiction* (Berkeley: University of California Press, 1988), and Martha Nussbaum, *Love's Knowledge: Essays On Philosophy and Literature* (Oxford: Oxford University Press, 1990) and *Poetic Justice: The Literary Imagination and Public Life* (Boston: Beacon Press, 1995). Most especially, I owe a deep debt to the thought of James Boyd White, whose portrayal of law and judging as forms of rhetoric and ways of speaking open a path toward an approach to legal criticism that is rigorous and exacting while not "methodical." See the works cited in notes 109 and 121, above, as well as *Justice As Translation: An Essay in Cultural and Legal Criticism* (Chicago: University of Chicago Press, 1990), 89-112.

Chapter 4

❖ ❖ ❖

"IT IS TIME TO ACT FOR THE LORD"
Toward a Hermeneutic for Progressive *Halakhah*

Peter Knobel

This paper[1] addresses three questions.
1) Is there a theoretical place within the *halakhah* for progressive *halakhah*?[2]
2) What are the principles within the *halakhah* that permit or prohibit changes in established norms?[3]
3) What is the role of *halakhah* or halakhic thinking in a movement that essentially defines itself as non-halakhic?[4]

Professor Menachem Fisch, in his book *Rational Rabbis* and in lectures delivered to the Beth Emet Israel Kallah, has argued that within the Talmud and therefore within rabbinic tradition as a whole there are two tendencies (1) traditionalist and (2) antitraditionalist. The traditionalist stance is characterized by a static understanding of Judaism. The new is permitted only where there are lacunae in what has been handed down. The antitraditionalist stance is characterized by an open understanding of Judaism. What has been handed down must be studied and taken seriously, but evaluation and decision making are the responsibility of the current generation. *Talmud torah* in Fisch's view should be analogized to scientific inquiry. The theories of the past are constantly being tested against new data. When the old theories do not adequately account for the data, then new theories are tested to discover if they more adequately account for the data. Nothing is ever considered finally settled. It is always open to revision. Fisch conceives of *talmud torah* as consisting of two phases, (1) the undergraduate education where the student acquires the knowledge of the past, and (2) graduate education, where the student submits the knowledge of the past to a process of testing. *Talmud torah* is not merely the rote repetition of the past but the constant reexamination in light of new circumstances.

In the following text from *Bamidbar Rabbah*, Moses corrects God and God acknowledges that Moses is not only correct but that he has taught God something. Fisch sees this as a classic example of the antitraditionalist attitude. It is especially important as a warrant for Progressive *halakhah* because, as in the case of the "Oven of Aknai,"[5] human interpretation trumps divine will and as a result becomes divine will.

> Another exposition of the text, "Then Israel sang" (Num. 21:17). This is one of the three things said by Moses to the Holy One, blessed be He, to which the latter replied: "You have taught Me something."
> (1) He said to Him (when interceding for Israel on the occasion of the making of the golden calf). "Sovereign of the Universe! How can Israel realize what they have done? Were they not reared up in Egypt? And are not all the Egyptians worshipers of idols? Moreover, when You gave the Torah You did not give it to them! They were not even standing near by: as it says, And the people stood afar off (Ex. 20:18)! You gave it only to me; as it says, And unto Moses He said: Come up unto the Lord (Ex. 24:1). When You gave the commandments You did not give it to them! You did not say, 'I am the Lord your God,' but 'I am the Lord your God'[6] (Ex. 20:1). You did say it to me! Have I sinned?" By your life,' said the Holy One, blessed be He, to him, ' you have spoken well! You have taught Me something! From now onward I shall use the expression, "I am the Lord your God."[7]
> (2) ' The second occasion was when the Holy One, blessed be He, said to him, "Visiting the iniquity of the fathers upon the children" (Ibid. 5). Moses said to him: "Sovereign of the Universe! Many are the wicked who have begotten righteous men. Shall the latter bear some of the iniquities of their fathers? Terah worshiped images, yet Abraham his son was a righteous man. Similarly, Hezekiah was a righteous man, though Ahaz his father was wicked. So also Josiah was righteous, yet Amon his father was wicked. Is this proper, that the righteous should be punished for the iniquity of their fathers?" The Holy One, blessed be He, said to him: "You have taught Me something! By your life, I shall cancel My words and confirm yours;" as it says, "The fathers shall not be put to death for the children, neither shall the children be put to death for the fathers" (Deut. 24:16). "And by your life, I shall record these words in your name;" as it says, According to that which is written in the book of the law of Moses, as the Lord commanded, saying: The fathers shall not, etc. (2 Kings 14:6).
> (3) The third occasion was when the Holy One, blessed be He, said to him:

"Make war with Sihon. Even though he does not seek to interfere with you, you must open hostilities against him'; as it says, Rise ye up, take your journey, and pass over the valley of Arnon. . . and contend with him [Sihon] in battle (Deut. 2:24). Moses, however, did not do so but, in accordance with what is written lower down, sent messengers (Deut. 2: 26). The Holy One, blessed be He, said to him: " By your life, I shall cancel My own words and confirm yours;" as it says, "When You draw near unto a city to fight against it, then proclaim peace unto it" (Ibid. 20:10).[8]

An even more dramatic and more directly relevant example is the Oven of Aknai. Professor Fisch sees this famous passage as a dramatic confrontation between R. Eliezer, whom he identifies as a traditionalist, and the antitraditionalists. The excommunication of a sage of R. Eliezer's prominence is unprecedented.[9]

> This was the oven of 'Aknai. Why [the oven of] 'Aknai? – Said Rab Judah in Samuel's name: [It means] that they encompassed it with arguments as a snake, and proved it unclean. It has been taught: On that day R. Eliezer brought forward every imaginable argument, but they did not accept them. Said he to them: "If the *halakhah* agrees with me, let this carob-tree prove it!' Thereupon the carob-tree was torn a hundred cubits out of its place – others affirm, four hundred cubits. "No proof can be brought from a carob-tree," they retorted. Again he said to them: "If the *halakhah* agrees with me, let the stream of water prove it!" Whereupon the stream of water flowed backwards – "No proof can be brought from a stream of water," they rejoined. Again he urged: "If the *halakhah* agrees with me, let the walls of the schoolhouse prove it," whereupon the walls inclined to fall. But R. Joshua rebuked them, saying: "When scholars are engaged in a halahkic dispute, what have ye to interfere?" Hence they did not fall, in honor of R. Joshua, nor did they resume the upright, in honor of R. Eliezer; and they are still standing thus inclined. Again he said to them: "If the *halakhah* agrees with me, let it be proved from Heaven!" Whereupon a Heavenly Voice cried out: "Why do ye dispute with R. Eliezer, seeing that in all matters the *halakhah* agrees with him!" But R. Joshua arose and exclaimed: "It is not in heaven."'(Deut. 30:12) What did he mean by this? – Said R. Jeremiah: "That the Torah had already been given at Mount Sinai; we pay no attention to a heavenly voice, because Thou hast long since written in the Torah at Mount Sinai, 'After the majority must one incline.'"
>
> R. Nathan met Elijah and asked him: "What did the Holy One, Blessed be He, do in that hour? – He laughed [with joy], he replied, saying, 'My sons have defeated Me, My sons have defeated Me.'" It was said: "On that day all

objects which R. Eliezer had declared clean were brought and burnt in fire." Then they took a vote and excommunicated him.[10]

Reform thinkers have long used this passage almost exclusively to justify openness in the rabbinic system. Fisch, who offers a detailed and sustained argument in support of the existence of the antitraditionalist element in talmudic writings, utilizes this passage as only one example. It is important to note that Fisch is addressing his argument not to Progressives, although his work is relevant for us. He is concerned to demonstrate that this view is legitimate for those who would identify themselves as Orthodox.

The Rashi to Hag. 3b makes clear that the *halakhah* is fixed by an assessment of the quality of the argument rather than by an appeal to tradition. The one important caveat is that those who are engaged in the argument are fully committed both to the process and to the theological principle underlying the process that they are trying to discern the divine will.

> "Make your ear like the hopper" For since the hearts of all the disputants are prudently directed to the heavens, therefore acquire an attentive ear, study [their words] and acquaint yourself with each of their [conflicting] opinions, when you are capable of discerning which of them is best suited [to the situation at hand], declare the *halakhah* to be as he says.[11]

This Rashi furthers the argument in asserting that differ times may require different answers.

> ... For when two dispute the views of one another, one of them claiming he said this and the other claiming that he said that, [at least] one them is lying [i.e., misrepresenting the truth]. But if two amoraim disagree on a matter of law, on which should be permitted and what should be forbidden, no lying is involved. Each of them is [merely] presenting his own opinion. One of them finds reason to permit, while the other finds reason to prohibit, one argues one way and the other argues differently. And in [such cases as these] we say "both are the word of the living God." For at times one particular line of reasoning may apply while at [other] times a different line of reasoning may apply. Indeed any reason could be wholly reverse at the slightest change of circumstance.[12]

If Fisch is correct, then openness to testing and verification is already built into the rabbinic concept of *Talmud Torah*.[13]

Before turning to an analysis of the principles and circumstances under which a rabbinic authority can abrogate matters, a topic to which Joel Roth devotes an entire chapter,[14] I want to share with you what I believe is at stake for the Reform movement in its attempt to revitalize halakhic thinking as a methodology of Reform Jewish decision making. At the beginning of its history in Europe, Reform Judaism sought to link its proposed changes to precedents found in the classical texts. Some of the early responsa and essays make interesting reading.[15] Reform in North America has come to understand itself as a non-halakhic movement. We often hear Mordecai Kaplan's famous statement quoted as follows: "The *halakhah* (the tradition, the past) has a vote but not a veto." This has encouraged the neglect of a serious examination of the sources as means of contemporary decision making. I know that my education at Hebrew Union College–Jewish Institute of Religion did not anticipate that I would need more than a cursory exposure to Talmud and codes. The responsa literature was ignored completely. I am told that rabbinic education has changed greatly since I was a student. The late Solomon B. Freehof, Walter Jacob, W. Gunther Plaut, Moshe Zemer, and Mark Washofsky and an active Central Conference of American Rabbis Responsa Committee deserve our gratitude for preserving and renewing halakhic thinking. While in recent years many responsa have been written, we are still at the beginning of efforts to explicate the theory behind our methodology.

Among the important questions that must be answered are: What distinguishes our methodology from that of the Orthodox? From that of the Conservative? Clarity on these questions will aid us to better understand the role of textual analysis as a source for decision making and enhance our ability to articulate the authority of Torah as an expression of the Divine will. The theological underpinnings of *halakhah* require explication. The lack of serious theological work on the meaning of revelation tends to reduce textual discussions to a semantic game. Text analysis is therefore taken seriously only by the Orthodox who have a commitment to a strong concept of revelation. Conservative Judaism, in spite of its commitment to *halakhah*, has also failed to make a sufficiently cogent theological case for the authority of the *halakhah*.

Primarily, I understand our work in progressive *halakhah* as a commitment to rigorous text- based thinking and reasoning, which means that we do not invent our Judaism out of whole cloth. We, however, are not merely inheritors, we are also innovators. Our purpose is ultimately to seek the "divine" as a source for action. Theologically we accept the rabbinic concept that being created in the divine image is the capacity of the human mind and heart to perceive or at least glance at the mind of God through an engagement with sacred texts.[16] In addition, halakhic reasoning will not be the only mode of reasoning which will influence serious Reform decision making.

In a community where the authority of the Torah and the *halakhah* in general is well established, there is a need to provide a method for amendment and/or abrogation. In a community like ours in which halakhic authority is practically nil, principles for abrogation and/or amendment can easily be misused to justify the establishment of any practice or to eliminate any practice. Historically we have often just made changes without necessarily engaging in rigorous systematic analysis. In addition, the emphasis upon individual autonomy divorced from some communally recognized authority or structure has limited the perceived need for a process. One colleague when asked why he agreed to perform same sex marriages said, "It just seemed right."[17]

In works that seek to establish Reform ethical practice, we frequently used theological concepts such as *b'tzelem elohim* (in the image of God), *mishpat* (justice), and *yetziat mitzraim* (exodus from Egypt) as the sole justification for a particular stance. How we utilize texts to create an authentic position requires the creation of a set of exegetical norms. Reform halakhic thinking can and should utilize aggadic texts in conversation with halakhic texts. If Bialik is correct that the *halakhah* is the crystallization of the *aggadah*, then it is time to reopen *halakhah* by the restoration of a primary role to *aggadah*. What renders a position Jewish is not the conclusion, but the fact that it is derived from a serious engagement with sacred texts. Joel Roth reminds us that "there are two theological assumptions entailed in a commitment to the halakhic process, and they are: (1) that the *grundnorm* is a reflection of the word and will of God; and that (2) the sages of the Torah are the sole legitimate interpreters of the *grundnorm*."[18] It does not commit us to a particular view of revelation nor does it limit who may be considered a sage. It does commit us to the concept that we are seeking to comprehend, however imperfectly, the Divine will through Judaic experts committed to this theological task. Progressive halakhic work places our practice, whether ritual or ethical, within the historical framework of Jewish decision making, whether it is accepted by our own community or other Jewish religious communities. It also becomes a resource for future decision making. Both Progressive responsa and Progressive reflections on methodology allow others to enter into the historical conversation. Professor Mark Washofsky's brilliant responsum "On Homosexual Marriage,"[19] with whose conclusion I strongly disagree, has permitted us to understand what is at stake. Allowing both majority and minority positions a full hearing enabled the CCAR to better determine how to take a position that upholds Torah. It is possible for us to consider whether resisting change or abrogating a previously established position upholds the will of God.

Rabbi Simeon Maslin in *Gates of the Season* declares that the burden of proof is upon those who wish to abandon a practice, not those who wish to maintain.[20] Like any legal system, the *halakhah* has inherent conservatism. Therefore, the purpose of amendment or abrogation should be undertaken only when necessary to make the whole Torah more authoritative.

The thrust of my current thinking may be summarized as follows: Our task is the recovery of a halakhic mode of thinking in which *aggadah* (narrative, theology, and ethics) is a primary hermeneutic tool rather than the recovery of *halakhah* per se. Fundamental to this is an examination of the authority and qualifications of the decisors and the principles that in the past were used to determine when amendment and abrogation were necessary and when it was appropriate to resist change.

The qualification of those engaged in halakhic decision making will perhaps be the most difficult and controversial aspect of any Progressive approach. Joel Roth posits three scenarios:

> (1) It is possible for two potential authorities engaged in identical behavior, the one of the reflecting a commitment to the halakhic system and that of the other reflecting an absence of commitment . . . the. . . The former qualifies as an authority but the latter does not. (2) It is possible for two potential authorities to engage in contradictory behaviors and for both kinds of behaviors to reflect commitment to the system . . . they both qualify as authorities. (3) It is possible for the behavior of a potential authority to reflect an ostensible commitment to the halakhic process while he lacks such a commitment. If he affirms, for example, that the *halakhah* is not normative and that its observance is dependent entirely on its meaningfulness to the individual, but that he, personally, finds almost all of *halakhah* meaningful, he would not qualify as an authority of the system.[21]

To raise the question of the qualifications of the authorities at this juncture may be counterproductive. However, the credibility of a process depends in part on the qualifications of the individuals who engage in it. Textual expertise is an obvious criterion. Institutional recognition, such as being a faculty member at a Progressive rabbinical school or being appointed to the CCAR Responsa Committee, is another obvious criterion. These are academic or institutional qualifications. Roth identifies a separate theological criterion *yirat hashem*, a behavioral commitment, which demonstrates that one is committed to living a life in response to the divine will.[22] While it is beyond the scope of this paper, it would be interesting to explore what role personal piety might have in making a Progressive *halakhah* creditable.

In chapter 7 of his book *Halakhic Process*, Roth examines in detail the right of sages to amend or abrogate norms that are considered de-oraita (toraitic). The authority of the decisor is extensive: in the most extreme instance, the principle *pe'amim she bitulah shel Torah zehu yesodah*– sometimes the abrogation of Torah, which is its foundation.

> When the ultimate goals of the Torah would be better served by its abrogation, even in its entirety, it is within the purview of the sages to take that step. The circumstances that might warrant such action are never defined. In the final analysis, the determination of the need for such action lies with the sages themselves. As Moses rendered the decision on his own, so too must the sages make the decision on their own.[23]

The Sages used medical and scientific sources to change the law. What counts is the specialist's expertise.

> It is a matter of record that the number of matters of law in the first sense stipulated in the talmudic sources and contradicted either by the expert scientific opinion of later ages or by the personal observation of later sages has produced many problems. How could it be that the talmudic sages had been mistaken? Surely it was not reasonable to suppose that the talmudic sages had misperceived their own reality. It was more reasonable to surmise that the reality had changed and once it became acceptable to make such a claim, medical/scientific sources that might result in the abrogation of previously held legal norms could be introduced without impugning the reliability or integrity of the talmudic sages. A new systemic principle referred to as *shinnui ha-itim*– change reality– became the vehicle that enabled later sages to make use of new medical/scientific knowledge without vitiating the smooth functioning of the halakhic system.[24]

Roth further writes:

> If new medical/scientific evidence indicates that a norm no longer applies to a majority of cases, and the norm itself was ground in earlier medical/scientific evidence that it did apply to a majority of cases, the extralegal sources allow the reopening of the question of the factual basis upon which the norm was predicated. In such a case, the extralegal sources allow the norm to be overturned by the claim of *shinnui ha-itim* if the evidence is strong enough.[25]

New information can also alter the meaning of a text. Archaeological, historical, and philological research is utilized to analyze a text. Such an analysis can potentially reveal that the text has been misunderstood. The most intriguing of the principles is *et la-asot ladonai heferu toratekha*.²⁶ Roth points out that the meaning of the final phrase of the verse *heferu toratekha* is clear: "they have violated [voided] Your Torah." The first phrase *et la-asot ladonai* can be understood in two ways: "It is time for the Lord to act" or "it is time to act for the Lord."²⁷

Roth cites Ber. 63a: "Rava said, "The verse may be explained both forward and backward. Forward: 'It is time for the Lord to act.' Why? 'Because they have violated Your Torah'. Backward: 'They have violated Your Torah.' Why? 'Because it is time to act for the Lord.'" Next Roth cites a text from *Sifrei Zuta* (ed. H. S. Horovitz) beginning of *parashat Pinchat*. It deals with the story of the request of the daughters of Zelophad to inherit their deceased father's property, in violation of the laws of inheritance, which stipulate that only sons inherit property.

> When did they (i.e., the daughters) stand before Moses? At the time that Israel was saying to him, "Let us appoint a leader and return to Egypt." Moses said to them (i.e., the daughters): "All of Israel is requesting to return to Egypt and you are seeking an inheritance in the land as it says: 'it is time for the Lord to act, they have violated his Torah.'" Do not read the [verse] thus. Rather: They have violated Your Torah, it is time to act for the Lord.

In this *midrash* the verse is used in both ways. The first interpretation requires God to act by bringing the people into the land and they want what they believe is justly theirs. The second interpretation justifies violating the law in order to serve God.²⁸ The following text permits the writing down of oral Torah, which is a violation of the letter of the law in order to prevent the Torah from being forgotten.

> Did not R. Abba the son of R. Hiyya b. Abba report in the name of R. Johanan: Those who write the traditional teachings [are punished] like those who burn the Torah, and he who learns from them [the writings] receives no reward. And R. Judah b. Nahman the Meturgeman of Resh Lakish gave the following [as exposition]: The verse says: Write thou these words and then says: For after the tenor of these words, thus teaching you that matters received as oral traditions you are not permitted to recite from writing and that written things [Biblical passages] you are not permitted to recite from

memory. And the Tanna of the School of R. Ishmael taught: Scripture says, "Write thou these words," implying that "these" words you may write but you may not write traditional laws! The answer was given: Perhaps the case is different in regard to a new interpretation. For R. Johanan and Resh Lakish used to peruse the book of *aggadah* on Sabbaths and explained [their attitude] in this manner: [Scripture says:] It is time for the Lord to work, they have made void thy law, explaining this as follows: It is better that one letter of the Torah should be uprooted than that the whole Torah should be forgotten.[29]

Et la-asot is both a radical and conservative principle. It can be viewed as supporting amendment or abrogation as well as preservation of Torah (i.e., what is essential to maintaining Judaism). When amendment or abrogation will call the system into question even if it might be justified on other grounds, then abrogation or amendment would be prohibited. I want to propose a thought experiment. Although the authors of the 1885 Pittsburgh Platform would not have understood themselves as violating the Torah in order to preserve it, it is possible to argue cogently that the history of Reform Judasim can be understood as the abrogation of major sections of *halakhah* sometimes on a temporary basis,[30] but often on what has been considered a permanent basis, to preserve Judaism and fulfill God's will.

If we return to Menachem Fisch's argument that there are traditionalist and antitraditionalist "parties" in the Talmud and that there is a twofold concept to Torah study, that is, as undergraduate education and graduate education, we discover that Torah is a potentially open system. One must master the fundamentals, and when those fundamentals are an adequate response to the world and seem to fulfill the divine wil, there is no need for abrogation or amendment. In fact, preservation is the order of the day. However, when 'traditional' practice no longer is consonant with the divine will, it is time to act for the Lord by abrogating or amending the understanding of Torah. In current historical juncture, Progressive Judaism is an interim period.[31] The age that created classical Reform and its immediate successors has passed and the new era, which is sometimes described as postmodernity, is just taking shape. One characteristic of this new age is the desire of Jews for authenticity and meaning, which they are increasingly finding in a return to an encounter with sacred texts. It is the responsibility of those who believe that God's will is manifest in a faithful and systematic approach to the study of sacred texts to demonstrate it in their writing and in their own lives.

Notes

1. This paper is also designed to serve as a tribute to Rabbi Moshe Zemer, who along with Rabbi Walter Jacob established the Freehof Institute for Progressive *Halakhah*. Rabbi Zemer's contributions have been immense. His vast knowledge and writing have deeply influenced the Progressive movement in Israel, demonstrating that Orthodoxy is not the final word on *halakhah*, and his halakhic writing challenges all of us in the worldwide Progressive movement to consider seriously the role that *halakhah* should have in our decision–making process. I pray that God grants him many more productive years as a primary teacher for all of us who want to renew and revitalize Progressive Judaism in a rigorous way.

2. My answer to this question depends heavily on the thought of Menachem Fisch, especially his books *Rational Rabbis* (Bloomington: University of Indiana Press, 1997) and *Da-at Hokhmah* (Jerusalem: Van Leer Institute, 1994) as well as a series of lectures that he presented to the Beth Emet the Free Synagogue Israel Kallot.

3. For this discussion I rely heavily on Joel Roth's book *Halakhic Process: A Systemic Approach* (New York: Jewish Theological Seminary of America, 1986).

4. As I will later argue, it is the rigor of textual analysis that is so characteristic of halakhic discourse that is most relevant. In another place I have discussed the possibility of a pluralistic *halakhah* where the discourse results in a range of answers about what is permitted and prohibited. For example, the proper time for lighting candles to begin Shabbat might be determined by the astronomical considerations such as, the setting of the sun, or sociological considerations, such as when the family gathers for Shabbat dinner; both would be proper in such as system. This is in contrast to the traditional halakhic system which provides only a single proper way of lighting candles. In an as yet unpublished essay on Jewish bioethics I have argued for an aggadic or narrative approach to Reform decision, making this a variant of my concept of a pluralistic *halakhah*..

5. *B.M.* 59b.

6. The text reads *elohekha* –, your God, using the singular suffix rather than *eloheikhem* – using the plural suffix.

7. The plural form so that the people are included.

8. *Midrash Rabbah*, Num. 19:33.

9. Fisch, *Rational Rabbis*, pp. 79-88.

10. *B. M.* 59b.

11. Rashi to *Hag.* 3b.

12. Rashi to *Ket.* 57a.

13. The full argument is presented in *Rational Rabbis.*

14. Roth, *Halakhic Process*, pp. 153-204.

15. They raise a question which we constantly confront today in our work: have we begun with a conclusion that we seek to dress up with texts, or are we genuinely examining texts under new lenses that cause us to view them differently. In the same manner, when traditional *poskim* are faced with unprecedented situations, we will turn to texts whose values illuminate the current situation, but it is also clear that we will hold up certain texts as authoritative which others will not. It is the quality of the argument and not merely the use of the texts that will make the position we articulate acceptable.

16. Jacob Neusner, *The Glory of God Is Intelligence* (Provo, Utah: Brigham Young University, 1978). This analogy may not be too distant from the concept of the physicists who understand their enquiry into nature as an attempt to read the mind of God.

17. We have both de facto and de jure autonomy. This pluralism and freedom can be very healthy and creative. Its greatest limitation is that it does not encourage an intellectually serious process before change is introduced.

18. Roth, *Halakhic Process*, p. 151.

19. CCAR Responsa 5756.8 (www.ccarnet.org).

20. Simeon Maslein, *Gates of the Season*, p. vii.

21. Roth, *Halakhic Process*, pp. 149f.

22. *Ibid.*, p. 151.

23. *Ibid.*, p. 180.

24. *Ibid.*, p. 237.

25. *Ibid.*, p. 244.

26. Ps. 119:126.

27. For a more complete discussion see Roth, *Halakhic Process*, pp. 169-76.

28. *Ibid.*, p. 171.

29. *Ter.* 14 b; Roth, *Halakhic Process*, p. 179.

30. The current reexamination of certain practices and principles suggests that the conditions that required amendment or abrogation of those principles and practices have passed. In a similar manner, our reconsideration of *halakhah* may be understood as a necessary corrective to past excesses.

31. Michael Morgan, *Interim Judaism* (Indianapolis: Indiana University Press, 2001). This small but important book details the breakdown of the philosophical consensus that was the underpinning of Progressive Judaism and sets the stage for a rethinking of the underpinning and the consequences for belief and ultimately practice.

Chapter 5

❖ ❖ ❖

HALAKHAH AND THE MODERN TEMPER

Jack Cohen

I have three objectives in mind in this essay. The first is to set forth the parameters of the *halakhah* as I see them. The second is to outline the components of the modern temper that I believe are common to liberal-minded persons. The third is to suggest the role that the *halakhah* might play in Liberal Judaism.

What Is the *Halakhah*?

My revered teacher and renowned Talmudist and expert in the whole range of Rabbinic literature, Professor Louis Ginzberg *z"l*, seems to me to be sufficiently authoritative as a source for an understanding of the nature of *halakhah*. Here are a few of his observations on the subject.[1]

We can all agree with Ginzberg's remark that, "the understanding of the Jewish past, of Jewish life and thought, is impossible without a knowledge of the Halakah."[2] We can also concur with his observation that historians who argued that there could be no history of a people without a state "could not but ignore the Halakah, a way of life that was rarely sustained by the power of the state but was frequently antagonized by it."[3]

Ginzberg is careful, however, not to define *halakhah*, except to say that, "its chief feature is education of oneself or training. Accordingly, the Halakah is a true mirror reflecting the work of the Jew in shaping his character."[4] Nonetheless, Ginzberg describes the *halakhah* as follows: "as its meaning 'conduct' indicates, {it} comprises life in all its manifestations – religion, worship, law, economics, politics, ethics, and so forth. It gives us a picture of life in its totality and not of some of its fragments."⁵ Or, as Professor Ernst Simon once said, "The *halakhah* is total but not totalitarian."

Ginzberg maintains that "it is only in the Halakah that we find the mind and the character of the Jewish people are exactly and adequately expressed. Laws which govern the daily life of man must be such as suit and express his wishes, being in harmony with his feeling and fitted to satisfy his religious ideals and ethical aspirations."⁶ In the end, Ginzberg confesses that, "it would be impossible within the compass of anything less than a substantial volume to present an analysis of the ideas comprised or implied in the term Halakah."⁷

Clearly, the *halakhah* as described by Ginzberg is a lifelong course of study for gifted scholars and for those men and women who are fortunate enough to have the time and resources that can enable them to devote themselves to mastering the vast halakhic literature. But the *halakhah* is more than an academic subject or an entire curriculum for graduate and postgraduate study. Ginzberg indicates as much when he tells us that it is a picture of life. He does not make clear, however, in what sense the *halakhah* is not a closed book. It is very much alive as the way of life of a significant number of Jews, and it underlies much of the behavior of millions of others who depart from one or another of its principles, forms, or contents. We cannot be satisfied with Ginzberg's hesitancy about evaluating the theological and ideological bases of the *halakhah*, its structure of authority, its parameters of freedom and pluralism, its role in the conduct of society and state and its handling of the spiritual and moral changes that characterize the human career in general and the Jewish career in particular.

The *halakhah* grew out of the belief in the authenticity of the Bible as the repository of God's will for the Jewish people and for humankind as a whole. Once the biblical text was canonized, the scholars who developed the *halakhah* were faced with the complex problem of interpretation and application of that text. They had to decide on a theory that would underlie their understanding of the divine commands and how to adapt them to the needs of the age. However, since the Sages differed in their perceptions and temperaments, it was inevitable that no single view could gain unchallenged authority. Nonetheless, one principle has never been questioned within the halakhic framework: the whole system rests on the assumption, indeed the dogma, that the Bible, the source of all authority, was revealed to the Israelites at Mount Sinai.

Until modern times, the rabbinical debate concerned the merits of the interpretation, development and application of the text, not whether it is the word of the living God. Even today, liberal halakhists might argue about whether a particular law is consonant with a modern ethic, but they protect the divinity of the text by attributing to it a built-in process of adaptation to new conditions. Thus, anyone who regards the Bible as a man-made document denies the theological foundation of the *halakhah*.

Until the modern settlement of Jews in *Eretz Yisrael* and the eventual establishment of the State of Israel, the polity fostered in and by the *halakhah* was a nomocracy, whose development rested in the hands of scholars recognized by popular consensus. That is to say, the halakhic authorities were not elected in a formal way by the community. Rather they were an aristocratic group who earned their status by virtue of their unquestioned scholarship, character and genius. Throughout halakhic history, Jews have been free to regard as their mentors, legislators, judges and decisors those recognized scholars whose opinions appear to them most representative of the divine will. In other words, until the creation of the Zionist *Yishuv*, the *halakhah* was basically a form of voluntary self-government made possible by the common acceptance of its system as divinely ordained.

The *halakhah*, of course, has its formal institutions, such as courts, *yeshivot*, whose leaders are often considered to be worthy of acting as *poskim* (decisors), and rabbis elected to act as local authorities *(marei d'atra)*. It has also given rise to communally elected civil servants, such as *gabbaim, shohtim,* and *parnasim*. But this entire enterprise has been able to thrive only to the extent that the basic principles of revelation and authoritative scholarship have been universally acceptable to the overwhelming majority of Jews. All this has changed during the last several centuries and especially since the establishment of the Jewish state.

The *halakhah* lost its hold over the Jewish mind in the wake of the modernism that I shall describe below. However, it is the existence of the State of Israel that has challenged the viability of the *halakhah* most acutely. The decision to found a democratic state pointed up clearly why the voluntarism of the *halakhah* could no longer satisfy even many of those Jews who believed in its divine origin but who also wanted a Zionist State.

The dream of all traditional halakhists, on the other hand, was and is the restoration of the halakhic system as the way of life of all Jews, individually and collectively. Individually, voluntary obedience to halakhic precepts seems to be unrealistic. Most Jews today follow only those portions of the halakhic tradition that accord with their outlook on life. Collectively, the conduct of a modern state is impossible under the halakhic conception of authority.

A modern, enlightened state is necessarily pluralistic, whereas the *halakhah* is inherently of, by, and for the Jews alone, except insofar as aliens fall under Jewish suzerainty. In a state that favors an open society, another feature of the halakhic mentality is also rendered obsolete. I refer to the halakhic insistence that even the ritual and cultic aspects of Jewish culture must be determined by halakhic authorities who use halakhic instruments. Every state, however, must establish standards and rules for the public observance of national holidays and days of rest, the determination of the legitimacy of marriage, divorce, and inheritance, and other matters of personal status. A state must also deal with rights of citizenship. In all these concerns, there is frequently a sharp difference between authority as wielded under democratic principles and polity and those of the *halakhah*. The struggle between these two social visions in Israel has led to the partial politicization of the *halakhah* and its conversion from a voluntary nomocratic instrument into a coercive set of laws dependent on the relative strength of political parties. Given a radical shift in coalition politics, even the limited areas of halakhic domination in Israel could be undermined or expanded by a single vote in the Knesset.

The *halakhah* is total. Nothing is exempt from its authority, although there has always been a difference of opinion concerning the authority of beliefs. But in all matters of law and practice, the *halakhah* is not subject to popular democratic vote. The reality of Israel has plainly eliminated most of the *halakhah* as a means of governing the Jewish state.

Those who still insist that *Hilkhot Melakhim* or some other halakhic version of statehood are still relevant and can be adapted to the needs of a Jewish people restored to its homeland have yet to come to terms with the fact that the halakhic system has in large part become anachronistic. This is particularly true of those who want to hold on to both ends of the string – both *halakhah* and democracy. Yet no one should dispute the fact that there are many democratic elements in the *halakhah*, from the rule of the majority in the *Beth Hadin, Beth Hamidrash,* and in town meetings on matters of charity, education and so on, to such values as the sanctity of life, concern for the needy and the stranger, and a host of other items that also enter into the democratic ethic. All this, however, cannot overcome the disparity between government by the people and government by the experts in a classic literature.

What Is the Modern Temper?

Whether we like it or not, we humans cannot escape completely from the circumstances into which we are thrust as a result of the time and place of our earthly existence. Of course, our environment is multidimensional, and much of our mentality depends on the influence upon us of our immediate surroundings, rather than on what is characteristic of the larger society. Thus, every age has its premodernists, modernists and postmodernists. They all interact, and as far as we can discern, the future is molded by the degree to which each mentality captures the truths of physical and human nature. Here, I examine and try to evaluate the temper or mood of modernity and its likely effect on the future of Judaism.

Unquestionably, modernity is intimately bound up with science. While science itself is subject to many, often conflicting interpretations, its overall mood is one of self-correction. It assumes that every phenomenon within the range of our experience can be explained. All phenomena are links in the chain of events that characterize what we call the cosmos or the universe. But all explanations are subject to the limitations of the human mind. The human mind, itself the outcome of natural developments, can with some degree of success learn about the connections between all immanent phenomena. With less authority, it can guess at what transcends the accessible data of nature: are there eternal laws of nature, for example, or are there other means of explanation for the connectedness, the movement, and the changes that occur in the world of our experience? This system of investigation is self-corrective, as new data widens or deepens our perception of things.

Modernity is not necessarily a rejection of the past or of tradition. However, it is inclined to favor standards and conceptions that are endemic to the thought and behavior of informed men and women of the present, when the tradition seems to retard the growth of the individual and the group. This is particularly true in regard to the mood of modernism in facing a tradition based on belief in an exclusive revelation and a supernaturally oriented theology. Inasmuch as our understanding of consciousness and thinking still retain elements of mystery, a modernist might argue, with some degree of justification, that discovery is a form of revelation. However, the modernist is hardly likely to follow the dictates of the strict constructionist of tradition who automatically grants superior authority to traditional norms of thought and behavior over those that commend themselves to liberal and scientifically oriented minds.

To the modern mind, the *halakhah* lacks the authority that induced Jews for more than two millennia to accept it as their ideology and their way of life. This blanket statement has to be qualified on two counts. Eliezer Berkowitz *z"l*, for example, whose mindset was undoubtedly modern in many respects, argued strongly for the validity of belief in historical revelation.[8] His defense of the possibility of supernatural revelation has to be dealt with seriously – something that I cannot do in this short essay – but even if we were to be convinced of the merit of Berkowitz's position, the fact remains that the overwhelming majority of Jews no longer think or live halakhically.

Second, the modern temper sees no necessary connection between the theological foundation of a culture and the way in which it is lived or not lived by its society. Men and women often adhere to traditional beliefs but depart from the observance of the pattern of life to which those beliefs gave rise. Thus, the deviations of many Jews in their practice of Judaism might not be an indication of their rejection of the *halakhah* as the legitimate guide to the culture of the Jewish people.

We should not be surprised at such contradictions. It is they that account for the cultural lags and the often slow pace of progress in every society. Nonetheless, the modernist chooses his or her path on the basis of probability. Given the evidence of the scientific study of the Bible, the modernist has two alternatives. He can either reject historical revelation altogether or argue that the scribes who prepared the biblical text and the scholars who interpreted and adapted it to their needs made mistakes that have no authority over our own intelligence. Therefore, their rules need not commit us to follow their demands. In either case, the *halakhah* can no longer possess the authority of old.

The modern temper is democratic, pluralistic, open-minded, and protective of the freedom of the individual. The *halakhah* protects the individual in many ways but places him or her in the straitjacket of a constricted view of personal status, worship, celebration, and esthetic preference. The modern temper, on the other hand, provides for a wide latitude of opinion and conduct in all these matters.

The modernist welcomes change, and he or she fashions the instruments that enable it as expeditiously as possible. Change that affects an entire population is not left in the hands of a single class of individuals, except insofar as they are chosen by all their peers. Every system of law has a certain amount of built-in restraint, but the modern temper enables outdated laws to be set aside by popular decision. The modern temper is experimental. Men and women of this temper are attuned to the notion that social changes of all kinds are very often the outcome of purposive action on the part of adventurers who set out to try new forms of behavior. These efforts are intended to improve the quality of life for all. However, since the results of such action are often unpredictable, many persons hesitate to engage in them, preferring the security of the known. Clearly, this spirit of adventure is largely absent from the *halakhah*.

Halakhah and Liberal Judaism

How should Liberal Jews view *halakhah*? If my analysis thus far is valid, several conclusions follow:
1. The *halakhah* is one of the greatest achievements of the Jewish people. It has enabled us to survive under circumstances of exile, oppression, and landlessness that are unmatched in the annals of history. It must therefore be continuously researched and studied for its many treasures and insights in all the areas of life, including those mentioned by Louis Ginzberg and others that he did not detail.
2. Nonetheless, as a system of governance and as a total way of life for contemporary Jewry in Israel and the Diaspora, the *halakhah* is

unworkable. However, it can be an invaluable source for the conduct of all kinds of Jewish communal organizations, from the Jewish state to the variety of voluntary associations that activate and perpetuate Jewish life all over the world. For the *halakhah* is a mine of wisdom that can and should become a primary resource for legislators, educators, ethicists, psychologists– indeed, for all Jews who wish to carry our tradition forward in a creative way. {Nor would it be far-fetched to recommend to non-Jews that they be encouraged to explore the *halakhah* for its suggestiveness in a wide range of matters, such as labor-management relations, medical ethics, worship, sane sex marriage, family harmony and countless other fields of human behavior.} Obviously, the use of the *halakhah* will have to be highly selective, but such is the case in every instance of learning from the past.

3. There is much talk today among liberal Jews about rescuing the *halakhah* from the constraints that traditional halakhists have placed upon it. Moshe Zemer's scholarly study, *Evolving Halakhah*, proves beyond a shadow of doubt that the *halakhah* has the necessary tools to overcome many of the inequities, and immoral and anachronistic stands taken by *haredi* and Orthodox scholars and which have alienated so many Jews. Moreover, I agree with Zemer that it is necessary to go beyond the *halakhah* in order to take proper advantage of its positive features.

In the first place, a clear distinction has to be made between the *halakhah* as a system of civil law and its role in ritual usage. In regard to the former, as stated above, the halakhic chain of authority is unacceptable in a democratic society. Liberal Jews have to make this point clear. Civil legislation does not belong solely in the hands of any rabbinic group, no matter how scholarly its members might be. On the other hand, it should be obvious that the *halakhah* is a mine of material that should be one of the main sources of inspiration for Israeli legislators and judges. Scholars of the rabbinic literature should be encouraged to make their research available to the officials who are responsible for the introduction of new legislation and for the judges and other governmental servants who have to administer the laws. Furthermore, liberals should accept the fact that the dedication to freedom demands that all matters of worship and ritual must be removed from the rule of law. Standards in these matters are desirable, and rabbis are qualified and obligated to take the lead in preparing their congregants to aim for the highest possible level of spirituality and respect for the heritage that has been bequeathed to us by our forefathers. But this is an educative function. As such, it cannot be a monopoly of halakhists. Each Jew must be encouraged to equip himself with the background that will enable him to choose that form of prayer and worship and those rituals worthy of a dedicated and spiritually alert Jew.

These considerations, if they represent liberal thinking, take us beyond the *halakhah*. However, let us remember that even those who have stepped beyond the *daled amot* of the *halakhah* live parts of it every day. Our holidays were molded in and by the *halakhah*; much of our ethical outlook is the product of the sensitivity of halakhic sages; our family ties owe much to the efforts of the halakhic scholars to preserve family purity and closeness; the intellectual bent and prowess of so many of our people can be traced to the educational outlook and the extraordinary dedication to learning that are built into the halakhic system. The tradition of self-help communal institutions is largely a carry-over from the *halakhah*. And so on. The point in all this is that Judaism can ill afford to lose the treasures imbedded in the *halakhah* and that we must find ways to extract them.

Liberal Jews, in my opinion, ought not to be spending valuable time and scholarly energy in trying to show that we can find better solutions, by means of halakhic interpretation and hermeneutics, than can traditional halakhists to problems that can be dealt with more proficiently by democratic means. Instead, we ought to be culling from the vast rabbinic sources those ideas, practices, and insights that can add to the quality of Jewish culture in our time.

In brief, Liberal Jews should convince themselves and try to convince their fellow Jews that the *halakhah* will be best honored by retiring it as a system of determining and conducting the Jewish way of life. The *halakhah* should become a kind of elder statesman, a source to which we can turn for advice and help in dealing with the problems of the Jewish people and the contemporary world.

Notes

1. The quotations below are from Ginzberg's *Students, Scholars and Saints* (Philadelphia: Jewish Publication Society, 1928 [reprinted in 1943]). In the quotations from Ginzberg, I have reproduced his spelling. The term "*halakhah*" is found in the literature in a variety of spellings and use of upper or lower casing. My preference is *halakhah* as a noun and halakhic as an adjective.

2. *Ibid.* 110.

3. *Ibid.* 113.

4. *Ibid.* 112.

5. *Ibid.* 114.

6. *Ibid.* 117.

7. *Ibid.* 109.

Chapter 6

❖ ❖ ❖

WRITING RESPONSA: A PERSONAL JOURNEY

Walter Jacob

Reform responsa have almost two centuries of tradition behind them. Despite the ambivalence expressed by some radical reformers in Europe and North America, responsa appeared from virtually the beginning, and we have seen ourselves as a continuation of the rabbinic tradition in a modern garb.[1] This literature, in our hands, has adapted the traditional patterns and been written in the vernacular as well as Hebrew.

My portion of this work has covered three decades, and my effort has been directed toward giving the *halakhah* a more central role within the Reform movement as a vehicle for setting standards and boundaries without eliminating the inherent flexibility of Reform Judaism. This halakhic approach will also bring us into a more focused discussion with the other branches of Judaism I have been aware of the positions taken by my predecessors in Germany, Hungary, and North America, especially the work of Solomon B. Freehof, my mentor and friend, who broadened the Reform interest in the *halakhah* beginning with his two volumes entitled *Reform Jewish Practice and Its Rabbinic Background* sixty years ago and continuing through a series of responsa volumes in English, without, however, writing about the theoretical basis for his efforts.[2] I have been interested both in writing responsa and going beyond responsa, which led to the founding of the Freehof Institute of Progressive *Halakhah*, a joint venture with Moshe Zemer. The volumes of the Institute complement the responsa literature as they provide a systematic discussion of issues. They differ from responsa as they do not present decisions but provide the basis for educated decision making.

For me interest in responsa began at the Hebrew Union College library in a very modest way. As a first- year rabbinic student

I earned some money by working in the library, shelving books and pre-cataloguing; I found the responsa collection difficult as the system had not taken into account the complexities of similar titles, various editions, and books that only vaguely belonged in that collection. My work brought me into contact with Herbert Zafren, the Director of Libraries, as well as Moses Marx and Isaiah Sonne, scholars in this field. The library had received a large number of books liberated from the Nazis, which were distributed to leading Jewish institutions throughout the world.[3] The library was short of help, so I was given tasks with much more responsibility than usually assigned to a beginner. Occasionally there was also an opportunity to purchase a duplicate old volume.

When I arrived in Pittsburgh at Rodef Shalom as a twenty–four–year–old, not yet ordained assistant rabbi in the winter of 1955, I had the opportunity of watching Solomon B. Freehof, who had begun seriously writing reponsa for the Reform movement.[4] Earlier he had prepared responsa for the armed forces of the United States, which had gotten him involved in writing responsa. My introduction that spring was very brief as I left for a two–year stint as a United States Air Force chaplain in the Philippines. Although this was a wonderful opportunity to become acquainted with the lands, cultures, and art of the Far East, the tropical Philippines were hardly a place for transporting a library, so I settled on the *Mishneh Torah* and continued to study it. This eventually led to a minor in rabbinic codes for my doctorate, however, upon returning to Pittsburgh I concentrated on a doctorate in the field of German Jewish literature. Daily contact with Solomon B. Freehof showed me the questions that were troubling our colleagues. He often asked me to read a newly minted responsum as he corrected it or checked some data. However, the tasks of this large congregation, establishing a family, and writing a doctoral dissertation did not leave much time for rabbinic literature. I was placed on the Responsa Committee of the Central Conference of American Rabbis (CCAR) in the 1960s, but as this committee never met and held no discussions,[5] it provided no additional exposure to scholarly debate, but I studied on my own and got to know the literature.

In the early 1960s a fire in a rabbinic library in Pittsburgh brought an insurance adjuster to Solomon B. Freehof for his estimate of the value of the books. It was a fine collection, mainly classical Hebrew books; Dr. Freehof inquired what would be done with the damaged volumes as they, like all Hebrew religious texts, deserved proper disposal. The company intended to destroy or bury them, but they were willing to sell them to Dr. Freehof, who had them delivered to a basement room in the Temple. We soon proceeded with the dirty work of going through this mountain of ash-covered books and sometimes were ankle deep in half-burned pages. After an hour we looked and smelled more like fire-fighters than rabbis; it was a dirty labor of love for two bibliophiles. Dr. Freehof selected some books for his library; we sorted dozens of cartons of *hidushin* for the Hebrew Union College; we sent copies of title pages of hundreds of other volumes to the Hebrew Union College, the Library of Congress, the Jewish Theological Seminary, and various universities to see whether they were interested in them. Finally we sent half a dozen cartons of fragments and loose pages to the Hebrew Union College. As several hundred volumes of responsa were duplicates of Dr. Freehof's library, they became the basis of my collection. All were in poor condition and constantly losing portions of their burnt binding edge. They needed to be wrapped before being shelved in my study. Through the next decade Solomon B. Freehof, whose hobby was bookbinding, bound all of them.[6] Many were rare early volumes. These books and those that I have purchased through the years make up my extensive responsa collection.

When Solomon B. Freehof retired as chair of the Responsa Committee, he suggested that I replace him. Before the ratification of that appointment, I wrote an initial responsum, simply to demonstrate some knowledge of the field and without an effort to provide a *hiddush*. For me responsa as well as my later halakhic efforts were a way of connecting the Reform movement more closely to the *halakhah*, which has always been the central expression of Judaism. Reform never abandoned the *halakhah*, as the discussions at the Central European and American conferences of the nineteenth and twentieth century among other things demonstrate. Even the radical meeting in Pittsburgh dealt with halakhic matters in some surprising ways.[7] Individualism and antinomianism had to be largely surrendered, despite theoretical debates, if one wished to be part of a community; I have treated this elsewhere.

Thus began a sixteen-year period in which I was heavily involved in the writing of responsa. Since then I have continued, but at a diminished pace and with more emphasis on halakhic essays, the founding and leadership of the Abraham Geiger College, and other interests.

My first task, as I saw it, was the reorganization of the committee into a functioning body for which there was no precedent. My colleagues were willing to participate but did not have the library resources in this period before computer references, or the inclination to devote a major amount of their time to this effort. I therefore suggested that I would prepare each responsum and they would comment via mail. This process worked reasonably well, although it was slow. In order to speed matters along we had some meetings, which we used in an attempt to create some general guidelines. As the funds of the Central Conference were extremely limited during these years, meetings were rare. In reality, it proved more useful to to use those few occasions to deal with the most difficult individual questions rather than to develop a general philosophy.

As the number of questions increased and as I sent an ever larger number of responsa to my colleagues for their comments, the return mail became slower; they were a bit overwhelmed and wanted to limit their work. We soon agreed that I should decide which responsa deserved committee attention and which should be answered by me, as chair, alone. The vast majority quickly fell into the latter category.

After a few years, I suggested that the committee prepare a collection of responsa that had been published by the CCAR so that our colleagues could refer to questions already settled rather than ask us again. Many of these responsa had been written under very different circumstances decades earlier and needed additional comments in order to be useful to our colleagues. I went through them, annotated them, and provided comments to which the committee responded, initially by mail and eventually, with the more difficult ones, through face-to-face discussions. This effort turned our attention to the different approaches of the chairs of the Responsa Committee. Some committee members proposed that we prepare position papers that I assigned, but nothing came of it.

Upon becoming chair of the committee, questions arrived from the first day. There was no time for philosophical contemplation or for lengthy discussions with the committee before undertaking the work. Colleagues and congregants were seeking answers, so I began, as most authors do of responsa and most judges in any jurisdiction, by writing and letting the philosophy work itself out as I proceeded, which undoubtedly produced some inconsistencies. Maturity and experience would play a major role.

Considerations and Assumptions

I have always considered writing responsa a religious task. The guidance provided must have a spiritual basis that needs to be clear in each answer. Occasionally I had to remind myself of this as I delved into the debates and details of the *halakhah*, which could wander far from their ultimate goal. As for my predecessors, it was my task to set boundaries to human behavior. In some instances this means narrowing the parameters, in others widening them. Many factors come into play as with earlier generations, though we perhaps are more conscious of them. My responsa continue to be written mainly for the American Jewish community; Reform communities in other lands often face different concerns and live in another environment, which may lead to different answers, especially in matters of status, ritual, and interfaith relations. I have always felt that the concern of those colleagues in Israel or Europe should be secondary and should not heavily influence American decisions. When, during the last years, I have written some responsa for the central European community, my answers take that environment and its *minhagim* into consideration.

My efforts have been based on an understanding of the *halakhah* which I shall briefly outline here; I have partially treated this topic elsewhere and will return to it. For me the origin of the *halakhah* is divine, but transmitted by human beings and therefore interpreted and reinterpreted by each generation from Moses onward and occasionally radically changed. This means that the ideas which lie beneath the specific human wording reflect divine inspiration. Each generation has interpreted the *halakhah* according to its understanding. That interpretation has been colored and molded by the times, the issues, and the environment.

I see rituals as less important than other aspects of the *halakhah*. Some, in a form different than currently practiced, can be traced to the Torah; others are *minhagim*, more significant in specific periods, or among *Ashkenazim* and *Sephardim*. They remind us of our ethical duties; they are important as they are an emotional and nonrational connection to Judaism.

The Talmud records a debate whether the *halakhah* was in human hands or should depend on divine guidance.[8] The fact that the debate took place shows that even on this fundamental matter there was disagreement. However, the majority of the talmudic scholars took as an underlying assumption that the *halakhah* was to be interpreted by human begins without divine interference. This has remained the basis of halakhic discourse from the Talmud onward. It was understood that 'divine revelation' had ended - with all the theological implications of that view: It meant that Christianity and Islam could be rejected on this ground alone. It made direct contact between human beings and God problematic and led to the development of Jewish mysticism. At times, as with Joseph Caro, the mystical path coalesced with the halakhic road.[9]

Succeeding generations have treated the *halakhah* in four ways. (1) Most scholars in all generations have seen themselves as only clarifying the tradition assumed to be unchanged since Moses. The entire *halakhah* was understood as a unified whole and all segments were forced into this position through any means possible – even when a simple reading would show tensions, contradictions, or radical shift from earlier decisions. The myth of a unified tradition was maintained. (2) Some scholars have stated that they wished to return to the original meaning of the tradition held in the days of Moses or by the talmudic 'giants.' (3) Still other scholars have understood that they were reinterpreting the *halakhah* to fit into a new age with due consideration for the past. (4) Some in many generations have sought to systematize and simplify the *halakhah* by creating 'codes' which summarized the *halakhah* as they understood it. This was also intended to make the *halakhah* accessible to the average Jews. Each codification has been vigorously opposed as its commentaries and super-commentaries show. (5) Finally *takanot* have always been used to deal with difficult issues, often, theoretically, on a temporary basis; yet many became permanent. The Reform movement has used this process to deal with status and other matters.

Those who have taken the first path, have spent vast energies adjusting and harmonizing the strands of the tradition and its contradictory statements from the Torah, through the two Talmuds, and the subsequent literature. Over the millennia, this task has become increasingly difficult. In the responsa literature it has often led to very long essays in answer to a simple question.

Those who have taken the second path, many in the generation immediately following the Talmud, sought the original meaning of the text and then the right path through the maze of later discussions. This was never easy as the scholars of the Talmud present a variety of opinions, often totally contradictory on virtually any matter. In scholarly debates, this made no difference, but for practical halakhic decisions it was impossible. The Talmud and the later gaonim were aware of the problem and established some rules for decision making; the fullest discussion is found in Avodah Zarah 7a. Later codes expanded these efforts. Joseph Caro used Alfasi,[10] Maimonides, and Asher ben Yehiel as his authorities for decisions and adopted the decision of two of those three, unless later scholars followed the opinion of the third. This was arbitrary, but practical.

The third path has been taken consciously in modern times, but not exclusively so. In the last two centuries scholars have become more aware of the outside sociological, philosophical, and political factors which have formed halakhic views and decisions. Scholars have looked for these factors in previous ages, so modern halakhic studies present a historical view.

In Orthodox circles the codification process has come to a halt since Joseph Caro in the 16th century. The Reform and Conservative movements have produced partial codifications of the ritual aspects of Judaism, but have not gone further.

For my writing I have followed the third and fifth path and have always been aware of the many internal and external influences which have shaped halakhic decisions. I am less interested in harmonization and more in the moral and ethical considerations which must lie beneath each decision. Several special consideration have also played a role: (1) As we understand that our decisions are the product of our age and its influences, then we may also see similar conditions in the past and accept decisions made long ago, but rejected by subsequent generations for reasons shaped by their times.

This means that the automatic reliance on one or another talmudic decissor – without thinking about the ethical basis as well as the historical and sociological reasons for that decision – may not be valid for us. Among the talmudic scholars, we may choose someone whom the tradition rejected. Among the 'codes, we may, on occasion prefer the path of Maimonides or Alfasi when there is a moral justification.

We are prepared to open old discussions and sometimes follow them to different conclusions – aware that the circumstances of our time may call for that direction. (2) The ethical imperatives of feminism, sexual orientation, disabilities lead us to a different view of the tradition. In these areas we have made a break with the past.

My decisions may agree or differ from some Orthodox decissors; either way, the underlying reasoning is often quite different as I, along with many others, consciously view the specific issue raised through the lens of tradition along with ethical concerns, history, sociology, economics, and related factors.

My view is that change is possible and that we must be open to experimentation. We link ourselves to the tradition and the past, but we do not replicate it. My colleagues and I reject Moses Sofer's assumption that all change is wrong. When conditions demand I am willing to embrace change even knowing that a later generation for its own good and valid reasons may reject it. This may well lead to more positive than negative halakhic decisions

For me the divine impulse underlying the *halakhah* remains the same. The past with its grand scholarship and literature is a vast reservoir from which we drink. We enter into debate with the scholars of previous generations, with due deference, but the decisions must reflect our own age. Reform precedent along with the resolutions of our movement, of course, always play a significant role in decisions.

Any decision, especially if made in writing places the author on the firing line. A safer path has been selected by many modern Orthodox scholars who state that their decisions represent academic discussions, but are not to be followed in practical life. Although this may avoid attack, allow a trial balloon, and permit a graceful withdrawal, it does not help the person seeking an answer. I would rather make a decision and have another generation of writers of responsa take a different path, than make no decision.

Some Practical Issues

There are a number of practical difficulties facing anyone who writes responsa. The first is the size of the literature and its state of disorganization. Most of the volumes of past centuries have no index or entries which are not helpful. That has been partially changed through the computerized responsa project undertaken in Israel which did not exist thirty years ago. A vast literature, along with its commentaries still lies outside the scope of the responsa project as does the secondary literature of books and periodicals, some of which are obscure.

The changing style of responsa writing that has developed through the ages brings its problems. During some periods responsa were direct and brief, though rarely as brief as some of Maimonides single–word replies. At other times the authors sought to display their erudition and cited every precedent along with their comments upon it. Another set of authors wished to create *hidushin* and traveled down numerous byroads to do so. It was necessary to sort out what was useful without neglecting the peripheral.

Questions come in every area of Jewish law and occasionally in rather obscure corners. Some issues that are of great significance to us were of little interest or peripheral in earlier ages, so responses had to be sought from analogous situations. The search in that direction can consume a huge amount of time and often with little to show for it. On the other hand, some issues loomed large in earlier periods and resulted in an enormous amount of literature that must be studied, although there is rarely time to master it. Some of the long–standing controversies that raged for a century in the traditional community have been of little interest to us.

A major problem for any writer is our modern impatience. Our inquirers want instant answers. How fortunate were the *gaonim* in Baghdad who received an inquiry from hundreds or thousands of miles away and had months, till the departure of the next caravan, to prepare a reply. Many questions come to me through urgent telephone calls. For example, a colleague calls about a *minhag* which has led to a dispute among mourners as a funeral is about to start; an immediate response is necessary and there is no time for research. I have always provided a tentative answer and indicated that it may need to be changed. My later detailed answer often demanded some modification, but at least the service could proceed peacefully. Even if the matters are not quite so urgent, a timely answer not one produced with academic leisure, is usually needed. This means that a committee process is a luxury for many questions, if we wish to truly help our colleagues. As both colleagues and lay individuals need guidance more or less immediately, I often have to place the background material into a later responsum to a related question.

There have been specific American considerations, such as the American Jew's emphasis on individualism and personal autonomy. We have created unique organizational structures that have led to new types of questions concerning charity, social aid, and education. Jewish religious bodies, both lay and rabbinic with their resolutions and *takanot*, are different from those of the past. The nature of the rabbinate has been redefined several times during the last two centuries. It has become professionalized, so that the traditional view needed adjustment.

It was not always easy to balance the task of writing responsa with the responsibilities of a large congregation with its numerous religious services, educational programs, pastoral duties, family crises, and communal tasks alongside a growing family and other interests. Only long evenings and early mornings of study along with tight personal organization has made it possible.

Specific Concerns

Our understanding of medical issues, particularly at the beginning and end of life, continues to change and so the traditional answers need constant review. Questions that deal with birth control, abortion, the status of the fetus, artificial insemination, surrogate mothers, and related controversial matters are among them. New medical procedures such as transplants, genetic tools, and experimental drugs have raised issues with little precedent. Our view of the status of women has us place many of these questions into a different framework.

In each of these instances, I have looked carefully at the traditional answers, usually given long before such advances were made, as well as those of contemporary colleagues. I have consulted medical experts, who have been helpful, but as some procedures remain controversial additional information is not always useful. Occasionally it has been necessary to qualify a response, but generally I feel that a definite answer is required. The questioner is not interested in an essay or a menu of choices but rather seeks help with a specific situation.

Our new relationships with the religions around us continue to bring a large number of questions. Ecumenism without syncretism and with a regard for the positive efforts of other faiths on social issues and theology has been my goal. Much material from earlier ages has not been appropriate; however, boundaries must be clearly drawn especially with intermarriage and issues connected with the extended family. For me the boundaries remain clear and there are limits beyond which it is inappropriate to involve non-Jews, no matter how friendly they may be. Usually the Jewish questioner has had more difficulty with this than the believing Christian.

In the matter of status we have taken a stand that remains somewhat controversial especially in Europe and Israel. It has enabled us to place more emphasis on education and personal involvement and less on lineage.

In matters of ritual in the synagogue or the turning points of life (birth, marriage, death) congregational independence has led to diversity which can often be justified through the endless variety of *minhagim* of the past, yet I have tried to help mold a consensus and not provide a menu of choices.

In these as well as other areas, I feel that generalizations will come after enough individual cases have been decided. It is wiser not to debate a general philosophical or theological approach in the abstract but to begin with specific situations that may lead to a broader policy.

Some Concluding Thoughts and Another Path

The fascination of responsa lies in many areas. For example, the questions reveal what is in the mind of our people, especially as larger numbers of questions come from congregants. These inquiries, perhaps more than questionnaires and surveys, provide an insight into the religious development of the Reform community. Clearly there is a rising interest in seeking a halakhic grounding.

For whom are we writing? This question faces all Jewish groups. Reform, Orthodox, and Conservative respondists write for those in their community who are committed. None write for their entire community. Certainly those in each group who ask the questions are likely to follow the path demanded and I have written for them. Our problem is less with Orthodox and Conservative co-religionists and more with secular Jews and who stand at the periphery of the *halakhah*. In our long history we have faced this problem before and have taken the attitude that we will eventually persuade the community to follow us. As I am generally optimistic, rather than lament, I prefer the path of *Pirkei Avot*: "It is not incumbent upon us to complete the work, but neither are we free to desist from it."

The disadvantage of being responsible for the responsa committee of the CCAR is that there is little time to study issues deeply. It means that one must suddenly shift attention to an inquiry in what may be new and unknown territory. This was pleasant for a time but also frustrating. Although I have continued to write responsa as well as halakhic letters, which are less formal, I do so on a selective basis and often refer individuals to the Responsa Committee and its chair.

As I wished to concentrate more on specific issues and also wanted to provide a more systematic background for the modern problems that confront us, I sought a way of preparing major position papers along with practical guidance for aspects of modern Jewish life. A new committee of the CCAR seemed like an appropriate vehicle. It was appointed but proved difficult as the organizational nature of the CCAR imposes restraints on committee membership and publications.

Even as I was thinking of a separate organization for this purpose, Moshe Zemer came along with his thoughts. It seemed logical to combine our efforts and to create a worldwide organization, which would also help Israeli Reform Judaism. The pattern which has developed gives Moshe as Director a free hand to do what he wishes in Israel with modest American financial backing. I hope that he will develop matters further in Israel. Our main effort has been concentrated in North America with considerable joint planning. I have taken care of the major aspects of the symposia and everything connected with membership, book editing and publication, the triennial *Halakhah,* and all mailings. As I have become more involved in central and eastern Europe through the presidency of the Abraham Geiger College in Potsdam, I have worked to expand our efforts and membership in those lands. A very informal governing structure made all of this possible for both of us.

The Institute continues to flourish with the blessings of the Central Conference of American Rabbis. The Central Conference provides a site for a major portion of our symposia while others have been planned with the World Union of Progressive Judaism as well as independently.

The world of Reform *halakhah* is expanding among the laity and the rabbinate and I hope that this will continue. Writing responsa and halakhic essays has given me the opportunity to engage in dialogue with generations, past and present, a grand gift. In the spirit of Reform Judaism, I remain open and willing to take new roads, which has been a hallmark of Judaism through the ages. The *halakhah* has provided a path for the development of Judaism and its ability to deal with the ever changing world. It continues to be my good fortune to make a small contribution to this process.

Notes

1. See the reference in the "Introduction" to Walter Jacob, *Contemporary American Reform Responsa* (New York: CCAR Press, 1987), p. xv.

2. Freehof's rationale for halakhic decisions have been pressented in the essay of David Golinkin in this volume. Earlier American writers of Reform responsa made no attempt in this direction.

3. The Nazi regime had collected Jewish books from all parts of Europe in order to create a vast anti-Semitic library. Many had been assembled in a Rhineland castle, where they were discovered by some Jewish soldiers who were seeking a suitable headquarters for a military command. After the war, whenever possible books were returned to the libraries from which they came or to their private owner. As many communities no longer existed, an enormous number of books were made available to Jewish libraries throughout the world.

4. Freehof wrote some brief pieces akin to responsa for the *Temple Bulletin* beginning in 1937, but his serious responsa writing began through his efforts as chair of a committee consisting of an Orthodox and Conservative colleague; they answered questions for the American armed services at the behest of the Jewish Welfare Board. Those responsa were published in 1947 and 1953. Freehof succeeded his friend, Israel Bettan as chair of the Responsa Committee of the Central Conference of American Rabbis and totally changed the style of writing from his predecessor..

5. No meetings or exchanges of correspondence have been recorded for the chairs of this committee before Solomon B. Freehof. Dr. Freehof did not involve the committee members in his work. It was his practice to send the responsum that he considered sufficiently significant to serve as the official responsum of the Conference for that year to the members of the committee with a reply postcard. Only once did a committee member write a minority opinion.

6. Solomon Freehof learned bookbinding while in Pittsburgh as a way of maintaining his large library and relaxing. His responsa library, given as a gift to the Hebrew Union College in Cincinnati, has a joyful look about it as he used remnants of binding material from the professional bindery of the Carnegie Library. This led to odd combination of colors and two-tone bindings. First editions, however, were bound in leather.

7. Walter Jacob, "The Influence of the Pittsburgh Platform on Reform Halakhah and Biblical Study," *The Changing World of Reform Judaism - The Pittsburgh Platform in Retrospect*, (Pittsburgh:Rodef Shalom Press, 1985), pp. 25 ff.

8. B. M. 59b

9. R. J. Zwi Werblowsky, *Joseph Karo - Lawyer and Mystic* (Philadelphia: 1977, Jewish Publication Society).

10. For a fuller discussion and other sources see Walter Jacob, "The Sources of Reform Halachic Authority," *Rabbinic Authority* [ed. Elliot L. Stevens], (New York, 1982: Central Conference of American Rabbis), pp. 31 ff.

Chapter 7

❖ ❖ ❖

ETHICS VERSUS RITUAL

John Rayner

Deed and Creed

"Judaism is a religion of deed, not creed." That slogan, attributed to Moses Mendelssohn, has been repeated by writers about Judaism, in so many words, ever since. There is much truth in it, but also some exaggeration.

It was gently ridiculed by Israel Abrahams when he wrote: "Since the time of Moses Mendelssohn the chief dogma of Judaism has been that Judaism has no dogmas." He went on to concede, however, that "Dogmas imposed by an authority able and willing to enforce conformity and punish dissent are nonexistent in Judaism."[1]

That there is nevertheless *some* emphasis in Judaism on correct belief can easily be demonstrated. There is, for instance, the admittedly uncharacteristic statement of the Mishnah that three categories of people – those who reject resurrection, revelation, and morality – have no share in the world-to-come.[2] There are the various medieval attempts, based on that statement, to formulate a Jewish creed.[3] And there is the fact that one of these, by Maimonides, found its way into the prayer book. In any case, it is clear that the *shema* is a declaration of faith, and that, since Maimonides, converts to Judaism have been required to affirm *ikrei hadat*, "the fundamentals of the faith," which are the unity of God and the prohibition of idolatry.[4]

Belief, therefore, is not unimportant in Judaism; but it is certainly true that the *greater emphasis* in Judaism has always been on action rather than belief, on deed rather than creed.

Learning and Doing

If there is anything that rivals action in rabbinic thought, it is not so much belief as learning. A well-known passage, after listing various commendable actions states, *v'talmud torah k'neged kulam* – "But the study of Torah is equal to them all."[5] That, however, is a deliberate paradox, which modern commentators have rightly resolved by explaining that the study of Torah is equal to them all only in the sense that it *leads* to them all.

There are indeed many rabbinic teachings to the effect that study without action is useless, or worse than useless.[6] Characteristic is the saying of Rabbi Shimon ben Gamliel: *lo hamidrash hu ikar ela hama-saeh* – "Not study but action is the essential thing."[7]

Defining Ethics

If Judaism is primarily, though not exclusively, concerned with doing rather than believing, or even learning, what kind of doing are we talking about? It is here that we come to the dichotomy that is the subject of this paper. For there are two kinds of doing that Judaism, like other religions, expects of its adherents: ethical and ritual.

What, then, is "ethics"? That seemingly simple question is not easy to answer. Obviously, ethics deals with such concepts as good and bad and right and wrong. But the trouble is that these terms are also used in nonethical senses. For instance, a painting, a song, a car, and even the weather can be said to be good or bad! Similarly, there is a right and a wrong way to close down a computer, to eat spaghetti, and to address an ambassador. Yet in none of these cases is any ethical judgment implied. It would seem, rather, that ethical issues arise only where there is free will, hence in human behavior; and only when the intended or unintended effect of the action is to benefit or harm another person.

In terms of Jewish tradition, the realm of the ethical

corresponds to what the rabbis called *mitzvot bein adam lamakom*, the obligations of one human being to another – except that we need to add that ethical issues arise also in our treatment of animals, because they, too, are sentient beings, and of the environment, because that affects the well-being of future generations.

Defining Ritual

What we mean by ritual is also not easy to define. For different institutions of society – political, legal, academic, and so on – have different kinds of ritual. To address an ambassador incorrectly, for instance, is a breach of the protocol governing diplomatic ritual. But in the area of religion, which concerns us, rituals are essentially actions deemed to be required by, or conductive to, the relationship of the individual – or of the community – with God. They therefore correspond to what the rabbis called *mitzvot bein adam lamakom*, the obligations of human beings, not to one another, but to God.

At least most typical, we think of rituals as symbolic actions involving sight or sound or taste or smell or movement or touch, or any combinations of these. In a Jewish context, lighting candles, singing psalms, eating unleavened bread, smelling the *havdalah* spice box, performing *hakkafot* (circumambulations), and building a *sukkah*, are all obvious examples.

But there are other, less formal actions that also pertain to the individual's relationship with God. One we have already mentioned is learning: the study of religious texts. Another is private prayer. Even inward attitudes, when directed to God, belong to the *mishkan*. Maimonides, for instance, in his *Sefer ha-Mitzvot*, includes among the first few of the Positive Commandments, the obligations to love God, to fear God, and to cleave to God.

Clearly, as we move from the more regulated to the more spontaneous, the word 'ritual' becomes less and less appropriate. Therefore, it would perhaps be better to speak of 'devotional' actions.

But since the word "ritual" is so well established in the context that concerns us, let us continue to use it and understand it in the broad sense I have indicated.

What we want to investigate, then, is the relative importance assigned to ethics and ritual, first in traditional Judaism, then in Progressive Judaism.

The Priestly Tendency in the Bible

If we begin with the biblical period, we immediately notice two divergent tendencies: priestly and prophetic. They are not mutually exclusive but are nevertheless distinctive.

The priestly tendency is represented mainly by the so-called Priestly Code of the Pentateuch. From this point of view, ritual – represented almost exclusively by the sacrificial cult – is *enormously* important. This may be inferred from the minute detail in which the construction of the *mishkan*, the Tabernacle of the Wilderness, and its furnishings are described[8] likewise from the meticulous precision with which the mandatory sacrifices, and the priestly functions relating to them, are regulated.[9] It may also be inferred from the dire penalties that attended any infringement of the cultic rules. Nadab and Abihu, sons of Aaron, were struck down by a thunderbolt because they offered "'strange fire".[10]

One gets the impression that the Temple cult was viewed as a means of ensuring the continuation of God's benevolence, and hence of sustaining the cosmos. For instance, it is repeatedly said that the purpose of the burnt offerings was to provide *re-ah niho-ah* – a "pleasing odor" for God.[11]

Closely associated with the laws of sacrifice were the laws of ritual purity and ritual purification, such as the rite of *parah adumah*, the Red Heifer.[12] Ritual purity, in turn, was closely associated with holiness; indeed, it was the chief means to holiness. Holiness, in the priestly legislation of the Pentateuch, is not primarily an ethical concept. It is rather a condition attained by scrupulous avoidance of anything defiling, which may be contact with a corpse but may also be sexual misconduct. The nineteenth chapter of Leviticus, for instance, includes some sacrificial laws as well as laws concerning garments made of *shatnez*, mixed cloth, and shaving. But it also includes some laws of good behavior and social justice, such as "You shall love your neighbor as yourself."

Thus, ethical concerns are not absent from the priestly portions of the Pentateuch. But they occupy only a fraction of the space devoted to ritual matters, and when, as in Leviticus 19, they jostle each other, one gets no impression that from the standpoint of the author or editor they are of unequal importance – that it is, for instance, more important to refrain from stealing than to refrain from wearing garments of mixed cloth.

And even if we switch our focus to the Book of Deuteronomy, or to the Pentateuch as a whole, we have to say that there is at best only an approximate *balance* between ethics and ritual, without any systemic distinction between them.

The Prophetic Tendency in the Bible

Very different is the prophetic tendency, at least as represented by the Books of Amos, Hosea, Isaiah, Micah, Jeremiah, and Deutero-Isaiah. In these books hardly anything positive is said about sacrifices or any other rituals; on the contrary, they are frequently dismissed as irrelevant, or worse, from a divine point of view. Here are some of the key passages, with just a few comments.

Amos speaks sarcastically when he says, "Bring your sacrifices every morning . . . for so you love to do, O children of Israel, says the Eternal God."[13] People enjoy performing rituals, but they deceive themselves if they think that to do so is to please God. And Amos spells out his quintessential message when he says in God's name: "I hate, despise your festivals, and I take no delight in your solemn assemblies . . . But let justice roll down like water, and righteousness like an overflowing stream."[14]

Hosea, in the same vein, makes God say: "I love loyalty and not sacrifice, and the knowledge of God rather than burnt offerings."[15] To know God is to know that only righteousness matters from a divine point of view.

Isaiah speaks unequivocally:
> "What to Me is the multitude of your sacrifices? Says the Eternal One . . . Your new moons and your appointed festivals My soul hates . . . . Even though you make many prayers, I will not listen. . . . Cease to do evil, learn to do good; seek justice, rescue the oppressed, defend the orphan, plead for the widow."[16]

Micah is equally outspoken:
> "Will the Eternal One be pleased with thousands of rams, with ten thousands of rivers of oil? . . . Human beings have told you what is good; but what does God require of you? Only to do justice, and to love kindness, and to walk humbly with your God."[17]

Evidently the 'human beings' in question are priests, who have been telling the people what a good thing it is to offer sacrifices.

Jeremiah, in his Temple sermon, leaves no room for doubt:
> "In the day that I brought your ancestors out of the land of Egypt, I did not speak to them or command them concerning burnt offerings and sacrifices. But this command I gave them, obey My voice, and I will be your God. . . ."[18]

To obey God's voice is not to perform rituals but to behave morally.

Deutero-Isaiah ridicules the people's notion that the way to gain God's favor is to afflict oneself by fasting. Is not this, he says, the only kind of fast pleasing to God:
> "to share your bread with the hungry, and to bring the homeless poor to your house; when you see the naked, to cover them, and not to hide yourself from your own kin?"[19]

In God's eyes fasting is nothing, but social justice is everything.

I am aware that nowadays apologists for tradition tend to explain these passages away as mere hyperbole, but I am convinced they are mistaken. They argue that because there were cultic prophets in the ancient Near East, therefore *all* prophets must have been connected with the cult; but, of course, that is nonsense. Or they reason that because Ezekiel devoted several chapters to setting out a blueprint for the postexilic Temple, therefore all prophets must have shared his enthusiasm; but that is another nonsequitur. Most probably, these modern apologists simply cannot imagine religion without ritual; but that is only a failure of imagination on their part.

Sometimes they try to clinch their point by quoting Isaiah saying in God's name, "I cannot endure iniquity along with the solemn assembly,"[20] or again, "Even when you make many prayers, I will not listen: your hands are full of blood."[21] "Aha," they say, "these phrases go to show that what God disapproves of is not ritual as such, but only the combination of ritual with iniquity. Without iniquity, solemn assemblies are positively to be desired, and if the people's hands were not full of blood God would surely listen to their prayers."

In short, ritual plus righteousness is good, but either without the other is bad; in themselves, they are of equal value. But that, I submit, is a gross misinterpretation. It implies that the Prophets did not mean what they said; it makes an unwarranted assumption about what they did *not* say; and it involves imputing to them an utterly banal view: that God is not well pleased with those who offer sacrifices and then proceed to commit robbery or murder. Surely the greatest religious geniuses of human history would not have been guilty of such banality!

The revolutionary point the prophets wished to make was that ritual, far from being what religion is all about, as had always been assumed, is not essential to it at all. It is not what God requires of human beings; it is not a criterion by which God judges them; it is not a way of gaining God's favor. The God of Israel is a moral God who demands righteousness and nothing else. From such a point of view ritual is an irrelevancy!

I am not saying that the prophets were necessarily right. It may well be that they underestimated the importance of ritual. It may also be that if the proposition had been put to them that the ritual, even if not essential, is nevertheless useful as a means to an end, they would have assented. I only want to insist that we have no right to trivialize their revolutionary teaching by superimposing on it our own conventional understanding of what religion is all about.[22]

Ethics Versus Ritual in Rabbinic *Halakhah*

We have seen that in the Hebrew Bible there are two opposing tendencies: a priestly tendency, according to which ritual is all–important – or at least no less important than ethics – and a prophetic tendency, which considers ethics all-important and ritual irrelevant. Where does rabbinic Judaism stand in this matter? To answer that question, we need to distinguish between *halakhah*, its legal aspects, and *aggadah*, its theoretical aspects.

On the halakhic side, we need to remember that the founders of rabbinic Judaism saw it as their principal task to construct out of the commandments of the Bible – supplemented by the ancient oral traditions – a legal system governing every aspect of life. Since these commandments are to be found almost exclusively in the Pentateuch, it is to this that they devoted their foremost attention, interpreting it as lawyers interpret a constitution. And since the pentateuchal legislation makes no systematic distinction between ethics and ritual, therefore the rabbis did not, either. Whatever the Pentateuch expresses in the imperative was equally grist for the rabbis' jurisprudential mill.

This is not to say that the rabbis were not influenced by the ethical teachings of the prophets. The humaneness of much of their civil and criminal legislation undoubtedly owes much to their influence. Nevertheless, on the issue that concerns us, of the relative importance of ethics and ritual, rabbinic Judaism on its halakhic side stands essentially where the Pentateuch stood: it makes no systemic distinction between them; it does not subordinate one to the other; it regards both as equally expressive of the divine will.

To this two further points need to be added. One is that between biblical and rabbinic times a huge change occurred in the nature and scope of Jewish religious ritual. In biblical times it was largely confined to the Temple. When that was destroyed, and its place was taken by the synagogue and the home, these became the institutions in which Jewish ritual was henceforth carried on. At the same time there occurred a huge expansion in the number of such rituals. Ninety percent of what we think of as Jewish observance is rabbinic rather than biblical in origin.

The other point is that the external situation changed. In biblical times most Jews lived as a majority in their own land. In postbiblical times they became minorities in many lands. As such, they were surrounded by societies that differed from them religiously as well as in other ways. In these circumstances, Jewish ritual, in addition to all its other functions, became an expression of, and a means of maintaining, Jewish identity and distinctiveness.

Ethics Versus Ritual in Rabbinic *Aggadah*

If, on its halakhic side, rabbinic Judaism followed the Pentateuch in making no systemic distinction between ethics and ritual, on its aggadic side it followed the prophets in regarding ethics as immeasurably the most important.

One of the most telling illustrations of this fact is the celebrated story of how Hillel, when challenged to sum up the entire Torah in a few words, said: "What is hateful to yourself, do not do to others; that is what the Torah is all about; the rest is a commentary on that principle."[23] In the same vein is Rabbi Akiba's comment on the Golden Rule of the nineteenth chapter of Leviticus, "You shall love your neighbor as yourself," *zeh k'lal gadol batorah* – "This is the greatest principle of the Torah."[24]

Equally significant is the talmudic passage[25] in which Rabbi Simlai, after asserting that the Torah comprises 613 commandments, shows how they were progressively subsumed under ever fewer general principles, all of which turn out to be of an ethical or general religious nature. Isaiah, for example, reduced them to six: to walk righteously, to speak uprightly, to reject oppression and bribery, and to refuse to listen to bloodshed or to look on evil.[26] Micah reduced them to three: to do justice, to love kindness, and to walk humbly with God.[27] And Habakkuk reduced them to one: "The righteous shall live by their faith."[28]

It is also noteworthy that what the rabbis called *sh'losh esreh midot*, the Thirteen Attributes of God,[29] are all more or less synonymous with compassion, and that, accordingly, the 'Imitation of God' was understood by the rabbis as requiring that quality on the part of human beings. For instance, on the phrase "to walk in God's ways"[30] the rabbis commented:

> "As God is called merciful, so you should be merciful; as God is called gracious, so you should be gracious; as God is called righteous, so you should be righteous; as God is called faithful, so you should be faithful."[31]

If any further evidence were needed, it might be supplied by the *vidui gadol* or "Great Confession" of the Yom Kippur liturgy, which employs the formula *al het shehatanu l'fanekha* – "For the sin we have committed before You . . . . " Dating from the Gaonic Age, the number of its confessions has grown in the course of the ages from 6 to 12 to 24 to 36 to 44.[32] Yet even the longest version lists exclusively sins of an ethical kind.[33] You will not find in it, for instance, "For the sin we have committed before You by eating forbidden food."

The Position of Progressive Judaism

We may then say that the general pattern, briefly summarized, is as follows: In the Priestly Code the primary emphasis is on ritual. In the Pentateuch as a whole there is a parity of emphasis on ritual and ethics. In the prophets the emphasis is almost exclusively on ethics. Rabbinic Judaism, on its halakhic side, follows the Pentateuch, but on its aggadic side, follows the prophets. The question we now need to ask is: which of these positions holds good for Progressive Judaism?

Of course there is no simple answer, for Progressive Judaism has undergone change and development in the two hundred years since it began, and not least in the area that concerns us. It is nevertheless clear that in its earlier phases, it emphasized the prophets rather than the Pentateuch and ethics rather than ritual. More precisely, it maintained that the "Moral Law" is primary and immutable whereas the 'Ceremonial Law' is secondary and alterable. However, since then a renewed appreciation of the values of ritual has slowly asserted itself. Let me illustrate this developing trend with a few quotations from the "platforms" that Progressive Judaism has from time to time adopted.

At Philadelphia in 1869, the first generation of American Reform Rabbis dismissed the sacrificial cult as having only historical significance, and went on to declare that "inner devotion and ethical sanctification are the only pleasing sacrifices to the All-Holy One."[34]

At Pittsburgh in 1885, the second generation of American Reform rabbis declared: "We accept as binding only the moral laws and maintain only such ceremonies as elevate and sanctify our lives . . . ." And they reiterated this ethical emphasis, with special reference to its social implications, when they added: "We deem it our duty to participate in the great task of modern times, to solve on the basis of justice and righteousness the problems presented by the contrasts and evils of the present organization of society."[35]

At Posen in 1912, the Liberal rabbis of Germany issued their *Richtlinien zu einem Programm für das liberale Judentum* {Guidelines for a Program for Liberal Judaism},[36] in which they began by stating, "the eternal truths and fundamental ethical principles of the Jewish religion." But they went on to declare:

"In view of the great significance of external forms for the religious life and the maintenance of Judaism, all those institutions and customs should be maintained and revitalized which . . . still have the capacity to bring the individual into a living relationship with God; to remind him again and again of the moral purpose of his life . . . which sanctify the life of the family . . . reinforce loyalty to the faith community and awaken Jewish self-respect."[37]

At Columbus, Ohio, in 1937, the Central Conference of American Rabbis (CCAR) declared:

> "In Judaism religion and morality blend into an indissoluble unity . . . Judaism seeks the attainment of a just society . . . It champions the cause of all who work and of their right to an adequate standard of living, as prior to the rights of property . . . Judaism as a way of life requires in addition to its moral and spiritual demands, the preservation of the Sabbath, festivals and Holy Days, the retention and development of such customs, symbols and ceremonies as possess inspirational value. . . ."[38]

In London in 1992, the Union of Liberal and Progressive Synagogues published its Affirmations of Liberal Judaism, which declared:

> We affirm the ethical emphasis of the prophets, that which what God chiefly requires of us is right conduct and the establishment of a just society. Religious observances are a means of cultivating holiness. As such, they are also important, but not of the same order of importance. . . . We affirm the need for sincerity in observance. Therefore observances must accord with our beliefs, and individual Jews must be free in this area to exercise informed, conscientious choice.[39]

In 1999 the CCAR issued *A Statement of Principles for Reform Judaism*, popularly known as the New Pittsburgh Platform, which stated:

> We are committed to the ongoing study of the whole array of *mitzvot* and to the fulfilment of those that address us as individuals and as a community . . . . We bring Torah into the world when we strive to fulfil the highest ethical mandates in our relationships with others and with all God's creation . . . . We reaffirm social action and social justice as a central prophetic focus of traditional Reform Jewish belief and practice.[40]

In 2001 the Union Progressiver Juden in Deutschland, Österreich und der Schweiz issued its 35 *Grundsätze des Liberalen Judentums,* which stated:

> "We feel obligated to lead a life of *mitzvot*. At the same time we insist . . . that the observance of *mitzvot* must be in harmony with the freedom of the individual conscience."[41]

Later it continued with the statement: "We affirm the universal ethical teachings of the prophets. The Torah demands that we conduct ourselves responsibly so as to bring about the establishment of a peaceful and just society, inclusive of all human beings."[42]

An Evaluation

From this survey it is clear that Progressive Judaism, throughout its history, has clung to the prophetic view that Judaism is first and foremost about ethics, in the double sense of personal right conduct and the promotion of a just and peaceful society. To that extent, the self-description of Progressive Judaism as prophetic Judaism is justified.

It is clearly in the evaluation of ritual that a gradual but definite shift can be observed: from an initial ambivalence to strong affirmation. To that extent the dual emphasis on both ethics and ritual of the Pentateuch and the rabbinic *halakhah* has reasserted itself, sometimes even to the point of obliterating or obscuring the distinction between them. And that is where, in my opinion, the trend has gone too far.

A reasonable view, I submit, would be as follows. The prophets, followed by the rabbinic *aggadah*, were right. The God of Judaism is a moral God; therefore, the only ultimate values are moral values; therefore the way to serve God, to please God, to merit God's favor, is to emulate the divine attributes of justice, compassion, and so on., and to create a society characterized by these values. Everything else is secondary.

Nevertheless, the secondary is also important. The Jewish faith community needs ritual in the broad sense in which we have been using the term, including learning and prayer as well as ritual in the narrower sense. All these things are a means to an end, but not in any simple and straightforward sense.

Learning, for instance, serves a double purpose. On the one hand, the study of religious texts is for the individual who engages in it a spiritual exercise. On the other hand, religious education is an indispensable tool for the transmission of the tradition from generation to generation.

Likewise, private prayer is a spiritual exercise for the individual; but public worship has, additionally, a social function. It binds the individuals together into a community, and is at the same time a corporate act of self-dedication on the part of the community, to its collective task.

Similar remarks apply to the rich variety of rituals in the narrower sense, which constitute so much of what people mean when they speak of the "Jewish way of life." In their totality they promote 'holiness', not in the sense of the Priestly Code with its emphasis on ritual purity, but in the sense of "God-consciousness." And the more conscious we are of God's presence, the more likely we are to respond to God's ethical demands. Ritual, we may then say, is a devotional exercise that promotes spiritual and therefore also moral fitness in much the same way as physical exercise promotes physical fitness.

At the same time, many rituals serve a more specific purpose. Some, like the Passover *seder*, evoke Jewish history and may therefore be described as educational. Some, like the recitation of the *halahma inya*, inculcate a particular virtue such as, in this case, hospitality. Some, like the blowing of the *shofar*, awaken repentance. Some, like the blessings before and after meals, instil a sense of gratitude. All of them help to sanctify individual, family, and communal life.

In addition, ritual helps to maintain the distinctiveness of the Jewish people, especially in the Diaspora, where the non–Jewish majority exerts a constant pressure on them to conform to its ways, and so to lose their identity.

This preservative or counter–assimilatory role of ritual should not be underestimated. But it also holds a danger. The danger is that we may come to value only those things that differentiate us from others, and only for that reason. That way of thinking leads to ghettoism, exclusiveness, and holier-than-thou arrogance. It also distorts Judaism. It obscures the fact that the essence of Judaism is in its ethical values, and if these have come in large measure to be shared by other traditions, that does not make them either less important or less Jewish. On the contrary, everything else is a means to that end. It is in the ethical sphere that we Jews have a contribution to make to the life of humanity if we have any contribution to make at all; and if not, our survival is a matter of no great interest except to anthropologists.

Implications for Progressive *Halakhah*

If this evaluation of the relative importance of ethics and ritual is more or less agreed, it remains only to consider what the implications are for Progressive *halakhah*. It would seem to follow that Progressive *halakhah* should concern itself mainly, though not exclusively, with ethical matters, because these alone relate directly to what God requires of us. Also, we might add, because unless the ethical problems of humanity are solved, there will be no future for the Jewish people or any other people in which to indulge in the luxury of performing rituals.

The facts, however, do not entirely bear out that expectation. For the literature of Progressive *halakhah*, as of *halakhah* generally, consists to a large extent of *she-elot uteshuvot*, responsa, so that the subject-matter of the literature is largely determined by the questioners. It is, in other words, reactive rather than proactive. And a glance at the literature reveals that a very large proportion of the questions concern matters of ritual rather than of ethics.

Of course, many of these questions have ethical aspects, so that it is not easy to draw a clear line of demarcation. To give only one example, the question of whether a *kohen*, such as a man claiming priestly descent, should be allowed to marry a divorcée raises ethical questions about the democratic nature of the Jewish people and the respect due to divorced women.

Nevertheless, when one looks through the collected responsa of the CCAR as well as those of individual Progressive rabbis, [43] one cannot but notice how many of them concern questions of ritual. Of course the same would be true, less surprisingly, of modern Orthodox responsa. And that, in turn, is partly due to the fact that the whole corpus of Jewish civil law has been much neglected since the emancipation because the human relations it deals with have largely become the province of gentile courts and governments. There, in traditional Judaism, the scope of the *halakhah* has shrunk and nowadays concerns itself mainly with *kashrut*, *shabbat*, conversion, marriage, and divorce.

But to this we may add that there is a general tendency for people involved in organized religion to become excessively preoccupied with matters of ritual. In addition, the differences in ritual practice between Orthodox, Conservative, and Progressive communities, and even between different branches of Progressive Judaism, inevitably create uncertainly and anxiety and cause questions to be asked.

But there is also a proactive Progressive halakhic literature, and there ethical issues are much more to the fore. That is true of Moshe Zemer's *Evolving Halakhah*,[44] which, for instance, devotes a whole section to the relations between Jews and gentiles in the State of Israel. Even more significant for our purpose is the work of the Freehof Institute of Progressive *Halakhah*, which, in the space of eleven years, has produced, under the joint editorship of Walter Jacob and Moshe Zemer, no fewer than twelve volumes of essays and responsa. These are: a general introductory one followed by *Rabbinic-Lay Relations* (1993), *Conversion to Judaism* (1994), *The Fetus and Fertility* (1995), *Death and Euthanasia* (1995), *Israel and the Diaspora* (1997), *Aging and the Aged* (1998), *Crime and Punishment* (1999), *Marriage and its Obstacles* (1999), *Gender Issues* (2001), *Re–Examining Progressive Halakhah* (2002), *The*

Environment in the Halakhah (2003).⁴⁵ As the titles indicate, every one of these volumes is concerned primarily with human relations and hence with ethical issues. And that, I submit, is exactly as it should be.

Differential Treatment

It remains only to consider whether ethical and ritual issues call for differential treatment on the part of a Progressive *halakhah*. I believe that the answer is yes.

Ethical matters are of the utmost importance. In the rabbinic phrase, they are *d'varim ha-omdim b'romo shel olam*, "matters that stand at the height of the world." That is both because they are the only things God really cares about and because on them the well-being of individuals and societies, and ultimately the survival of civilization, depends. Therefore they demand the most strenuous efforts to establish, as far as we humanly can, what is right and what is wrong.

Ritual matters are very different. They do not belong among God's primary demands, and they do not directly affect human welfare. Indeed, they do not generally raise questions of right and wrong in an ethical sense. Of course there is, according to Jewish tradition, a right and a wrong way of doing everything – of blowing a *shofar*, building a *sukkah*, affixing a *mezuzah*, and so on. But these are matters of etiquette, protocol, or *minhag*, custom, rather than morality. Therefore they need not, and should not, be taken with the same seriousness as ethical matters. As Rabbi Ignaz Maybaum once remarked, "The 'Thou shalt' of the moral code must not be spoken where ritual is concerned."⁴⁶

In ethical matters the argument from tradition carries no weight at all if what the tradition demands – for instance, that we should discriminate against women – is plainly wrong. But in ritual matters, because they do not generally raise an ethical issue, the argument from tradition carries a lot of weight. Certainly it would be foolish and perverse to deviate from the tradition for no good reason.

And yet the argument from tradition is not always decisive. For there have always been varieties of practice in Judaism, with considerable emphasis on the duty to follow *minhag hamakom,* local custom. And if in Progressive Judaism there is even greater diversity of practice than there has traditionally been, that is not necessarily a bad thing. If, for instance, some congregations stand and some sit for a particular prayer, no great harm is done. And in addition, Progressive Judaism recognizes individual differences that a ritual that works for one person does not necessarily work for another. Therefore it is right that in ritual matters Progressive Judaism should allow, respect, and even encourage individual choice.

Mitzvot in Progressive Judaism

In the light of everything that has been said, let us, in conclusion, take a fresh look at the word *mitzvah*, and note that it is traditionally used in three different senses.

In the strict sense of "commandment" it applies, first of all, to the 613 imperatives, the *taryag mitzvot* that the Pentateuch is traditionally said to contain. But if the prophets – who lived mostly before the Pentateuch was compiled – are right, only those of an ethical nature can strictly be said to be divinely commanded.

Secondly, the word *mitzvah* is sometimes used in the sense of a "good deed," that is, an act of *g'milut hasadim*, of practical kindness, such as visiting the sick, especially when performed spontaneously and *lifnim mishurat hadin* – "beyond the call of duty."

But then there is a third sense in which the word *mitzvah* refers primarily to devotional acts such as religious study, prayer, worship, and ritual, especially ritual. Indeed, it is precisely before the performance of such acts that the tradition prescribes the recitation of those blessings, known as *birkhot mitzvot,* which praise God *asher kidshanu b'mitzvotav v'tzivanu* as having "sanctified us by His commandments and commanded us" to perform the action in question – which may be to recite Hillel, to listen to the shofar, to dwell in the sukkah, to kindle the Hanukah lights, to eat matzah, or any one of the many acts of ceremony that constitute the Jewish devotional life.

This is, of course, a paradoxical usage in view of the prophetic teaching that ritual is the very thing thath God does *not* command. And it is even more paradoxical when the action in question is of postbiblical and uncertain origin. The kindling of the Sabbath lights, for example, was an innovation of the Pharisees, strongly opposed by the Sadducees; and the blessing stating that God has commanded us to do it is first attested as late as the ninth century.

Nevertheless, the usage has come to stay, and nobody has suggested, or would suggest, that it is a mistake. Let us therefore continue to speak of *mitzvot* in this sense but be clear what we mean. These are not actions that are in any ultimate sense commanded by God. Rather, they are practices which our tradition has devised to remind us of our history, to symbolize particular values, to evoke a sense of God's presence, to sanctify family life, to lend rhythm and pageantry to the succession of the seasons, to celebrate life cycle events, to bind us together as a community, and to perpetuate our religious heritage from generation to generation.

Although we cannot truthfully say that any one of these *mitzvot* is divinely commanded, I nevertheless believe that in their totality – provided that they are sincerely carried out – they constitute a way of life that must have God's approval. If there is any truth in the concept of the Covenant; if we Jews have a providential task to perform in human history; then it must be God's will that we should preserve and transmit our heritage; and if the doing of *mitzvot* can serve that end, that is their justification. In that sense we can justifiably recite the formula *asher kidshanu b'mitzvotav v'tzivanu*; and I suspect that most of us would do well to become more, rather than less observant in our devotional lives.

And yet we need to remember that all these acts of ritual,

however important they may be, and however much we may enjoy them, are only a means to an end. The end is what it has always been. The end is that we should learn to respond to the prophetic demand *asot mishpat v'ahavat hesed v'hatzne-a lekhet im eloheykha* – "to do justice, and to love kindness, and to walk humbly with God." Nothing else has ultimate value, and by no other standard does God judge us.

Notes

1. Israel Abrahams, *Judaism* (London: Constable, 1917), p. 26.

2. *San.* 10:1.

3. See Solomon Schecter, *Studies in Judaism* (Philadelphia: Jewish Publication Society, 1945) First Series, chapter 6, "The Dogmas of Judaism."

4. *Mishneh Torah, Hilkhot Issurei Bi'ah* 14:1.

5. *Tamid* 5:1.

6. *Avot* 3:17; ARN 24; *Lev. Rabbah*, 35:7.

7. *Avot* 1:17.

8. Ex. 25, 17, 35-40.

9. For example, Num. 28.

10. Lev. 10:1-3.

11. In Leviticus and Numbers the phrase occurs 34 times.

12. Num. 19: 1-22.

13. Amos 4:4.

14. Amos 5:21-24.

15. Hosea 6:6.

16. Is. 1:11-17.

17. Mic. 6:7.

18. Jer. 7:21-23.

19. Isa. 58:3-7.

20. Isa. 1:13.

21. Isa. 1:15.

22. Any readers who are still in doubt about the point that has been made should read Israel I. Mattuck's *The Thought of the Prophets* (London: George Allen and Unwin, 1953), especially chapter 9, and Sheldon H. Blank's *Prophetic Thought, Essays and Addresses* (Cincinnati: HUC Press, 1977), especially chapter 1.

23. *Shab.* 31a.

24. *Sifra* 89b to Lev. 19:18.

25. *Mak.* 23b-24a.

26. Isa. 33:15.

27. Micah 6:8.

28. Hab. 2:4.

29. Derived from Ex. 34:6-7; *R.H.* 17b; *Pes.*.57a.

30. Deut. 11:22.

31. *Sifrei* Deut. 49; cf. *Sotah* 14a.

32. See Macy Nulman, *The Encyclopedia of Jewish Prayer* (Northvale, N. J. and London: Jason Aronson, 1996), pp. 18-19.

33. *Service of the Synagogue*, 18th ed. (London: Routledge & Kegan Paul, 1955) Day of Atonement, vol. 1, pp. 8-10.

34. David Philipson, *The Reform Movement in Judaism* (New York: KTAV, 1967), pp. 354-55.

35. *Ibid.*, pp. 355-57.

36. *"Die ewigen Wahrheiten und sittlichen Grundgebote der jüdischen Religion."* *Richtlinien.." Richtlinien . . . nebst den Referaten und Ansprachen . . .* (Posen, 1912), pp. 56-67.

37. *Angesichts der grossen Bedeutung der Erscheinungsformen für das religiöse Leben und die Erhaltung der jüdischen Religion sind ... .alle diejenigen Einrichtungen und Bräuche zu bewahren and neu zu beleben, die noch heute den einzelnen in lebendige Beziehung zu Gott setzen, ihn immer wieder an seine sittliche Lebensaufgabe erinnern . . . .die das Familienleben heiligen...die das Band der Glaubensgemeinschaft festigen die Glaubenstreue stärken und ein edles jüdisches Selbstbewusstsein wachrufen."* W. Gunther Plaut, *The Growth of Reform Judaism*, (New York: World Union for Progressive Judaism, 1965) pp. 68-73.

38. *Central Conference of American Rabbis Yearbook* [ed. Isaac Marcuson] (Cincinnati, Central Conference of American Rabbiss, 1937), vol. 47, pp. 418-22 ff..

39. *Affirmations of Liberal Judaism* (London: Union of Liberal and Progressive Congregations, 1992)

40. *Central Conference of American Rabbis Yearbook* [ed. Elliot L. Stevens] (New York: Central Conference of American Rabbis, 2003), vol. 109, p. 110.

41. *"Wir fühlen uns einem Leben nach den Mitzwot verpflichtet. Dabei fordern wir...dass die Beachtung der Mitzwot im Einklang mit der Freiheit des einzelnen Gewissens steht."*

42 *"Wir treten für den universalen, ethischen Anspruch der Propheten ein. Die Tora fordert von uns verantwortliches Handeln zur Errichtung einer friedlichen, gerechten und alle Menschen umfassenden Gesellchaft.*

43. Solomon B. Freehof, *Reform Responsa* (Cincinnati: HUC Press, 1960) [50 responsa]; idem., *Recent Reform Responsa*, (Cincinnati: HUC Press, 1963) [50 respnsa]; idem., *Current Reform Responsa* (Cincinnati: HUC Press,, 1969) [60 responsa], ideam., *Modern Reform Responsa* (Cincinnati: HUC Press, 1971) [54 responsa]; idem. , *Contemporary Reform Responsa* (Cincinnati: HUC Press, 1974) [58 responsa]; idem., *Reform Responsa for our Time* (Cincinnati: HUC Press, 1977) [56 responsa]; idem., *New Reform Responsa* Cincinnati: HUC Press, 1980) [53 responsa]; idem., *Today's Reform Responsa* (Cincinnati; HUC Press) [51 responsa], Walter Jacob (ed.), *American Reform Responsa* (New York: CCAR, 1983) [172 responsa]; Walter Jacob, *Contemporary American Reform Responsa* (New York: CCAR, 1987) [202 responsa], Walter Jacob, *Questions and Reform Jewish Answers* (New York: CCAR, 1992) [246 responsa]; W. Gunther Plaut and Mark Washofsky, *Teshuvot for the Nineties* (New York: CCAR, 1977) [72 responsa].

44. Woodstock, Vt: Jewish Lights Publishing, 1999; previously published in Hebrew by Dvir, Tel-Aviv.

45. The earlier volumes were published by Rodef Shalom Press, Pittsburgh, Pennsylvania; the latter ones by Berghahn Books.

46. Ignaz Maybaum, *The Jewish Mission* (London: James Clarke, 1949), p. 39.

Chapter 8

❖ ❖ ❖

ON THE STANDARD OF HOLINESS IN JEWISH LAW

Jonathan Cohen

In his recent *Evolving Halakhah*, Moshe Zemer issues a direct challenge to a conventional understanding of the religious function of halakhic observance. As he explains:

> The possibility of attaining *kedushah* [holiness] is one of the criteria for the observance of a commandment. Precepts such as prayer, Torah study, philanthropic deeds, and others should lead to sanctification. The litmus test of holiness should determine the value of every religious act in the daily life of Jews in our generation.[1]

Beyond the suggestion that observance of the commandments does not necessarily lead to holiness, Zemer contends that observance should be selective and regulated so that holiness may be achieved.

Other scholars and practitioners of Jewish law confirm the potential of *mitzvot* to elevate observant Jews toward holiness. This quality of *halakhah* is sometimes illuminated by those who affirm that Jewish law is divinely authored.[2] However, personal and collective holiness are also advertised by others who do not. Theodore Friedman, writing on behalf of the Law Committee of the Rabbinical Assembly of Israel, asserts "that it is in the power of *halakhah*, as it is interpreted by us, to guide the nation dwelling in Zion toward its divine destiny, to be 'a kingdom of priests and a holy nation.'"[3] Also, David Golinkin, outlining several reasons for observance, explains that "*mitzvot* lead us to holiness, sanctify our lives and bring us closer to God."[4] J. Guttmann identifies holiness as the core, or origin, of the "commandment, imperative form" that characterizes Judaism. Addressing Jews who reject the claim of divine authorship of Torah, he explains that commandments express the notion of the sanctity of life and are the means to realizing it. He also proposes that religious Jews who cannot accept the claim of divine authorship may recognize the commandments as a product of prophetic revelation. Thus, he promotes observance of the commandments, albeit in a new way that advances their purposes and highlights their religious value.[5]

Yet, according to Zemer, holiness is neither inherent in the commandment nor consequent upon observance. In fact, by presenting holiness as a criterion for observance, Zemer establishes it as an extra–halakhic standard to assist the observant in selecting and ranking commandments, rejecting those that fail to generate the intended result.

The use of holiness as an extra-halakhic measure to regulate the conduct of observant Jews is not new. One prominent example of such use of a standard of holiness occurs in a responsum that is attributed to Rashi. The document contains both a question and a response and appears in printed editions of Rashi's response.[6] The question that is sent to Rashi outlines a dispute that arises from the attempt to dissolve a partnership. Rashi employs a requirement of holiness to influence the actions of the parties and prepare his correspondent toward dispute resolution. The following are the salient features of the question:

Reuben and Simon were brothers and business partners. Each held 50 percent of the (money lending) enterprise, and both were working to support their venture. At a certain point, they were approached by Levi and his mother, who became partners. From that time onward Reuben and Simon each held a third of the business, and so did Levi and his mother. As Levi was young, and his mother was not accustomed to commerce, most of the work continued to be carried out by Reuben and Simon until Levi grew older. There was an understanding among the partners that those who worked in the partnership (at the time, Reuben and Simon) could draw their working expenses from the general partnership account proportionally. With time, Levi started learning the trade working alongside Reuben and Simon, and earning money. Then, when the partners had started dividing some of the profits among themselves (as they had agreed to do), Levi expressed the wish to dissolve the partnership and asked to divide all of its capital and funds among the partners.

At that point a dispute arose between Simon and Levi. Simon explained that a number of gentiles still held money owed to the partnership. The partners could, according to Simon, divide among themselves all that they held at the time and dissolve the partnership, but they could not divide among themselves a sum of money that was still owed to the partnership and, therefore, not yet at hand. Simon, therefore, suggested that each partner should acquire a right to claim his share of the debts owed to the partnership, and that, if Levi wanted to dissolve the partnership immediately, he should go among the gentiles and collect his own portion of the debts when they mature. Levi was not willing to go and collect his portion of the debts from the gentiles and claimed that they did not know him and would not recognize him as their creditor. As Simon was the one who made the loans to the gentiles in the first place, Levi suggested that he should be the one to go out and collect the debts, and that the money collected should then be divided among the partners. Simon was, under such circumstances, not willing to dissolve the partnership. He pointed out that his expenses would no longer be covered, since the partnership would no longer be in existence, and warned Levi that he would claim a share of his profit if he (Levi) tried to start working on his own while there were still outstanding debts requiring collection. Levi, on the other hand, argued that the partnership is now dissolved since the parties have already started to divide the partnership funds, and claimed his share of the debts remaining in the hands of the gentiles from Simon. Levi proceeded to express the concern that Simon would delay in collecting the debts outstanding and warned Simon that he would claim his share of the monies collected from the partnership account after Levi had expressed his wish to dissolve the partnership.

The question presented before Rashi was whether Levi was entitled to dissolve the partnership and require Simon to pay him his share of the money collected following the dissolution, or, alternatively, whether Simon was authorized to continue functioning as if the partnership still existed, collect his share of Levi's profits, and be reimbursed for expenses incurred while collecting outstanding debts.

Rashi's response opens with an elaborate greeting to his correspondent, Rabbi Abraham, and proceeds to present the core, or rationale, of his ruling:

> Regarding their question, I have listened with full attention and am responding according to my humble opinion and the words [that I have heard]. My mind tends that Simon is speaking incorrectly in suggesting to lay his burden upon the widow and her son against their will. We find no authority allowing a partner to delay the apportioning requested by his fellow partner unless he had set him a [specific] time from the start; as there is no practical value in selling – since the matter has been brought into the open – let them split.

Having ruled in Levi's favor, Rashi, outlines three potential courses of action that Simon may take and offers an assessment of each. The exposition of these three scenarios represents the bulk of the text and aims to help Rashi's correspondent appreciate the implication of Simon's potential arguments and react to them appropriately. They also aim to facilitate Rabbi Abraham's efforts to persuade Simon to act in a way that is consistent with Rashi's ruling, rather than oppose it and engender sanction. The three potentialities are presented in order below:

> (1) With regard to that which is already in the hands of Levi – if Simon were to say: "It is inconceivable that you should profit instead of using my contacts – so I will pay you from my own part, and as for the interest accrued to this point, when I collect it, I will give you your share, and from now onwards it [the business] is all mine" – his words would be true.
>
> (2) But for Simon to say to Levi: "if you wish – go out and collect your own part yourself, and if you

do not succeed it will be lost among the gentiles" – this is not the way for a holy nation who follow the Torah of the holy. The people of Israel are bound by the commandment "thou shalt . . . bring them back to your brother" and are warned "thou mayest not hide." He [Simon] cannot say "mine comes first," as there is no added cost (or damage) in collecting his and his friends' portions at the same time. For who distributed these funds to the gentiles? There is not a penny that is disputed which does not have a rightful owner.

(3) And even if Simon were to say "Let me die with the Philistines" – meaning [I will not go out and collect any debts at all and] we will both lose out, he cannot be heeded, because he delivered the money into the hands of the gentiles and on that day he became a paid bailee; partners are governed by the laws of paid bailees. Now, one may say, the depositor does not have to return [money] from his own [funds] when the owners claim [the money back]. Now that [the money] is in Simon's care, Levi should wait until Simon collects from the gentiles, and they will distribute their profit in equal shares. But it is upon Simon to make the effort and retrive it, because even in cases of loss in which a paid keeper is not held liable, we learn that if the thief is identified and he [the paid keeper] can retrieve from his hands, he will once again try to retrieve [that which was stolen] from the thief. In cases where the thief is identified, Abaye says the unpaid keeper either swears or pays [the owner] and the paid keeper does not swear, while Rava says they both pay and neither swears, and with the exception of six *halakhot*, the law is always according to Rava. But Abaye and Rava agree with regard to the paid keeper.

> In this case we deal with a paid keeper, and he himself [Simon] has deposited them [the coins]; therefore, he certainly has to retrieve them, even from bears and lions and he may no longer claim payment for them unless it is the custom of the city that he who lends money through a friend leaves a third or a fourth or a fifth [of the interest] to the agent, and Simon must distribute the interest according to the custom of the city.

Rashi concludes the responsum with a short section that complements the first few lines of the response. While the first phrases of his text address the core issue of dissolution, this last section adds detailed information in response to other questions presented by Rabbi Abraham. Rashi's instructions are:

> But [regarding] other ventures in which they have both earned [money], one has no claim against the other from the day that Levi said "I am no longer interested in the partnership." And all that Simon has spent in the form of expenses that Levi is entitled to he must return to him. And if he should allow his heart to rely on his friend's money, he should seek his rates [to practice his trade] somewhere else.[7]

Simon's three hypothetical reactions are presented by Rashi in order of preference or desirability. Rashi's first scenario reveals the possibility that Simon may accept responsibility for collecting the debt and concede to the dissolution of the partnership. Under such circumstances, Simon's demand that Levi undertake not to compete with him using Simon's clients or contacts should be met. This first case presents Simon in a very positive light. According to Rashi, Simon may offer Levi the principal owed to him of his share of the money. In other words, Simon would pay Levi the principal of the debt in advance and assume the risks entailed in such credit transactions. Should the costs of collection increase, or the likelihood of collecting the principal (let alone the interest) decrease, Simon would bear the consequences.

The implications of such a course of action are not unknown

to Rashi. The Hebrew word he employs to describe Simon's commercial contacts is specifically used in relation to priests and Levites.[8] In one Talmudic passage, the term is used to identify priests who are popular and have many acquaintances.[9] There, it is used in connection to R. Joseph's teaching, allowing priests to assign their gifts to poor students before the gifts are received. This ruling is said to apply only to those priests who are known to be "popular," or who have many acquaintances, and who have predictable levels of income. Only such priests may assign part of their future income to deserving students. While Rashi uses the term to express Simon's demand that Levi restrict his commercial activities, the parallel between the first scenario he describes and the teaching of R. Joseph is revealing. In both cases, those who are deemed in a position to assist the less fortunate are prompted to do so and assume a risk. While an implied juxtaposition of Simon with a popular priest may be flattering to Simon, it also serves to remind him that Levi is still a needy protégé, rather than an equal competitor. Rashi must recognize that for Simon to act generously with Levi and enable him to work independently, Simon requires the confidence that he can, and should, assume the risk.

The second possibility envisioned by Rashi is far less positive. In this scenario, Simon decides to collect only his portion of the debt and force Levi to deal with the debtors on his own. Under such circumstances, Levi may fail to collect his share. Consequently, the money he is entitled to will remain in the hands of gentiles. As Rashi makes clear, such action would entail a denial of responsibility toward Levi and would be particularly offensive because Simon would not incur any added expense if he collected his share along with Levi's simultaneously.

If Simon chose this path, his actions would be judged against the standards set by the Positive Commandments to restore lost property and not to evade responsibility when seeing lost objects. The finder's responsibility to return such items arises at the moment of finding or seeing the lost object. Needless to say, the finder is not held responsible for the circumstances of the loss so the positive duty to restore lost property is not associated with any negligence or wrong committed by the finder's encounter with the lost object. Unlike the duty to restore misappropriated objects,[10] this commandment assumes no pre-existing relationship between the owner and the finder. Rashi's message in explaining Simon's responsibility in this context is that regardless of the preexisting relationship and dispute between Simon and Levi, Simon should at the very least treat Levi as a co-religionist to whom he owes a duty to restore lost objects. Also, Rashi implies that he does not consider Levi capable of collecting his share of the debt. If Levi is unable to collect his share, any money not collected by Simon would be as good as lost. Indeed, the core of Rashi's argument in this regard relates to Levi's dependence upon Simon and the latter's sense of solidarity. His statement that "this is not the way for a holy nation who follow the Torah of the holy" is immediately followed with the explanation: "The people of Israel are bound by the command "thou shalt . . . bring them back *to your brother*,"[11] and are warned "thou mayest not hide."[12] In short, when Simon collects his own portion of the debt, he faces a choice: He may either collect Levi's share at no added cost (since he is already collecting his own debt anyway), or leave Levi's portion in the hands of the gentiles. To Rashi, the possibility that Simon would prefer to see the money owed to Levi remain in the hands of undeserving gentiles reveals a lack of national and fraternal solidarity with Levi. Thus, Rashi's entreaty constitutes a warning that Simon has forgotten to whom he owes a duty of allegiance. In this case, Rashi associates the commandment to restore property with "the way for a holy nation that follow the Torah of the holy." Rashi's holiness does not entail spiritual elevation toward the numinous or closeness to God. Rather, it reflects a sense of unity and fellowship among Jews, particularly in their dealings with gentiles.

The third scenario envisioned by Rashi is the most disturbing. In this case Simon decides to abandon his own share of the debt.

Otherwise put, Rashi fears that Simon would not go out to collect any money, and that gentiles should be left with both portions of the debt (that Simon and Levi are owed). Such a course of action would reflect Simon's strength of feeling and willingness to sacrifice money for the sake of principle. Thus, Rashi fears that such an act of defiance may be presented as a positive act of self-sacrifice akin to martyrdom.[13] His reference to Samson's last utterance "Let me die with the Philistines" reveals the absurdity of this position: According to the Biblical narrative, Samson desires to die with the Philistines having confronted the consequences of his failings, in order to exact revenge from his gentile captors. In contradistinction, Simon would sacrifice his earnings to deny responsibility toward a fellow Jew, defy rabbinic authority, and financially damage a former partner. Ultimately, only gentiles would benefit from his protest. In other words, if Simon were to offer to "die with the Philistines," the only "Philistine" he would "die with" is Levi. Not only would such a course of action reflect lack of fraternal allegiance or solidarity on Simon's part, it would reveal Simon's identification with his gentile associates and his perception of Levi, along with those members of the Jewish establishment who support him, as adversaries.

According to Rashi's ruling, if Simon reacted in this way, he should be compelled to go out and collect Levi's debt as if he were a paid keeper, or bailee, who lost a deposit. This ruling reflects an understanding that while partners are empowered to deal with each other's property, they are also bound to each other by a duty of care that characterizes the relationship between paid keepers and their depositors.[14] According to a Talmudic dictum, if an item is stolen or taken from the keeper's possession, even when the circumstances of the loss indicate that the keeper is not liable,[15] if the thief is later identified, the paid keeper is bound to compensate the owner[16] and pursue the thief himself. As Rashi explains, since Simon knows precisely where he can find Levi's money, he is bound to try to return the money to Levi as if he were a paid keeper. He also clarifies that under these circumstances Levi should wait until Simon collects his portion of the debt, but Simon must make every effort to extract the money on Levi's behalf, even if it is in the hands of bears and lions.[17] Also, Simon may not collect any further payment or remuneration for his efforts to recover the money, unless local practice allows him to do so. Rashi's proposed reaction to this third scenario does not entail blame, or condemnation of Simon's role in the partnership, or of his disposition of partnership funds. However, it does create a clear link between Simon's association with the gentile debtors and his duty to recover the money owed to Levi on his behalf. It also places the burden of collection on Simon, regardless of the financial consequences.

Rashi's reaction to this last potential situation is harsh by comparison to the second scenario and deserves closer scrutiny. If Simon were inclined to collect his share of the debt, Rashi would demand that Simon treat Levi in a brotherly way, and assume responsibility for the collection of Levi's portion, regardless of their preexisting relationship. Rashi's presentation of the second case entails two assumptions. The first is that Simon is interested in collecting his own share of the debt, and the second is that he would bear no added cost in collecting Levi's share. Under such circumstances, Rashi's demand that Simon collect Levi's money would aim to convince Simon that his duty of allegiance to a fellow Jew should override his instinct not to assist his young competitor. Rashi would try to impress upon Simon the implications of the choice between collecting the money on behalf of a Jew to whom the money is owed at no added cost, or leaving the money in the hands of gentiles who have no legitimate claim to it. However, Simon's abandonment of the debt would generate an entirely different reaction: Rashi's ruling would compel Simon to act in the "Jewish interest" to his financial detriment, in spite of his intention to write off the debt, his preference for gentile associates over his former partner, and his fear that the young entrepreneur would compete with him over clients.

The punitive aspect of this ruling highlights the failure of the analogy between the case of these partners and the relationship between bailor and bailee. As briefly explained above, Rashi's argument relies on the Talmudic example of a paid keeper who is not liable for the loss of a deposit.[18] Such a bailee would be required to compensate the depositor if the thief were identified. Commenting on this dictum, Rashi writes: "In spite of the fact that he [the bailee] is not liable in [a case of loss through confrontation with] armed brigands here – since the thief has been identified, *and [as] he [the bailee] would lose nothing*, he must toil and pursue it [the deposit]."[19] Rashi's commentary reveals sensitivity to the position of the keeper, and confirms that he should not bear the costs of collection.[20] In this responsum as it appears before us, Rashi seems to depart from that position. The issue of costs figures prominently in the question, and Rashi's assertion of Simon's responsibility leaves little room for doubt as to his position.[21] If the text before us accurately reflects Rashi's position, then it reveals an interesting discrepancy between his Talmudic commentaries and this responsum.

This text sheds light on Rashi's application of the notion of holiness in the context of dispute resolution. Rashi employs holiness as a value in assessing the second scenario in order to persuade Simon to act appropriately. Holiness is not used in relation to voluntary action to support the needy, nor in the context of strict, punitive law enforcement. Rather, its function is to highlight Simon's halakhic obligations. Rashi's holy nation follows the Torah of the holy, and the commandment to restore lost property to one's brother in particular. A brief study of this responsum suggests that Rashi's decision is a product of appropriate, lawful conduct, rather than a criterion utilized by individuals to determine the value of religious duties.

Yet it also functions as a standard that entails fraternal solidarity and allegiance. Rashi's use of holiness in association with the obligations relating to lost property adds a new layer of meaning to this concept. While a number of midrashic texts link holiness with all the commandments,[22] it is not explicitly or specifically associated to the commandment to restore lost objects. It is commonly associated with rules relating to idolatry,[23] the fringes of garments,[24] the separation of clean and unclean animals,[25] and sexual relations and 'successful' procreation.[26] Commenting on the biblical requirements to be holy, Rashi specifically associates the commandment with sexual propriety.[27] While the concept is often associated with separation, including the separation of Jews from non–Jews. I can find no evidence suggesting that it is used to describe or require solidarity among Jews, nor a certain code of conduct in their dealings with non Jews, Rashi's use of holiness in this text transcends the strict halakhic definitions of the term and sets a new objective or rationale to the observance of the commandment to restore lost property. His use of holiness is clearly designed to inform, guide, or regulate the observance of the commandment, rather than impose a halakhic obligation on the basis of established dicta.

While Zemer's perception of holiness is very different from Rashi's, it also entails a departure from, or extension of, halakhic definitions and aims to set a standard, or rationale, for the observance of commandments. The text before us suggests that Rashi injects new meaning, or understanding, into the notion of holiness, to inform the correspondent of his expectations of Simon. Whereas definitions of holiness may change and norms evolve, the rabbinic reinvention of holiness to regulate *halakhah* does not. In this respect, Zemer's teaching forms yet another part of a rich, creative tradition.

Notes

1. *Evolving Halakhah* (Woodstock, Vt: Jewish Lights Publishing, 1998), p. 50. The book was first published in Hebrew under the title *The Sane Halakhah* (Tel Aviv: Dvir, 1993).

2. For a recent example, see the introduction to R. Joseph Baer Soloveitchik's responsa *Beit Halevy, Oz V'Hadar* (Jerusalem, 1995-96).

3. Theodore Friedman, *The Rabbinical Assembly of Israel Law Committee Responsa* 5746

(Jerusalem: The Movement of Masorti Judaism in Israel, 1985-86), p. 1 (Heb.).

4. David Golinkin, *Halakhah for Our Time* (New York: United Synagogue Youth, 1991), pp. 11-12.

5. J. Guttmann, *Religion and Knowledge* (Jerusalem: Magnes Press of the Hebrew University, 1955), pp. 273-75 (Heb.).

6. The text is partly translated below. The translation is from the Hebrew version that appears in Elfenbeim's *Teshuvot Rashi* [The Responsa of Rashi] (New York:,1943; Jerusalem, 1966), pp. 103-07. The responsum occurs in section 80, concerning the law of partnerships.

7. In transliteration from the Hebrew: *ve-yivror lo she'arim mi-makom aher*. Elfenbeim comments that this is a unique phrase in Rashi's writings. See his *Teshuvot Rashi*, pp. 107. A similar phrase is quoted by Rashi in his responsum #231 (Elfenbeim,. *Teshuvot Rashi*, p. 258). There, Rashi comments that he does not understand the meaning of the sentence. This translation has been suggested to me by the late Haim H. Cohn.

8. In transliteration from the Hebrew: *bimekirei*. See particularly 2 K. 12:6, *Git.*, 30a., *Hul.* 133a.

9. *Hul.* 133a and Rashi's commentary starting at *u-dehikah leh milta*. Elfenbeim also refers to this passage in his *Teshuvot Rashi*, p. 106.

10. For example, Lev. 5:21.

11. Deut. 22:2 (my emphasis); and see Rashi on *B.K.* 108b cf. *oseh*.

12. Deut. 22:3.

13. Elfenbeim points out a variant on this text that reads, "Let me die the death of martyrs," rather than, "Let me die with the Philistines." See Elfenbeim's *Teshuvot Rashi*, p. 106.

14. For example *B.B.* 42b, and Rashi's commentary cf. *ve'na'asin ke-shomrei sachar zeh la-zeh*.

15. For example, if the item were taken by force. See *B.K.* 108b, and Rashi's commentary cf. *nignevah be-ones*.

16. In transliteration from the Hebrew *oseh imo din*, and see Rashi's commentary.

17. The Hebrew text reads: *miyad dubbim va-arayot*, literally: from the hands of bears and lions. However, in another responsum regarding the laws of partnership, Rashi refers to packs of animals and brigands (transliterated from the Hebrew: *gedudei hayot ve-listim*). See Rashi's

Sefer Ha'Orah, ed. S. Buber (Lvov, Jerusalem, 1967), part 2, no. 140, p. 223. See also Elfenbeim's *Teshuvot Rashi*, p. 107.

18. *B.K.* 108b.

19. Rashi on *B.K.* 108b cf. *ve-im shomer sachar hu* (my emphasis).

20. Rashi's commentary to Samuel's teaching is also sympathetic to the partner who loses partnership property through theft. In *B.B.* 42b cf. *ve'na'asin ke-shomrei sachar zeh la-zeh* Rashi explains that in such a case, the partner must pay (his colleague) as if he were a paid keeper, and his reward, or payment, is that his colleague will also be placed in the position of a bailee for the same period of time – *ve-zehu sekharo she-gam havero yishmor ha-kol ke-shi'ur zeman she-meshamer zeh akshav*. This passage does not specifically address loss for which the partner and keeper is not liable. Yet, Rashi's's comment is conciliatory and emphasizes the reciprocal nature of the partners' duties.

21. Toward the end of the third scenario Rashi writes that Simon must retrieve the money but may no longer claim payment for his services. Further, in the concluding phases of the responsum he asserts that Simon must return to Levi all expenses drawn from Levi's share of the account. See above.

22. See note 25.

23. For example, *Sifra Kedoshim* 10:9.

24. for example, *Sifrei* (Num.) 115.

25. See, for example, *Sifra, Shemini* 10:12, and see Rashi's commentary on Ex. 22:29.

26. See, for example, *Sheb.* 18b, and *Shab.* 86a.

27. Rashi's commentary on Lev. 19:2. However, see also the first chapter of *Sefer Ha'Orah* [attributed to Rashi, edited,and interpreted by Salomon Buber] (Lemberg, 1905; Jerusalem, 1966), pp. 3-6.

Chapter 9

❖ ❖ ❖

TZEDAKAH: ASPIRING TO A HIGHER ETHIC

Daniel Schiff

I dedicate this article to my dear friend and mentor, Rabbi Dr. Moshe Zemer. Moshe's scholarly accomplishments and his extensive contributions to the pursuit of a "sane *halakhah*" are detailed elsewhere in this volume. Beyond these considerable achievements, I cherish even more Moshe's personal qualities that have meant so much to me through the years. It was Moshe's infectious enthusiasm for the responsa literature that first started me on the path that led toward my interest in the field; it was Moshe's unending academic curiosity and careful intellectual rigor that proved so very inspirational; and it was Moshe's love for the Jewish people, for our rich heritage and for *Medinat Yisrael* that provided such a wonderful model. I am deeply indebted to Moshe for all his wisdom, guidance, patience and encouragement. Perhaps more importantly, the Jewish people are indebted to Moshe for having taken us "beyond the letter of the law" in seeking to understand the *halakhah* in a way that is compassionate, coherent and fully consistent with the Jewish heritage.

❖ ❖ ❖

In 1993, archaeologists unearthed a fifth–century mosaic synagogue floor at Zippori in the Galilee. Alongside a host of rich symbolic representations, the mosaic included the following inscription: "May he be remembered for good, Yudan son of Isaac the Priest and Paragri his daughter, Amen, Amen." Scholarly speculation holds that the tribute was probably designed to offer recognition to a generous donor who helped the synagogue financially. It is, of course, impossible to ascertain what type of *mitzvot* this alleged donor performed beyond that of contributing to the communal construction project. However, on the reasonable assumption that the other commandments he fulfilled did not exceed those of his compatriots, the inscription likely testifies that the practice of providing special honors for those individuals whose distinctive contributions to society are monetary in nature is an age-old one within the Jewish world.

The question, though, that ought to be of concern – to Jews in particular – is whether this practice, despite the fact that it is embraced across the Jewish spectrum, is just. Is it altogether harmless to Jewish standards of justice and equality to offer wealthy donors extraordinary recognition, including naming rights, plaques, gifts, or access opportunities to events and personalities, that are unavailable to lesser givers? While such practices have become so common in contemporary Jewish life that they have become the *sine qua non* of organizational fund–raising, their near-universal employment does not offer assurance that these measures comply with the highest aspirations of Jewish ethics. Nor should the reality that such techniques are extensively utilized by numerous institutions renowned for Jewish learning, or for Jewish religious commitment, be seen as any guarantee that these methods are in full conformity with the traditions that these organizations espouse.

An oft-repeated lesson of fundamental Jewish education is that the Hebrew term "*tzedakah*" should not be translated as "charity." Whereas charity denotes a voluntary gift – one given from the heart – the mandate to engage in *tzedakah*, Jews are regularly reminded, is an obligatory commandment. The Hebrew root "*tzedek*," the lesson proceeds, is best rendered as "justice" or "righteousness," behaviors that are demanded of a Jew. In other words, a Jew who wants to live as part of a community has no choice other than to participate in the creation of the just society through the utilization of his or her resources of money and time.[1] There is a powerful logic behind this requirement: the attainment of wealth – however great or small in measure – is in part due to the talents and industriousness of the individual concerned, but also owes a great deal to the community's preparedness to utilize the products or the services that person offers. Wealth, clearly, does not strictly correlate with individual giftedness or even commitment to hard work. It does, however, depend heavily upon communal participation and the community's preparedness to support a particular service or product.

Hence, it follows that, since wealth attainment is dependent upon the privilege of being afforded a welcome place within the communal structure, justice demands that each person be required to contribute money and time to support the community from which he or she has benefited. This is, after all, the philosophical premise underlying taxation: according to one's means, we require everybody to participate in the establishment and maintenance of communal infrastructure that seeks to establish a society of opportunity, dignity, and safety for all its members. If participation in taxation were made voluntary, it would probably lead to the creation of certain services and institutions perceived to fulfill a variety of self-interests, but the societal outcome, at best, would be uneven, certainly not a result that would be regarded as "just" in anybody's terms.

It is, then, important to observe that the Jewish notion of *tzedakah* is far more akin to that of contemporary taxation than to that of contemporary charity. The *tzedakah* commandment connotes that contributing toward the ideal of a just society is a requirement that is incumbent upon all those who want to partake in that society. But the Jewish vision of what constitutes a just and righteous society extends beyond what is normally subsumed by the realm of taxation. Not satisfied with basic societal structures and support systems, Jewish law advocates that it is the duty of the individual to help in such a way as to maximize the shared communal enterprise and to raise the bar of human dignity. The Torah's injunction to "love one's neighbor as oneself,"[2] institutes the predominant theme: Jews are expected to stretch themselves toward enhancing their neighbors' lot, and not to be satisfied with simply helping in a perfunctory fashion.[3]

To balance the equation, conversely, Jewish tradition does not expect an individual to be so subservient to communal needs that he or she is required to undergo a substantial alteration in the financial well-being that he or she has come to enjoy. It is for this reason that the rabbis state that while there is an expectation that upstanding members of the community will give at the rate of twenty percent,[4] one is not to give at a rate of more than twenty percent, lest *tzedakah* begin to affect the giver adversely.[5] If, after all, *tzedakah* did in fact come to effect the giver's financial standing materially, compliance with the mandate would become an even more problematic proposition.

Tzedakah, then, from a Jewish perspective is a requirement that is like taxation in that *all* members of society are to be "*tzedakah* taxed" at a rate of ten to twenty percent, without regard to financial status.[6] Unlike taxation, however, where the direction of tax proceeds is a matter for communal decision, the use of one's *tzedakah* allocation is left in the hands of the individual. Judaism, to be sure, offers guidance as to how this money might most appropriately be apportioned,[7] but ultimately the allocation choice rests with the giver.

Given this context, it is readily apparent that when a particular Jewish communal institution honors a "big" donor, the honoring, from a Jewish perspective, cannot be because the donor has given a large amount of money – this is, after all, the donor's obligation; rather, it is because said donor chose that particular institution upon which to lavish funds rather than some other institution. By way of illustrating the point, we do not hold ceremonies to honor those who pay a large amount of tax or publish the names of those whose tax contribution has exceeded a certain limit, even though without these families many bridges, schools, and hospitals would never be built. We do not honor them specially, because we view taxation as just as much a requirement for them as for any other citizen – though the amount they might contribute might be large, they are not in fact doing anything that is considered unusually praiseworthy. Moreover, the fact that any particular bridge or school might be constructed is not a result of their decision to pay tax but is a communal choice.

Within the Jewish system, though, it is certainly easy to understand the gratitude of any institution that has been fortunate enough to receive a large gift. It is, moreover, highly appropriate that such an institution should express its profound appreciation to the giver for voluntarily deciding to support it. If, however, it is the voluntary decision to choose that institution which is being recognized, rather than the size of the gift itself, then there is no reason why institutions would not be *equally* grateful to any individual who voluntarily chooses to give to that establishment, no matter what the size of the gift.

While some Jewish institutions might make the claim that they are indeed *equally* grateful for all gifts, no matter the size, their behavior will usually eloquently belie this assertion. In virtually all cases, "big givers" are recognized in ways that "small givers" are not. If it is in fact true that the institution is *equally* grateful for all gifts simply because the giver has voluntarily chosen that institution, then the only way to communicate this reality is to acknowledge all gifts in precisely equal fashion. The fact that this is almost never done goes beyond simple inequality. It is unjust. And it is un-Jewish.

The reasons why it is unjust and un-Jewish require explanation. There are five specific rationales why offering wealthy givers *tzedakah* inducements, which are unattainable for the less affluent, does not conform to the Jewish *tzedakah* ideal. The first has to do with the specific expectations of the mandate to fulfill the *mitzvah* of *tzedakah* in its financial form. Given that every Jew is expected to give at least ten percent to *tzedakah*, consistency with Jewish ideals would demand that if it were Jewishly appropriate to honor a particular sub-group, it would be the group that meets and exceeds the *tzedakah* requirement, i.e. the group that indeed does give between ten and twenty percent in a given year.

Reality, however, works differently. Imagine an extraordinarily wealthy individual who has an annual income of five million dollars. Consider further that in one given year this individual gives all of his *tzedakah* money to one place: a one hundred thousand dollar gift to his synagogue rebuilding campaign. Compare him to a woman who belongs to the same congregation who, because she cannot work full–time, has an annual income of eight thousand dollars. She, too, gives all of her *tzedakah* money in that year to the synagogue rebuilding campaign, a gift of nine hundred dollars. If this is the totality of each of their commitments to *tzedakah* in one year, then, from a Jewish perspective, who has done better? Clearly, the woman has fulfilled the *mitzvah* of *tzedakah* by exceeding the ten percent level, whereas the man's contribution is dramatically short of this obligation. What, though, will be the actual outcome? The man, if he so desires, will be able to name the social hall, or some other part of the institution, in honor of his family, and he will be publicly celebrated. The woman will get a letter of thanks, and may get her name posted in a long list of soon-forgotten "also-ran" donors, even as the man's name is enshrined in stone and spoken about for decades.

This, of course, is Judaism inverted. One should not assume for a moment that those who give large gifts regularly fall short of their *tzedakah* obligations. One should certainly, however, appreciate that fulfilling the ten percent mandate, rather than providing some extraordinary dollar figure, is what we say really matters in Jewish life. Hence, even if the man's gift had been six hundred thousand dollars, it would be no more Jewishly worthy than the woman's nine hundred dollars. As a matter of fact, in terms of virtue, one might make the argument that her gift, which may have been far more difficult for her to do without, could actually have been the more meritorious and hence the more worthy of recognition. The Jewish system suggests that all who fulfill their *tzedakah* mandate should be respected alike. To honor "big givers" in unique ways, whether or not their *tzedakah* mandate has been fulfilled, is to treat those of lesser means, who have nevertheless given greater percentages, unjustly.

The second reason why offering inducements to those of extensive means leads to unjust application of *tzedakah* norms stems from what we might call pooling. Consider the following circumstances: If I have thirty thousand dollars to give to *tzedakah*, and I donate the entire sum to the local Jewish day school, that school will doubtless offer me a range of different honors or naming opportunities. If, however, I take the same thirty thousand dollars and divide it into fifty equal gifts of six hundred dollars, and I send those gifts to fifty worthy communal institutions, each of those places will acknowledge my kind donation, but not one of them is likely to offer me a special honor of any type. Yet the question must be asked: in which instance have I behaved better or served the interests of the community in a more desirable fashion? The answer is that this is an impossible call to make. The broader interests of the community may be better served by one institution getting all the money. It is possible, though, that the future of a number of places may be more assured if people were encouraged to spread their wealth more evenly among various institutions. Since, then, it is not plausible to state that one who concentrates his or her giving on one institution has done something better than one who spreads small amounts further, why should one be honored and the other not? The fact that it is quite possible that honors are being distributed to individuals who pool substantial amounts in one place, while those who give even larger sums to multiple addresses go entirely unrecognized, is clearly unjust. Moreover, it is yet another reason why a smaller donation might well deserve equal recognition with a larger one, since it is certainly plausible that it represents but a fraction of that individual's *tzedakah* commitment.

The third problem behind treating the rich differently is the unpleasant reality that it can, and at times does, lead to unseemly inequalities in other areas. Assume for a moment that you are the executive director of a large synagogue. Mr. Cohen, who last week was feted as a million–dollar giver to the synagogue capital campaign, in which he has so far given the first installment of a five-year gift, is on the telephone. His son is becoming a Bar Mitzvah at a service a month from now, and Mr. Cohen is calling to ask whether the service could start a half hour earlier than normal because it fits in better with the family's postservice plans. Is this possible? Now if Mr. Cohen were just some "ordinary giver" you would immediately, politely, tell him that there is a policy as to when services begin, and you cannot start to deviate and make exceptions. But you know that Mr. Cohen is no "ordinary giver." He is one of your million–dollar givers. You do not want to upset him and potentially threaten his gift. You swallow hard, and you tell him that you need to consult further and you will get back to him. The consultation process will be relatively straightforward. If it is deemed likely that denying Mr. Cohen his request might in any way threaten his gift, the starting time will be moved, rather than risk offending such an "important donor." This is, of course, a relatively trivial example. One could think of countless ways in which the knowledge that somebody might provide a large amount of money can open up possibilities for special treatment – even rule-breaking exceptions – for that individual that would be unthinkable for others.

The fourth reason why putting the rich in a separate category can have invidious outcomes is, counterintuitively, because it disrespects the rich. This becomes clear when one considers the strategy that is so frequently used in fund-raising campaigns: Imagine that you are a solicitor who is visiting a "prospect" from whom you can reasonably expect a one thousand dollar gift. Since, in this particular campaign, the first level at which you can offer inducements of special parties, room-naming rights, public awards, access to distinguished scholars, and the like is that of a ten thousand dollar gift, you have no tangible incentive available to you with which to entice the person you are now visiting. "Why should I give one thousand dollars to your institution?" your fund-raising target asks. Given that you have no enticements to offer, you stress the worthiness of your cause, the great *mitzvah* of *tzedakah*, and the fact that your "target" has the capacity to give at this level, such that he or she would be playing an important role in a critical communal endeavor in a fashion that is commensurate with his or her capacity. Impressed both by the nature of the fund-raising cause, as well as the ethical argument that a person should contribute to communal causes to the extent that funds allow, your prospect – with a measure of self-satisfaction – writes a one thousand dollar check.

The next day you visit somebody from whom you are expecting a twenty–five thousand dollar gift. This time the conversation is altogether different: "Why should I give twenty–five thousand dollars to your institution?" this fund-raising target asks. Again, you utter some worthy words about the importance of the cause and the *mitzvah* of *tzedakah*, but these items by no means form the focal point of your presentation. Instead, this time you talk extensively about the opportunity to name a classroom in honor of the giver's family, about the special "wall of merit" that is planned for big giver's names, and about the unique one-on-one opportunities on offer to meet with the special personality who will be attending the dedication.

The salient difference between the two presentations is obvious. To the less wealthy individual, the reasons you provide for giving amount to: it is a good cause, you should participate in communal projects of this type because it is the right thing to do, and you have the capacity to give at this level. To the wealthy individual, the major reasons for giving amount to: this is a great deal for you because we are putting forward distinguished honors, gifts and access in return for your donation.

While the contrast depicted between these two events is a stark one, the picture is close enough to reality to represent a reasonable approximation of real-life events. The implicit assumption revealed by these vignettes is telling. With the less wealthy, when there are no incentives to offer, the prevailing assumption is that the sheer worthiness of the cause should be enough to merit the requested gift. With the wealthy, however, the prevailing assumption is that this will not suffice. The wealthy, according to this logic, will only give if offered sufficient trinkets, trophies, or slices of immortality to attract them. Why, though, it must be asked, should this be the case? Why is it unreasonable to expect that the wealthy will give to the campaign if presented with precisely the same arguments as the less wealthy? Why is there a belief that the wealthy have to be induced to give with tangible items, when we expect gifts from others without such inducements? Is it not implicitly disrespectful to the wealthy to convey that they will only give donations at levels appropriate to their capacity if they are offered gifts in return, as if to suggest that attempts to persuade them to do that which is ethically right for its own sake will never resonate with them? There is, then, a very real sense in which treating the wealthy in special ways diminishes their chances for altruistic giving, discounts their capacity to do what is proper, and unjustly treats them as if they were inextricably beholden to the heady drug of recognition.

There is yet a fifth reason why putting the wealthy in a distinctive category may have deleterious outcomes. This reason has to do with expectations that are sometimes sparked in the donor that he or she will be able to influence the shape of the project or the direction of the program that has benefited from his or her large gift, according to his/her personal vision. More than occasionally, donors who provide major gifts expect to be consulted on the manner in which their gift will be used, and seek to shape structures or steer organizational directions according to their own personal ideas. If the sponsoring institution balks at this desired involvement, there are times when the donor's indication that the money could be directed elsewhere is enough to provide the donor with the sought-after participatory role. Indeed, in burgeoning numbers, disinterested in others setting priorities or directions for them, "big givers" simply establish and fund their own foundations or organizations so that they can pursue their own interests and direct their own legacies entirely as they see fit, without the slightest regard for communal priorities. "There are now in the Jewish community some families of such extraordinary wealth that their own private foundations have become players on the Jewish scene," observed one expert on contemporary Jewish philanthropy.[8] This phenomenon has begun to reshape Jewish communal priorities in significant ways. As one editorial writer stated it bluntly, the Jewish world has become witness to

> the rise of the mega-donors, that handful of billionaire philanthropists who are becoming a sort of ruling aristocracy in communal life. The mega-donors whose gifts become the life's blood of key institutions, and who believe they've bought the right to dictate decisions. The mega-donors who create new institutions to address a pet crisis, ignoring cash-starved agencies that have been struggling with the problem for years. The mega-donors who insist on micro-managing the work of scholars and activists with years of experience and expertise. The mega-donors who suddenly lose interest in a cause and walk away, leaving the institutions they created to go begging, or simply collapse.
> Most mega-donors would take exception to their portrayal as robber barons. . . . These are, after all, voluntary donations of private cash. Other millionaires are buying yachts, while these individuals are supporting Jewish life. The criticism smacks of ingratitude.But that's the point. In a voluntary community, private donations are the tax base that keeps things going. Jewish culture survived for centuries through a delicate balancing act, in which voluntary donors agreed to act as though they were under obligation. The community was treated as an entity that was entitled to demand members' money and spend it as the community saw fit."[9]

Allowing donors through the use of their funds – even those who have considerably less than the billionaires – to influence decisions beyond the ability of others to do likewise directly undermines the fabric of community. Indeed, there is increasing evidence that the "fabric of community" is already seriously fraying. There has been a noticeable "trickle–down" effect from the wish of the wealthy to establish their own *tzedakah* priorities: more and more Jewish communities are assisting those who – at all financial levels – wish to establish family funds that can be targeted as the donor's interests dictates.[10] While this may have a few positive outcomes, like ending the lifespan of Jewish organizations that have lost relevance while encouraging new and creative ventures to come into being, there are also real costs associated with this individualization of *tzedakah*. Perhaps the most worrying issue is that as individual givers become more attracted to new, "cutting-edge" projects, the "nuts-and-bolts institutions of Jewish communal life – the synagogues, family service agencies, and nursing homes" – see their critical needs erode.[11] Unable to compete in terms of appeal, the vital core communal institutions are no longer guaranteed support, while novel "niche" projects attract interest that exceeds their communal utility. Thus, the diminution of a sense of communal duty on the part of the wealthy has the potential to lead to a similar reduction at all levels and a consequent failure to maintain a coherent and well-balanced communal funding structure. Again, the analogy with taxation provides insight: if individuals were permitted to determine the type of projects to which their taxation would flow, there would probably be plenty of parks and grand bridges and monuments, but would there be enough roads and sewer systems?

Yet another regrettable way in which donor influence can become manifest is when positions of organizational leadership are, at times, offered to members of affluent families with the aim of keeping them "committed to the cause" and giving at their customary amount. The result, of course, is to overlook those who may have the same or even more managerial or leadership skills, but who cannot compete at the same giving level. Not only, then, does paying attention to wealth have the potential to distort communal priorities, it can distort the very structures that drive communal decision–making, as well.

By supplanting the democratic communal process and bypassing those who have accumulated wisdom to guide communal priorities, a sense of communal participation and communal ownership of institutions and projects is replaced by a sense that true power resides in the hands of an oligarchy. Not surprisingly, this can have a chilling effect on the *tzedakah* of those of modest means. Moreover, there can be no sense in which the dictation of communal direction by those who possess the most wealth is just. If the obligation to accede to communal wishes is voluntarily assumed in the same way by all, then decision-making divisions between the rich and the not-so-rich are the antithesis of the expectations of fairness subsumed within the *halakhah*.

Notwithstanding all these significant Jewish objections to providing the rich with special recognition, occasional discussions have explored *halakhic* justifications for affording the rich distinctive honors. A succinct illustration is provided in a brief piece by the contemporary ethicist Rabbi Dr. Asher Meir, in which Rabbi Meir answers the question, "Is it really proper to name buildings after donors?" This is an ancient question to which Jewish tradition gives an emphatic answer: It is proper and even desirable to acknowledge the generosity of donors by perpetuating their names.

Rabbi Shlomo Adret, a medieval rabbi who was one of the greatest Jewish legal authorities of all time, was asked about a man who donated a synagogue to the community. The man wanted to write his name on the entrance, but the community objected; in the end, they consulted Rabbi Adret.

The rabbi's answer was: "Who can stop someone who dedicates and builds from his own property, for the sake of heaven, from mentioning his name on what is his?" He continues, "And this is a trait of wise and experienced people, in order to give a reward to those who perform good deeds. Even the Torah itself adopts this trait, for it records and publicizes those who perform good deeds."

The main message of Rabbi Adret's answer is that there is nothing unethical or shameful about recognition. It is appropriate and even desirable to give people credit for their contributions.

However, it is still not proper to give in the first place in order to obtain recognition, or to draw excessive attention to our good deeds. The Talmud tells us that a person who gives in order to boast is in danger of losing all the merit of his gift; charity needs to be given in order to provide for the needs of the community.

What then is the reason that giving charity with improper intention is so problematic?

One answer is that there is a difference between using honor as a motivator and viewing it as a true goal. A person who excels in his studies in order to obtain recognition strives to eventually surpass this level, to discard this crutch. But if the *entire purpose* of the good deed is for honor, then there is no spiritual progress at all.

Another answer is that in the case of charity giving, an improper intention can actually contradict the entire concept of this important commandment. The Torah doesn't just tell us to provide the needs of the poor; the first thing it tells us is "Don't harden your heart" (Deuteronomy 15:7). A critical aspect of the commandment of charity giving is to open our hearts as well as our wallets and identify and commiserate with the recipient. A person who is giving out of a desire to boast and exalt himself is not only missing the point, he is accomplishing the exact opposite of the true object of this important mandate.

A charitable donor is certainly entitled to ask that reasonable recognition be provided in return for the gift, and the charitable organization may and even should acknowledge generosity in this way. However, the giver should be certain that his main objective is to identify with the needs of the recipient; his desire for recognition should be an encouragement, and not the reason for the donation. Boasting and basking in recognition work against this important condition.[12]

Rabbi Meir's response is highly instructive. He begins by giving the impression that naming a building for a major donor would be a reasonable act of acknowledging "the generosity of donors by perpetuating their names." However, his citation of Rabbi Adret's *teshuvah*[13] puts this permissive stance within a narrow context: one individual has provided the entirety of the funds for the given project.

This donor has, effectively, "bought" the building or the institution himself, and, hence, it is more difficult to argue with his privilege to name what amounts to "his" building. This, however, does not address the normative situation in which the donor offered naming rights is one among numerous donors who contribute to the project. In that circumstance, Rabbi Adret reminds us, "even the Torah itself adopts this trait, for it records and publicizes those who perform good deeds." In the case of multiple givers, then, "those who perform good deeds" clearly subsumes everybody who has made a *tzedakah* contribution; there is no suggestion that Rabbi Adret would advocate omitting those who gave smaller amounts from the Toraitic mandate to record and publicize their *mitzvah*. Hence, we might appropriately understand Rabbi Meir to be conveying that unless one individual has shouldered the entire *tzedakah* burden alone, the involvement of all who have participated should be recorded and publicized, without singling out one or another for special recognition.

But Rabbi Meir goes further. He communicates that "the giver should be certain that his main objective is to identify with the needs of the recipient" and that "his desire for recognition should be an encouragement, and not the reason for the donation." In other words, in matters of *tzedakah*, while giving is what counts, the motivation behind the giving ought not to be ignored. When the donation of a particular gift is wholly dependent on the recognition or reward afforded the donor, the "main objective" is subverted in a way that is unacceptable to Rabbi Meir. Moreover, when attractive inducements are known to be on offer to those who provide substantial donations, the determination of whether the "desire for recognition" is just an "encouragement" or has become the "reason" for the donation becomes difficult indeed. It seems fair to assert, therefore, that the only way to be certain that the line between the two is not crossed is to avoid offering special inducements to "big givers" from the start.

In the book of Leviticus, the Torah instructs "*lo teh'dar p'nei gado*l" you shall not honor [literally, "beautify"] the great [literally, the "big ones"].[14] Insufficient attention has been paid to this statement. The tradition has normatively understood this instruction to apply to the court system. Thus, Rashi specifies – based on the *midrash* – that one should not say, "This man is rich; he is the son of great men; how can I disgrace him?"[15] As *Sefer HaHinukh* explains,

> This means, then, that he should not honor him more than his opponent at the trial, who is not as great as he. It is therefore stated, *nor shall you favor the person of the great.*
>
> ... Among the laws of the precept, there is what the Sages of blessed memory taught: that one [of the parties to the lawsuit] should not sit and the other stand, but rather both should stand.[16]

From a narrow reading of the Torah's context, it is easy to understand why the oral tradition emphasized the legal milieu when discussing this *mitzvah*. For the injunction not to favor the rich comes in the midst of a variety of directives, and those that are proximate to the statement under consideration do indeed seem to relate to the judicial process:

> You shall not curse the deaf, and you shall not place a stumbling block before the blind; you shall fear your God – I am the Lord. You shall not commit a perversion of justice; you shall not favor the poor and you shall not honor the great; with righteousness shall you judge your fellow. You shall not be a gossipmonger among your people, you shall not stand aside while your fellow's blood is shed – I am the Lord.[17]

It becomes clear, then, from a broader view of the context, that while justice is certainly the object of the passage, it is not merely courtroom justice that is intended. Indeed, these verses, occurring as they do within the so-called Holiness Code of Leviticus 19, are really part of a series of regulations designed to elevate human interrelationships in a wide range of circumstances. Justice, they demand, is to be extended far beyond the legal process. It is supposed to permeate areas of social interaction thoroughly, such that one's speech and actions are fully oriented toward demonstrating that one truly aspires to the lofty goal of "loving your fellow as yourself."[18]

Consequently, perhaps a rigorous reading of Leviticus 19:15 should lead us to conclude that not favoring the poor and not honoring the great are, in actuality, not micro statements about sitting and standing in court, but are in fact macro requirements about the manner in which society should handle fairly the reality of economic disparities. The poor should not be afforded inequitable opportunities or exemptions simply because they are poor,[19] and the wealthy should not be honored simply because they are wealthy. As has been discerned, when the wealthy give of their material blessings in the same proportion as do others, the dollar impact can be remarkable, but they have done nothing out of the ordinary that is deserving of special honor. If we honor the affluent, we are "beautifying" their contributions simply because they are wealthy, and this is precisely the action that Leviticus 19:15, in its fullest sense, prohibits.

There has been much discussion among scholars of Jewish law and ethics about the nature of the textual principle *lifnim mishurat hadin*, the notion that it is worthy to act "beyond the letter of the law." This principle, to be found in a number of places in rabbinic literature,[20] suggests that there are times when going further than the law specifies is regarded as deserving of praise. Professor Louis Newman offers a fine description of this concept in his perceptive essay on the subject:

> It would appear that the concept of *lifnim mishurat hadin* parallels most closely notions of waiver in Anglo–American jurisprudence. While the concept of waiver arises in a wide range of legal contexts, the fundamental element is a "voluntary relinquishment or renunciation of some right, a forgoing or giving up of some benefit or advantage, which, but for such waiver, a party would have enjoyed. Specifically, the term denotes waiving a legal right to act, or to refrain from acting, in some specified manner. Whether we are concerned with an elder who has a right to refrain from unloading animals (but does so anyway), or a man who has the right to keep the property that has been sold to him (but returns it to the seller), the term *lifnim mishurat hadin* designates a willingness to waive voluntarily some benefit or right to which one is entitled by law. In each case it is implied that the party who waives the right in question does so out of a concern for the other party, who would be harmed or disadvantaged if the right were exercised. In this sense, *lifnim mishurat hadin* has a moral dimension that distinguishes it from other sorts of waivers that could be exercised for any of

> a number of reasons, including monetary gain or self-interest. . . ." As we have also seen, one who acts *lifnim mishurat hadin* invariably gives up something, whether tangible property or intangible benefit, for the sake of another. Often this loss is financial . . . In other cases, it is a matter of . . . foregoing honor . . . . More to the point, the personal sacrifice that invariably accompanies an act of this sort is an expression of compassion or generosity.[21]

The central discussion about *lifnim mishurat hadin* concerns whether an act deemed to be *lifnim mishurat hadin* is one that should be considered as an act of "extreme piety or supererogation," or an act to which one is actually halakhically obligated, or – a middle position – an act that represents a moral duty.[22] Though this debate is interesting, it is not directly germane to our current purposes. What is significant, though, is Newman's explanation that *lifnim mishurat hadin*, whether invoked as an act of worthy piety, legal requirement or moral expectation, is designed to direct individuals towards abstaining from taking a benefit that is available to them "out of a concern for the other party, who would be harmed or disadvantaged if the right were exercised." *Lifnim mishurat hadin*, then, has the effect of urging, or perhaps requiring, individuals to strive toward the highest possible ethical ideal in the name of others, even if it means renouncing a legally permitted potential gain.

There is no arguing that the current *din*, the law, of *tzedakah* allows for the honoring of the wealthy in whatever fashion might be thought suitable for a particular campaign. Were this not the case, the honoring phenomenon would not be acceptable across the *halakhic* spectrum as it plainly is. Perhaps, though, it is time to challenge Jewish communities to aspire to a higher *tzedakah* ethos. Perhaps the moment has arrived to urge individuals and institutions to give *tzedakah lifnim mishurat hadin*, in a manner that goes beyond what the law requires and stresses compassion, generosity of spirit, societal welfare, and justice in a way that contemporary norms ignore.

Of course, there will be staunch opposition to such a proposal. The fund-raisers and campaign strategists will no doubt forecast instant doom for anybody who is foolhardy enough to attempt such an approach. While such bleak predictions will probably prove exaggerated, the strategists will have a point. This will be all the more true if an isolated fund-raising effort attempts to go down this path while competing for dollars with surrounding campaigns that offer inducements; presumably the lure of the incentives will cause more than a few to simply gravitate toward projects with something to offer them in return. If, then, *tzedakah* is to be given in a *lifnim mishurat hadin* spirit that truly hopes to suppress inherent injustices and promote communal well–being, it will be important to garner broad local support.

However, even if such broad support proves difficult to muster, there are two points to be made in response to the fund–raisers' concerns. The first is that it is possible that their worries represent an overly cynical reaction to the inherent strength of the commitment to Jewish giving at all echelons. Is it not credible that, given effective leadership and educational guidance, Jews might well sense the virtue inherent in such an ethic and might indeed heed the call with classic Jewish dedication when challenged to aspire to the highest? Is it not conceivable that, after an initial dip in giving, as the shock of the new approach is absorbed, the dollar figures – though, admittedly, harder to obtain – might, before very long, approach previous levels?

The second response to the fund-raisers must be that, naïve as it may sound, Jewish priorities have always placed seeking justice ahead of dollar amounts. Let us imagine a Jewish Community Center (JCC.) that decides it would like to add a one million dollar extension. The fund-raisers advise that if the full range of incentives are offered to the "big givers," the million–dollar target should be reached. If these incentives are not provided, their estimate falls to eight hundred thousand dollars. What should the JCC do? Is aspiring to a higher ethic really worth the potential loss of two–hundred–thousand dollars and the scaled-back plans and fewer resources that would result?

These are important questions, and the answers to them are not trivial – indeed, it is no exaggeration to state that they speak to the nature of the mission of the Jewish people itself. When God chose Abraham for a special task in the world, God described the role of Abraham and his descendents in this way: "I have singled him out, that he may instruct his children and his posterity to keep the way of the Lord by doing what is just and right. . . ."[23] In other words, the Jewish people became the Jewish people charged with one preeminent divine purpose: the shaping of Jewish conduct to represent the finest model possible for what is "just" and "right" in the world so as to further divine aims ahead of human ones. The Hebrew that the Torah employs for "just" and "right" is *"tzedakah u'mishpat."* Jews are singled out, God declares, in order that their every act – to the extent that it is possible – should be characterized by the most refined manifestations of *tzedakah* – active justice – and *mishpat* – true judgment – imaginable. When inquiring, then, about which path a Jew or a Jewish organization should select, there is simply no competition: a Jew can only be fully faithful to the Jewish mission, and a Jewish institution can only be true to its ultimate raison d'etre, when behaving according to the best standards of justice and the fairest judgments available. As Abraham swiftly discovered, and as Jews have known through centuries of experience, commitment to these standards does have a cost, and sometimes the price is high. It is, however, a price worth paying in order to contribute to the significance of the Jewish odyssey through history. The JCC, then, has its answer: what a salutary lesson it would be to a world that is consumed by monetary pursuits for an institution to forgo income because of a commitment to an elevated pursuit of justice.

Lifnim mishurat hadin puts Jews on notice that there are times when seeking the finest ethical standards will demand an enhanced behavior that goes beyond the current stipulated requirements of the law. Perhaps, then, it is time for Jewish authorities to call for a *tzedakah* environment that transcends the law as written and ventures *lifnim mishurat hadin*, placing a renewed focus on critical issues of justice and communal integrity. *Lifnim mishurat hadin*, after all, should not be left as just a historic concept that once in the past lifted Jewish eyes higher. It could serve the Jewish people in a renewed fashion if it were rabbinically applied to contemporary circumstances wherein a greater measure of virtue might be attainable. For the model it might provide to surrounding societies, as well as for the way it might dignify the Jewish landscape, maybe it is indeed time to aspire to a finer *tzedakah* ethic.

Notes

1 There is no question that *tzedakah* is more than just a financial requirement. The commandment to be engaged in *tzedakah* implies setting aside time to serve the community in a myriad of ways. However, this time requirement in no way relieves one of one's financial *tzedakah* obligations. Hence, while many Jews – at all levels of wealth – are involved in worthy acts of *tzedakah*, this paper focuses on the justice associated with *tzedakah*'s monetary aspects.

2. Lev. 19:18.

3. Assuming that most individuals have a high regard for themselves, the requirement to love one's neighbor in a similar fashion is, after all, an exceptionally demanding one. It suggests that we should attempt the extraordinarily righteous undertaking of being as assiduous about the well-being of other members of our society as we are of those in our own household.

4. There is a common misconception that the expected rate is ten percent. In fact, the rabbinic tradition regards ten percent as merely satisfactory, while twenty percent is seen to be the true fulfillment of the commandment. A giving rate of less than ten percent is unsatisfactory. See Maimonides, *Hilkhot Matanot Aniyim* 7:5.

5. *Ket.* 50a.

6. *Ibid.*

7. Maimonides, *Hilkhot Matanot Aniyim* 7:13-14.

8. David Altshuler, President of the Trust for Jewish Philanthropy, as cited in S. Fishkoff, "The Jewish Money Culture," in *Moment*, vol. 28, nu .1, (February 2003), p. 56.

9. Editorial in *The Forward*, November 29, 2002, p. 10.

10. "The Jewish Money Culture," pp. 56-57.

11. *Ibid.*, p. 79.

12. Taken from internet page: http://www.besr.org/ethicist/namebuilding.html

13. *Responsa of Rashba*, 1:581.

14. Lev. 19:15.

15. Rashi to Lev. 19:15.

16. *Sefer HaHinukh* (New York: Feldheim Publishers, 1984), vol. 3, p. 65.

17. Lev. 19:14-16. Translation adapted from that of *The Tanach* (New York: Artscroll, 1996), p. 293.

18. Lev. 19:18.

19. In Jewish law, for example, even the poorest member of the community is expected to participate in the requirement of *tzedakah*.

20. For a representative sampling and interpretation, see L. E. Newman, *Past Imperatives – Studies in the History and Theory of Jewish Ethics* (Albany: State University of New York Press, 1998), pp. 17-33.

21. *Ibid.*, pp. 29-30.

22. *Ibid.*, pp. 34-37.

23. Gen. 18:19.

Chapter 10

❖ ❖ ❖

RABBI ELIYAHU GUTTMACHER ON CONVERSION

David Ellenson

Rabbi Moshe Zemer has displayed a consistent attitude of care and concern for the proselyte throughout his distinguished career. His erudition as a scholar and his sensitivity as a rabbi have been employed to ease the plight of the stranger and to welcome the gentile who would come "under the wings of the *Shekhinah*" into the Jewish community. In his writings and in his deeds, Rabbi Zemer has embodied the words of our sages, who taught, "He who wounds the feelings of a proselyte transgresses three negative injunctions [of the Torah], and he who oppresses him infringes two." Thus Scripture states in Exodus, "Thou shalt neither wrong a stranger, nor oppress him, for you were strangers in the land of Egypt" (B.M. 59b). This essay will therefore present an analysis of the often-overlooked yet enduringly relevant halakhic writings of Rabbi Eliyahu Guttmacher (1795-1874) on issues of conversion as an appropriate way to pay tribute to Rabbi Zemer on the occasion of this *festschrift*.[1]

Guttmacher the Man

Eliyahu Guttmacher was a well-known mid-nineteenth century central European rabbi who was born in Borek, Posen. As a youth, he studied with the famed Rabbi Akiva Eger, and throughout his lifetime Guttmacher regarded Eger as his most outstanding teacher. During his adult years, he served as rabbi of Grodzisk in what was then Prussia. Guttmacher was open to the influences of Kabbalah and *hasidut*, and his fame in these areas caused Hasidim living in western Europe to send him hundreds of *kvitlich* (notes) asking for guidance on personal problems as well as requests for amulets that would provide cures for medical illnesses. In addition, he was a great proponent of the then embryonic movement for Jewish resettlement in *Eretz Yisrael*. Guttmacher was a significant halakhic authority ,as well, and his responsa are contained in his *Aderet Eliyahu*. His opinions reflect an absolute command of traditional Jewish sources as well as a subtle turn of mind, and the several rulings he issued on matters of conversion command modern-day attention because of the creativity he displayed in this area of Jewish law. It is to a description and analysis of these writings that the paper now turns.[2]

The Guttmacher Responsa on Conversion

Writing in 1838-39 in *Aderet Eliyahu, Yoreh Deah,* #33, Rabbi Guttmacher responded to a rabbi who asked whether it was appropriate to accept an individual for conversion who intended to marry a *kohen*. He noted that Jewish law brooked no compromise on this matter -- the rule prohibiting a priest from marrying a convert was clear. As marriages between Jews and gentiles were still extremely rare at this time, there was little need – in light of the rule – for him to employ this responsum – as later responsa by diverse *poskim* often would – as a vehicle to inveigh against intermarriage and the threat it might pose to Jewish continuity. He obviously felt no necessity at this point in modern Jewish history to issue a policy statement on this matter. Consequently, R. Guttmacher wrote a brief and straightforward responsum in this instance. There was no extended discussion. He simply stated that the rabbi should not perform the conversion.[3]

However, two decades later the situation concerning intermarriage between Jews and gentiles had changed and R. Guttmacher began to formulate a stance on these matters. Writing in a more expansive manner in *Aderet Eliyahu, Yoreh Deah,* #87, in 1858, he dealt with a case where a gentile man in Meizeritsch desired to convert so that he could marry the young orphaned Jewish woman whom he loved. The rabbi who posed the question to R. Guttmacher reported that the prospects were good that the young man would be pious. The prospective *ger* had studied and apparently accepted the Thirteen Principles of Maimonides as the authoritative beliefs of Jewish faith, and he had familiarized himself with the *siddur* and the traditional order of Jewish prayer. The rabbi was therefore inclined to carry out the conversion. However, he wanted R. Guttmacher's approval before performing this ritual act.

R. Guttmacher initially noted that while it was permissible for the rabbi to accept this young man as a proselyte, he further advised that the young man was required to produce a secular legal document asserting that it was legally permissible for him to do so before the rabbi could conduct the conversion. This was simply a matter of secular law, and Guttmacher was clearly concerned to comply with the regulations of the secular authorities. Conversion could be conducted only on the condition that the secular government allowed it.

Guttmacher then turned his attention to the substantive matter of Jewish law in the issue before him, and he focused the first part of his discussion on the passage (Yev. 109b) that asserts that evil befalls those who convert gentiles to Judaism. Guttmacher quickly limited the scope of this ruling by claiming that this judgment applied only to those who converted gentiles to Judaism precipitously or to those who sought out gentiles in order to seek their conversion. In his opinion, active proselytization on the part of Jews was forbidden.

In the case of individual gentiles who sought admission on their own into the Jewish people, R. Guttmacher adopted a different attitude – even when this request for entry was attached to a yearning for a Jewish mate. Indeed, he claimed that there was greater "accountability" *(aharayut)* for those rabbis who "rebuffed" *(dehiyah)* such would-be converts than for those rabbis who accepted these persons into the Jewish faith even if their motives were not pure and even if legitimate doubt remained about the sincerity of their claim that their intent was to become completely observant following their conversion. R. Guttmacher stated that the law (*din*) supported this stance because even if the potential convert misled the rabbinic court about his intent to observe the commandments, the conversion was still valid once the appropriate rites of entry were performed under the supervision of a qualified *bet din*.[4]

Furthermore, if the candidate for conversion was worthy and the rabbinic court rejected him, the damage that might be done to the Jewish people was potentially catastrophic. R. Guttmacher based this position on the talmudic tale in Sanhedrin that relates a case concerning Timna and the patriarchs of the Jewish people – Abraham, Isaac, and Jacob. According to this legend, Timna approached the patriarchs and beseeched them to convert her to Judaism. However, the patriarchs refused her request to convert because they believed her desire was not pure. They felt she was motivated to enter Judaism by her love for the patriarchs alone.

R. Guttmacher asserted that the patriarchs were wrong in rendering this judgment and he even condemned their refusal to accept Timna as a proselyte as a great sin with horrific consequences for future generations of the people Israel. As a result of their rejection, Timna was prevented from building a *bayit ne'eman* in Israel. Instead, she married a non-Jew and the Jewish people were ultimately severely punished. For, according to Jewish legend, Timna bore Amalek, the person whose hatred for Israel was such that he ultimately emerged as the eternal archetype for all those who would persecute and attack the Jewish people.

R. Guttmacher went on to state that the patriarchs would have better served the Jewish people when Timna approached them for conversion had they adopted the lenient example set by Hillel, the great Tanna who accepted candidates for conversions whose initial motives were apparently not selfless.[5] Those rabbis who would be stringent in regard to conversion should therefore recognize that the potential accountability (*aharayut*) for rejecting "a good soul" (*nefesh tov*) constitutes a graver threat and danger to the Jewish people than the responsibility involved in accepting an individual "who was not worthy" (*eino ra-ui*).

As a result of these considerations, R. Guttmacher asserted that the rabbi should certainly be lenient in this case and accept this gentile man as a convert to Judaism. He stated that it was of little import whether this man had an orphaned Jewish girl in mind as a future marriage partner. Despite the stricture in *Yoreh Deah* 268:3 that decreed that conversion prompted by an "ulterior motive" was not to be allowed, R. Guttmacher did not regard this "ulterior motive" as a decisive ground for rejecting this man. Instead, he was aware that there were contrary precedents in Jewish law that would permit such conversions and he stated that the conversion of this man and his subsequent marriage to this girl would constitute the fulfillment of a "great *mitzvah*" for the Jewish people.

To be sure, nothing in this Guttmacher responsum indicated that R. Guttmacher expected anything less than complete Jewish observance from this man. Nevertheless, R. Guttmacher concluded by stating that he rendered an explicit judgment on this matter precisely because his rabbinic colleagues as well as the Jewish people needed to be aware that potential dire consequences might result from a refusal to accept a potential proselyte. In the contemporary period, there was no reason to fear that converts would cause Israel to stray "from the correct path." Israel does that without them! Hence, all negative statements about converts do not apply in our day, one in which, "on account of our many sins, lawless violators (*peritizim*)" lead our people. Indeed, given the observance of many converts, "would it only be (*halevi*) that we should learn from them."[6]

Seven years later, Guttmacher adopted a similar position in another case that came before him. Writing in *Aderet Eliyahu, Yoreh Deah*, #85, in 1865–66, Guttmacher observed that the Hungarian government now permitted civil marriage between Jewish men and non-Jewish women (see the article on Hungarian law). These couples had no intention to dissolve their bonds, and many of these unions had already produced children. The question that Guttmacher addressed in this responsum was whether these women could be converted, as these non-Jewish women now "desired to enter into the religion of the Jews," and the Jewish "husbands also awaited . . . this [act of] *hesed*." In framing the question in this way, it is apparent that R. Guttmacher was inclined to rule leniently in the case before him and accept this young man into the Jewish fold. Of course, both R. Guttmacher and his rabbinic interrogator knew that there were halakhic obstacles to the conversion of such women. Indeed, R. Guttmacher cited these problems at great length.

At the same time, R. Guttmacher recognized in this responsum – as he had in the previous one – that other precedents could be employed that would permit the conversion and subsequent entry of these women into the Jewish community. He observed that these couples had already fulfilled "their desire," that is, consummated their union, and he acknowledged that these husbands would surely not divorce their gentile wives. As a result, there could no longer be grounds for claiming that their aspiration for conversion was prompted by an ulterior motive. Therefore, R. Guttmacher stated that, in his "humble opinion," the conversions should be performed for these women. It could even be said that the desire of these women to convert to Judaism "was an act done for the sake of God (*davar hashem*)."

In a vein that would later be adopted by other modern Orthodox rabbis, R. Guttmacher further contended that each woman should be converted to Judaism "in order to save the husband" from violating a legal prohibition that forbade a Jew from having intercourse with a gentile. According to Jewish law, the punishment for a Jewish man having intercourse with a gentile woman was that he would suffer *karet*, excision from heaven.

R. Guttmacher felt that the rabbis were duty-bound to prevent such transgressions inasmuch as they had the legal right to do so in these instances. Clearly, the task of the rabbi – insofar as he was able – was to "grant merit" *(lizkot)* to Jews.

Finally, R. Guttmacher observed that if each woman converted, then all future children that would issue from her husband and her would possess Jewish status. He also stated that the older children who had been born prior to the conversion of their mother should be converted as well. Undoubtedly, Guttmacher was concerned with the unity of the family as well as the status of the non-Jewish spouse and the religious state of the man's children. These values clearly informed the halakhic stance he adopted in these cases. In championing this posture, R. Guttmacher expressed a position that other like-minded Orthodox authorities would adopt who also favored an inclusionary posture in regard to conversion as the optimal policy for the Jewish community to adopt in view of the reality of intermarriage between Jews and gentiles in the modern setting.[7]

In *Aderet Eliyahu, Yoreh Deah*, #87, Guttmacher reconfirmed this lenient stance yet again in another case regarding a potential convert and his family. In this instance, the individual who wished to convert had a Jewish wife who had previously apostatized from Judaism and embraced Christianity. Currently pregnant, this woman already had given birth to a son and daughter fathered by this gentile man. She had stated that she and her children now wanted to return to Judaism, and her gentile husband expressed a desire to convert. However, the rabbi who posed this question to R. Guttmacher stated there was apparently an ulterior motive that prompted this longing to return to and enter the Jewish fold. For the Jewish mother as well as the siblings of this women had stated that they would share the family's apparently considerable wealth with their daughter and sister as well as her husband and children only if the entire family embraced Judaism. Thus, R. Guttmacher was being asked not only whether to convert this gentile man to Judaism. He was being asked to deal with an entire family seemingly prompted by the base motive of financial gain. His decision on this issue of pressing concern for the Jewish people would clearly demonstrate the priority he would assign "constituency retention" as a decisive factor in directing his judgment in this case.[8]

R. Guttmacher began by pointing out that the children were already Jewish from the viewpoint of *halakhah*. After all, Judaism simply does not – in a technical sense – recognize the possibility of apostasy. The reason for this is found in the rabbinic dictum put forth in Sanhedrin, "A Jew, even when he sins, remains a Jew." While the Jewish woman in this case clearly had committed a sin by "marrying" her husband and "converting" to Christianity, her "lawlessness" could not remove her status as a Jew. Therefore, her children – in light of the traditional rule that matrilineal descent is determinative of Jewish status – were Jewish.

R. Guttmacher defined the children as *anusim* (compelled ones), a term reserved in halakhic literature for Marranos and others who were not allowed to express their Jewishness publicly through no fault of their own. If the rabbinic court did not accept their father as a Jew, the children could not be rescued from their "gentile state," albeit that they were – strictly speaking – Jews. If the father was not accepted as a convert, it would be as if the rabbis had "pushed the children away with two hands from the community of Israel."

R. Guttmacher contended that the rabbinic court was therefore obligated to rescue the children from this fate by accepting the father as a convert, even if this act was "a bit contrary to the law – *ktzat neged hadin*."

The rabbinic dictum (Shab. 4a) "Do not say to a man, 'Sin so that your friend will gain merit,'" was not legally actionable in this instance. While the *bet din* might be faulted for committing a "minor sin" in accepting such a candidate as a proselyte, the subsequent *mitzvah* that would flow from this act of acceptance would offset this "minor transgression." For should the father convert, he would actually fulfill the commandment of Genesis, "Be fruitful and multiply."

R. Guttmacher then returned to the same passage (Yev. 109b) that states that great evil befalls those who accept gentiles to Judaism, which he had cited previously, and he again dismissed it as irrelevant R. Guttmacher once more asserted that this rule was applicable only if two preconditions were involved. The first was that there were active efforts at outreach – "to mix strangers (*zarim*) among the Jewish people." The second condition was that the rule should be actionable only when there was no compelling reason to accept the gentile candidate into Judaism. However, neither of these conditions applied in this case. First, there had been no outreach efforts to convert the Jewish father. He had come of his own accord and approached the rabbi concerning conversion. Second, "in this instance, there is good cause and reason *(ta'am usevara)*" to perform the conversion. Consequently, Guttmacher reasoned that "it is a commandment to do so." Furthermore, the rabbinic principle "Everything depends upon the judgment of the rabbinic court" provided an additional warrant for performing the conversion. For, if the rabbinic court decided that such a conversion constituted a "benefit"*(tovah)*, for the Jewish people, then it was imperative -- there was a "need" *(tzorekh")* – that the conversion be conducted and that this man and his family be ushered into the Jewish community.

In his final paragraph in the responsum, R. Guttmacher fully explained why he felt conversion in this instance constituted such a "benefit." At the outset of this paragraph, R. Guttmacher observed that in the contemporary era no rabbinic court possessed the stature that a rabbinic court possessed in ancient days. After all, each contemporary rabbinic court is one composed of *hedyotot*, understood here to mean persons who are not actually ordained.[9] Basing himself on his interpretation of a passage found in the *Mishneh Torah*, R. Guttmacher claimed that courts composed of *hedyotot* are permitted to accept converts whose motives are less than pure (*Hilhot Issurei*

Biah 13:16). Only the *Bet Din Gadol* of ancient times refused to accept such persons as proselytes.

R. Guttmacher therefore maintained that the court in question had an obligation to "rescue" the woman and her children – as they were Jews – from the "sin" and "negative influence" of living with a husband and father who was a non-Jew. Therefore, it was "permissible to accept him" as a convert. While the rabbi and the rabbinic court had good cause to be suspicious as to whether the man would be an observant Jew subsequent to his conversion, it could not be known with certainty that he would return to his former ways. Indeed, he might become an observant Jew.

Therefore, for the sake of his family and in light of the precedent concerning Timna (San. 109b) cited above, R. Guttmacher concluded by maintaining that the conversion of this man would constitute a "benefit" *(tovah)* for the Jewish community. The man should therefore be accepted as a proselyte and the family should be welcomed back into the Jewish people. By converting the father, a "blemish" *(pisul)* would be removed from the family.

Afterword and Final Thoughts

In writing on conversion in his *Evolving Halakhah*, Rabbi Zemer observed that his analysis of Jewish legal literature on this topic reveals that there is a "dynamic interplay between Torah law and the demands of life." This interplay leads rabbis to issue inclusive rulings on this matter that Rabbi Zemer labels as "bold and moral."[10]

In this paper, the responsa of R. Eliyahu Guttmacher on conversion display this spirit. R. Guttmacher clearly believed that Jewish law contained resources that allowed for the admission of persons who came for purposes of intermarriage into the Jewish people and he assigned priority to the unity of the family as a primary consideration in rendering his decisions. This analysis of the Guttmacher responsa on conversion only supports the notion of an ethical and sensitive *halakhah* that Moshe Zemer has always championed. It has been a privilege to offer this essay as a gift of gratitude to him. May he merit many more years of scholarly productivity and life.

Notes

1. For his writings on the topic of conversion, see Moshe Zemer, *Evolving Halakhah: A Progressive Approach to Traditional Jewish Law* (Woodstock, Vt.: Jewish Lights Publishing, 1999), pp. 121-176.

2. For an analysis and description of Guttmacher and his life as a "Hasidic leader," see Victor Reinstein, "By the Merit of a Tzaddik," M.A. thesis, Hebrew Union College–Jewish Institute of Religion, New York, 1978.

3. The prohibition forbidding a *kohen* from marrying a convert is found in *Even HaEzer* 6:1. For a concise English language summary of this prohibition, see Isaac Klein, *A Guide to Jewish Religious Practice* (New York: The Jewish Theological Seminary, 1979), pp. 383 and 387-388.

4. See *Hilkhot Issurei Biah* 13.14-18 for a digest of the sou4ces upon which R. Guttmacher relied, as well as *Shulhahn Arukh, Yoreh Deah* 268.12. Avi Sagi and Zvi Zohar proide a masterful account of the role of *kabalat mitzvot* in the process of conversion in their *Conversion to Judaism and the Meaning of Modern Jewish Identity: A Study of Halakhic Sources from the Talmud to the Present Times* (Jerusalem: The Bialik Institute and the Shalom Hartman Insitutue, 1994) (Hebrew), pp. 171-210.

5. See Shab. 31a where Hillel accepts an individual as a candidate for conversion whose ulterior motives are initially responsible for prompting his desire for conversion.

6. In making this argument R. Guttmacher displayed a sensibility similar to an 1864 responsum concerning the conversion of children born to Jewish fathers and gentile mothers, R. Kalischer wrote, "At a time like this there are many who do not conduct themselves according to Jewish law. Nevertheless, we should circumcise the son with joy. For, God forbid, we should not push him away." Indeed, R. Kalischer even stated that "with children such as these, there is sometimes the possibility that great leaders of Israel will arise from among them." The Kalischer responsum is found in R. Esriel Hildesheimer, *She'ei'lot U'teshuvot Rabbi Esriel, Yoreh Deah*, #229. For an English translation of parts of this responsum, see Robert Levine and David Ellenson, "Rabbi Zvi Hirsch Kalischer and a Halakhic Approach to Conversion," *The Journal of Reform Judaism* (Summer, 1981), pp. 49-57.

7. For a Discussion of this lenient *tendenz* regarding conversion among Orthodox *poskim* in the modern era, see David Ellenson, "The Development of Orthodox Attitudes to Conversion in the Modern Persio," *Conservative Judaism* (Summer, 1983, pp. 57-73).

8. In arriving at this posture, R. Guttmacher foreshadowed the rulings of Rabbi David Zevi Hoffmann of Berlin on this issue. This term is employed by Daniel Gordis to describe the approach taken by Rabbi Hoffmann to the issue of conversion. See Daniel Gordis, "David Zevi Hoffmann on Civili Marriage: Evidence of a Traditional Community Under Siege," *Modern Judaism* 10 (1990), pp. 85-103.

9. On the question of *semihah* (ordination) in Jewish law and its cessation in the fifth century, see Menachem Kellner, *Maimonides on the "Decline of the Generations" and the Nature of Rabbinic Authority* (Albany: State University of New York Press, 1996), pp. 89-90.

10. Zemer, *Evolving Halakhah*, pp. 175 f.

Chapter 11

❖ ❖ ❖

THE RESPONSA OF RABBI SOLOMON B. FREEHOF
A Reappraisal*

David Golinkin

We have learned in the tractate of Ta'anit (29a): *Mishenikhnas adar marbin b'simhah* – " when Adar enters, our joy increases". It is hard to say that this year, due to the ongoing violence and terrorism in the State of Israel. Nonetheless, I am happy to participate in this symposium for three reasons. I am happy to see that so many Reform rabbis have come to Jerusalem for the CCAR Convention despite the Intifada. I am happy to see the growing interest in *halakhah* and *mitzvot* within the Reform movement, as is evident from the new Pittsburgh Platform of 1999. Finally, I am happy to honor my friend, Rabbi Dr. Moshe Zemer, who has had an important impact on Israeli society through his articles in *Ha'aretz* and *Davar* and through his book *Halakhah Shefuyah* (*Evolving Halakhah*). He has also had an important impact on the Reform movement through these symposia and through the series of volumes published by the Freehof Institute of Progressive *Halakhah*. May it be God's will that Moshe continue to study and teach *ad meah v'esrim*.

I shall divide my remarks about the responsa of Rabbi Freehof into six sections: his biography; the breadth of his interest and knowledge; his responsa and other halakhic works; his attitude to *halakhah* and rationale for writing responsa; a comparison of the responsa in *Reform Responsa* – his first volume of responsa – to his stated rationale and conclusions.

A Biographical Sketch[1]

Rabbi Solomon B. Freehof, a descendent of Rabbi Shneur Zalman of Ladie, was born in London in 1892 and brought to Baltimore by his parents in 1903. He graduated from the University of Cincinnati in 1914. He was ordained by Hebrew Union College (HUC) in 1915 and served briefly as a chaplain in the American Expeditionary Force during World War I. Freehof served as Assistant Professor of Medieval Liturgy and Rabbinics at HUC from 1915- to 1924, where he received his D.D. degree in 1922. In 1924 he became rabbi of Kehillath Anshe Ma'arav in Chicago and in 1934 he became rabbi of Rodef Shalom Congregation in Pittsburgh, where he was named rabbi emeritus in 1966.

Aside from the chairmanship of the Responsa Committee of the Central Conference of American Rabbis, Freehof held a number of national and international positions within the Reform movement. He became chairman of the Liturgy Committee in 1930; that committee published the *Union Prayer Book* in 1940-45. In 1942, he became Chairman of the Commission on Jewish Education, a position he held until 1959. From 1943 to 1945 he served as President of the Central Conference of American Rabbis, and from 1959 to 1964 as President of the World Union for Progressive Judaism. Rabbi Freehof passed away in 1990 *b'sevah tovah* at age 98.

Renaissance Man

In his student days at Hebrew Union College, Freehof was the favorite pupil of Professor J. Z. Lauterbach (1873–1942).[2] In 1952, Freehof published an appreciation of Lauterbach entitled "Jacob Z. Lauterbach and the Halakah" in which he wrote:

> The Talmud makes its children flexible, alert and many-sided .... Any modern Jewish scholar who began his scholarly life in his boyhood with a thorough grounding in the Talmud is likely to be somewhat of a polymath, certainly a many-sided author competent to deal with a surprising variety of

subjects; almost never is he a limited specialist, and certainly never a narrow mind.[3]

Freehof could have been describing himself, for he too was such an *ish eshkolot*[4] or renaissance man. The *festschrift* in his honor, published in 1964, already lists 783 items, and this was 26 years before his death![5] He published 21 books all told. In addition to *halakhah* and responsa, which we shall discuss below, he published books in four main areas:

(1) Literature: *Books of Thirty Years*, published in 1964, contains the lectures he gave to his modern literature class between 1934 and 1963.

(2) Bible: As a result of his serving as chairman of the Commission on Jewish Education, Freehof published *Preface to Scripture* (1950) along with a series of popular commentaries on Psalms (1938), Job (1958), Isaiah (1972), Jeremiah (1977), and Ezekiel (1978).

(3) Liturgy: In addition to teaching liturgy at HUC, he published *Blessing and Praise* with Rabbi Israel Bettan (1924); *The Small Sanctuary: Judaism in the Prayerbook* (1942); *The Union Prayerbook* (1940–45) as mentioned above; *The Union Home Prayerbook* (1951); and *In the House of the Lord* (1951). He also served as editor of the Liturgy Department of *The Universal Jewish Encyclopedia* in the 1940s.

(4) Homiletics: Freehof published *Modern Jewish Preaching* in 1941, and he was an excellent preacher who spoke without any notes.[6]

Freehof's Responsa and Other *Halakhic* Works

It seems quite clear that Freehof became interested in responsa and halakhah as a result of the influence of Rabbi Lauterbach, who wrote a number of seminal works on *halakhah* and served as chairman of the Responsa Committee of the CCAR (1922–33), for which he wrote some important responsa.[7]

Freehof joined the Responsa Committee of the CCAR ca. 1923. He began to publish responsa in the *Rodef Shalom Temple Bulletin* in 1937, where he tackled topics such as "Is Visiting the Cemetery a Fixed Jewish Custom?", "Why Are the Candles Lit on Friday Night?", and "Why Is It Customary to Refrain from Celebrating Marriages Between Passover and Shavouth?"[8] In 1944, Freehof published the first volume of *Reform Jewish Practice and Its Rabbinic Background*, which is an apologetic work explaining the talmudic and rabbinic background of Reform Jewish practice. The second volume appeared in 1952.

Beginning in 1942, Freehof served as chairman of the Responsa Committee of the Commission on Chaplaincy of the National Jewish Welfare Board, along with Rabbi Milton Steinberg (Conservative)[9] and Rabbi Leo Jung (Orthodox). Freehof authored all of the responsa, though occasionally there is an Orthodox alternative answer at the bottom of the page. The first volume, *Responsa in War Time*, appeared in 1947 and the second volume, *Responsa to Chaplains*, in 1953.

It is worth noting that Freehof's first volume of responsa appeared in 1947 when he was 55 years old, though he later made up for lost time! It is also worth noting that all of his responsa were written in English, a phenomenon I have discussed elsewhere.[10]

In 1955, Freehof became the chairman of the CCAR Responsa Committee, a position he held until 1976, and this position led to his major publications on responsa, which continued for the next 35 years until his death. In 1955, he published *The Responsa Literature*, which remains the best English introduction to that vast literature. In 1961, he published his supplement of 570 titles to Professor Boaz Cohen's classic bibliography *Kuntress Hateshuvot*.[11] In 1963, Freehof published *A Treasury of Responsa*, which is an English translation of selected responsa culled from 1,500 years of responsa. Finally, he published eight volumes of his own responsa between 1960 and 1990.

In an address delivered in 1961, Freehof says that he received 300 questions per year.[12] This means that he may have answered as many as 15,000 questions over the course of 50 years![13] Be that as it may, he published 59 responsa for the Commission on Chaplaincy, 30 for the CCAR Responsa Committee (which also appear in his volumes of responsa,) and 450 of his own responsa, for a total of 539 responsa.[14] This is a corpus comparable in size to many Orthodox *poskim* in the modern era.

Freehof's Approach to *Halakhah* and Rationale for Writing Responsa

Rabbi Freehof published a number of important essays and introductions in which he expresses his attitude to *halakhah* and explains why he wrote responsa. We shall concentrate on two such essays. In "Reform Judaism and the Legal Tradition", which was delivered as an address to the Association of Reform Rabbis of New York City in February 1961, Freehof explained that the *halakhah* is no longer viable today for three reasons: "It has the power of interpretation, but no longer has the power of *takanah* or legislation; it is paralyzed by the Orthodox fear of all change; and it is also inhibited by *yirat hora'ah*, or fear of making halakhic decisions due to self-deprecation.[15]

As a result of these phenomena, early reformers such as Rabbi Samuel Holdheim, who was a *talmid hakham*, revolted like an eighteen-year-old revolts against his parents. But now that we have achieved independence from the law, we can work our way back "to understanding the parent form of Judaism."

> In the beginning of the Reform Movement, we thought that the Bible and the Prophets, especially the Prophets, would be sufficient. But now. . . we are coming to see that we cannot hope for an integrated religious personality if we are permanently alienated from fifteen hundred years of the supreme

Jewish intellectual effort. I do not mean that we are alienated from the entire rabbinic literature. We have always used the *Haggadah* and the *Midrash*.

But the real intellectuality of our people, their real brilliance, their full sounding of the depths of human ability to think and to reason, is in the halacha. It is not an exaggeration to say that never in the story of mankind's intellectual effort has so large a proportion of one people produced so brilliant a succession of intellectual works. Among what other people would some little man in a little village devote his whole life to producing a book of brilliant *hiddushim*, legal ideas which demand our best brains to understand and to follow? Such achievements by minor scholars were created by the thousands in every generation and in every land of Jewish residence! How can we be integrated as a Jewish movement, if we remain permanently alien from the great, creative Jewish legal tradition? We declared our independence and *are* independent. Now we must find a way, as a son finds his way, to remain independent, to remain free, and yet to be understanding and to get the benefit of whatever will be helpful to us in the legal tradition. . . . .

In general I have arrived... at a rule-of-thumb rather than a *doctrine* of legal authority. We make our contact with the great rabbinic intellectual tradition, see wherein it can help us. If we find cases in which the rabbinic tradition does not fit with life, then those cases will have to take their chances with life as everything else does. *I follow the tentative formula that the halacha is our guidance and not our governance.* I do not claim this as an adequate principle. I claim it as a rule-of-thumb, useful as we go along.[16]

A year earlier, Freehof explained the Reform attitude towards *halakhah* and his rationale for writing responsa in his Introduction to *Reform Responsa*:

It is clear why halachic questions come up, but it is not clear what, in Reform, should be the basis of the answers . . . . Of this much we are sure, that whatever authority the *Halacha* has for us is certainly only a selective authority. There are vast sections of law about which we are never questioned . . . . [such as] the mixing of meat and milk, *mechirat hametz*, or the construction of the ritual bath.[17]

Later on, Rabbi Freehof asks: if rabbinic law does not have God-given authority, what does it mean to us? He replies:

To us the law is human, but nobly human, developed by devoted minds who dedicated their best efforts to answering the question: "What doth the Lord require of thee?" *Therefore, we respect it and seek its guidance. Some of its provisions have faded from our lives. We do not regret that fact. But as to the laws that we do follow, we wish them to be in harmony with tradition.*[18]

... In other words, the law is authoritative enough to influence us, but not so completely as to control us. *The rabbinic law is our guidance but not our governance.* Reform responsa are not directive, but advisory ... Our concern is more with the people than with the legal system ....[19]

A Comparison of the Responsa in *Reform Responsa* to Freehof's Stated Approach and Rationale

Thus far we have seen that Rabbi Freehof basically says that *halakhah* has a voice but not a veto. But if we carefully examine the responsa in his first volume of responsa – *Reform Responsa* – published in 1960, we must agree with Rabbi Gunther Plaut that "the overwhelming weight of Freehof's conclusions is based solidly on Tradition."[20]

First of all, Rabbi Freehof's responsa are organized in the traditional fashion, according to the order of the *Shulhan Arukh*. Second, in terms of his *sources*, Rabbi Freehof does indeed utilize what he called "fifteen hundred years of the supreme Jewish intellectual effort."[21] He quotes the Bible, *Mishnah, Tosefta, Bavli, Yerushalmi, Midrash*; codes such as Rambam, *Tur, Shulhan Arukh* and *Arukh Hashulhan*; dozens of responsa from the Maharam of Rotenberg and the Rashba to the *Hatam Sofer* and *Melamed L'ho'il*; and halakhic journals such as *Hamaor, Hapardess, Haposek*, and *Vay'laket Yosef.*[22]

Indeed, if one looks only at his *sources*, one could easily surmise that these responsa were written by an Orthodox rabbi. In eight places, he quotes or refers to books and articles that could be categorized as *Wissenschaft des Judentums*,[23] and on four occasions he consults with doctors, a lawyer, and a librarian regarding the subjects he is discussing.[24] Yet frequently he does *not* use *Wissenschaft* and other sciences when he *could* have or *should* have. For example, in Responsum no. 14 regarding the use of Jewish symbols on synagogue floors, he *rejects* the evidence from ancient synagogues even though he is aware of it. In Responsum no. 28 regarding whether Jewish doctors should inform patients that they are dying, Rabbi Freehof consults neither doctors nor medical journals. In Responsum no. 33 as to whether a Jew may be buried in a Christian cemetery, he consults neither archaeologists nor archaeological journals. Most blatantly, in a responsum on smoking published in 1977, he says that "if [smoking as harmful to health] is proved to be a fact," then Jewish law would be opposed.[25] Had Rabbi Freehof consulted doctors or medical journals, he would have known that fact had been established long before 1977.[26]

Thirdly, the responsa themselves are much more traditional than one might expect. Of the 57 responsa in *Reform Responsa*, 46 have a clear *psak halakhah* (legal decision).[27] Among those 46 responsa, 36 (78 percent) are lenient and 10 (22 percent) are strict. This is not surprising. What *is* surprising is that 24 of the 36 lenient responsa (66 percent) are based on sources.[28]

Thus, for example, Rabbi Freehof allows a memorial service on Shabbat (no. 2), basing himself on *Shibolei Haleket*, Responsa *Tzapihit Bidvash,* and the *Kol Bo*. And he allows a congregational meeting on Shabbat provided no minutes are taken (no. 8), basing himself on Shab. 150a, Rambam, Rosh, *Shulhan Arukh*, and *Responsa Lekha Shelomo.*

On the other hand, five of the lenient responsa contradict the halakhic sources.[29] Thus, for example, after quoting many sources that say that a husband should *not* recite *kaddish* and *yizkor* for his first wife (no. 39), Rabbi Freehof states that a husband should not do so. But he then adds: "If, however, his first wife had no children and there is no one to say *kaddish* for her, then the husband may say *kaddish* in the absence of his second wife, but may have no *yahrzeit* light in the house."[30] In a responsum regarding the adoption of non-Jewish children (no. 47), he rules against the *halakhah* and requires no immersion or circumcision, basing himself on the CCAR position, which he himself authored in 1947.³¹ In Responsum no. 49 regarding the custody of children, he surveys the *halakhah* and then states: "As far as Reform Judaism is concerned, all of the above has comparatively little bearing. In general, we accept the validity of civil divorce and therefore must accept the decision of the civil courts as to custody of the children." ³²

Reform Responsa also contains eight responsa that are stringent on the basis of sources.³³ Thus, for example, no. 4 forbids a Sunday Bar Mitzvah since there is no Torah reading on Sunday and the blessings would be a *brakhah l'vatala*. No. 11 explains that a *sukkah* built on the *bimah* of a synagogue is merely a decoration and cannot be regarded as a legal *sukkah*. In Responsum no. 18, Rabbi Freehof was asked if a convert to Judaism may retain his church membership. He concludes "on the basis of both common sense and the Jewish law . . . [that] such an arrangement as suggested is utterly unacceptable under Jewish law and tradition."³⁴ And in Responsum No. 26 Rabbi Freehof was asked if a Jewish boy may sing in a church choir and wear a cross. He explains that Christians are allowed *shittuf* (i.e. to believe in God along with "the Son and the Holy Ghost" – cf. *Tosafot* to San. 63b), but *shittuf* is forbidden to Jews and therefore the boy may not participate in any trinitarian worship.

Finally, two of the responsa are stringent on the basis of ethical considerations.³⁵ No. 20 deals with a fifteen-year-old Christian girl who wants to convert to Judaism without her parents' consent. Rabbi Freehof admits that it is halakhically permissible. But he explains that in the past Christians snatched away Jewish children and converted them to Christianity. If we start doing the same, "we are destroying a moral decency which we have maintained . . . . All of this is based rather on the spirit of Jewish tradition than on its actual letter."³⁶

Conclusions

A Conservative rabbi who reviewed Rabbi Freehof's *Recent Reform Responsa* published in 1963 doubted whether the answers are really responsa. He says that in the first half of each responsum, Rabbi Freehof surveys the vast legal literature, while in the second he judges the case on the basis of the mood and mores of the modern Jewish community. "The problem lies in the fact that there seems to be no organic relationship between the two parts of each responsum. It is clear that the study of the past fascinates him. However, he considers only his judgement of the present relevant in reaching a decision."[37]

This assessment is true regarding the five lenient responsa mentioned above, but it is *not* true regarding *most* of the responsa in *Reform Responsa*. A more accurate assessment of most of Rabbi Freehof's responsa is contained in his own assessment of Rabbi Lauterbach's responsa: "Thus, except for the fact that his decisions are liberal, giving contemporary needs greater weight than an old fashioned *Moreh Hora'ah* might give, he is, in method at least, in line with the historic tradition of legal interpretation and decision."[38]

Indeed, we have already seen that most of Rabbi Freehof's responsa in *Reform Responsa* fit this description. He follows the order of the *Shulhan Arukh*. He primarily quotes classic halakhic sources. He quotes very little *Wissenschaft* or modern science. Though he is clearly lenient, most of his *kulot* are based on sources. Only five of his 46 responsa with a clear *pesak* (11 percent) clearly contradict *halakhah*.

There is no question that Rabbi Freehof's fifty years of writing responsa and fourteen volumes of *halakhah* and responsa had a profound effect on the Reform movement, forcing it to confront "fifteen hundred years of the supreme Jewish intellectual effort". He inspired others, including Rabbis Jacob, Zemer, Plaut, Ellenson, and Washofsky to follow in his footsteps, and his halakhic activity may have even helped lead to the positive approach toward *mitzvot* found in the revised Pittsburgh Platform of 1999.

It is also clear that his halakhic writings will continue to influence Conservative and Reform *poskim* for many years to come. And in that sense Rabbi Freehof continues to speak to us, as we have learned in the tractate of Yev. 97a: *kol talmid hakham shomrim devar shemua mipiv ba'olam hazeh siftotav devevot bakever* – "Any sage who has a teaching cited in his name in this world, his lips murmur in the grave." *Yehi zikhro barukh*!

Notes

*In memory of Eve and Avid Boaz *z"l.* 21 Tevet and 2 Shevat 5762. "Beloved and cherished in life; even in their death, they were not divided."

1. This section is based on *The Universal Jewish Encyclopedia* (New York: Universal Encyclopedia Press, 1941), vol. 4, p. 433; Walter Jacob et al. [editors], *Essays in Honor of Solomon B. Freehof* (Pittsburgh: Rodef Shalom, 1964), hereafter: *Essays*; *Encylopaedia Judaica*, vol. 7, col. 121; Rabbi Walter Jacob in Rabbi Solomon Freehof, *Reform Responsa for Our Time* (Cincinnati: Hebrew Union College Press, 1977) pp. ix-xxvii; *The New York Times*, June 13, 1990, p. B20; *American Jewish Yearbook* (New York: 1992,) vol. 92, pp. 594-595; Kerry Olitzky et al. [editors], *Reform Judaism in America: A Biographical Dictionary and Sourcebook* (Westport, Conn.: 1993) pp. 62-64.

2. According to Rabbi Walter Jacob in his introduction to Rabbi Solomon Freehof, *Today's Reform Responsa* (Pittsburgh: Rodef Shalom Press, 1990), before p. 1.

3 *Judaism* vol. 1, no. 3, (July 1952), p. 270. Regarding Freehof's close relationship to Lauterbach, see also his dedication to *Reform Jewish Practice* (Cincinnati: Hebrew Union College Press, 1944) ["to the memory of my revered and beloved teacher"], his introduction to *Recent Reform Responsa* (Cincinnati: Hebrew Union College Press, 1963), p. 12 ["my revered and unforgettable teacher"] and his introduction to Lauterbach's *Rabbinic Essays* (Cincinnati: Hebrew Union College Press, 1951) pp. xiii-xvi.

4. The expression *ish eshkolot* is used to describe two early Sages in Sotah 9:9. Samuel Sotah 47b) explains the term as a *notarikon* of *ish eshkolot* – "a man who contains everything."

5. *Essays*, pp. 53-93.

6. Rabbi Frederick Schwartz in *Essays*, pp. 3-32; and a personal communication from Rabbi

Dr. Ruth Langer, March 6, 2002. Rabbi Langer interned at Rabbi Freehof's synagogue in the 1980s.

7. See a bibliography of Lauterbach in his *Rabbinic Essays,* pp. 3-20. For a survey of his responsa, see Walter Jacob and Moshe Zemer [eds.], *Dynamic Jewish Law* (Tel-Aviv and Pittsburgh: Rodef Shalom Press, 1991), pp. 98-101.

8. See *Essays,* pp. 58-59.

9. He was replaced later on by Rabbi David Aronson.

10. See my introduction to *The Responsa of Professor Louis Ginsberg* (New York and Jerusalem: Jewish Theological Seminary Press, 1996), p. 24.

11. *Studies in Bibliography and Booklore* 5 (1961), pp. 30-41 (Hebrew section). In December 1957 and November 1959, Freehof wrote to Boaz Cohen urging him to publish a new, enlarged edition of *Kuntress Hateshuvot.* (The letters are preserved in the Boaz Cohen Archives, Rare Book Room, Jewish Theological Seminary, Box 9, "Freehof, Solomon.") Cohen must have replied in the negative, leading to the publication of Freehof's list.

12. *Reform Judaism and the Legal Tradition – The Tintner Memorial Lecture,* (New York:Association of Reform Rabbis, 1961), p. 10, hereafter: *Legal Tradition.* In the introduction to *Recent Reform Responsa,* p. 7, Rabbi Freehof says that the Responsa Committee has received 200 questions per year for the last decade.

13. By way of comparison, Rabbi Shlomo ben Adret (1235-1310), who was considered to be one of the most prolific responders of all time, was rumored to have written 6,000 responsa of which 3,373 have been published. See S. Z. Havlin in *Teshuvot Sh'elot L'harashba(* Jerusalem: 5737 [1977]), p. 8, note 4.

14. The responsa written for the Responsa Committee are found in Walter Jacob [ed.], *American Reform Responsa* (New York: Central Conference of American Rabbis, 1983). Rabbi Jacob (above, note 2), says that Rabbi Freehof published 433 of his own responsa, but some of the responsa deal with a few different topics, hence the total of 450.

15. *Legal Tradition,* pp. 2-5.

16. *Ibid.,* pp. 7-10.

17. *Reform Responsa* (Cincinnati: Hebrew Union College Press), 1960 [hereafter: *RR*], p. 19.

18. *Ibid.,* p. 21.

19. *Ibid.,* p. 22. For the phrase "guidance but not governance," cf. pp. 75, 218.

20. Rabbi Gunther Plaut in Jacob and Zemer , *Dynamic Jewish Law,* p. 113.

Chapter 12

❖ ❖ ❖

THE RABBINIC RIDDLE

Louis Jacobs

Examined here is a minor, though not insignificant, genre of rabbinic literature, the puzzles or riddles to which the reader is invited to supply the solutions. More specifically, to be examined here are the collections of such riddles compiled by various authors, ostensibly with the aim of providing a stimulus to the mind engaged in the study of the Torah but with an incidental recreational purpose, the sheer enjoyment obtained in arriving at the correct answer to a difficult problem.

From Talmudic times the setting of problems was an established practice among the Jewish teachers. The *baya*, the purely academic problem, is a ubiquitous form in the Babylonian Talmud.[1] More directly relevant to the phenomenon discussed here are the instances in the Talmud[2] where the third-to fourth-century Amora, Rabbah, is said to have encouraged his disciples to sharpen their minds by making statements contrary to the law in order to see whether they were sufficiently on their toes to challenge him. This method of "alerting the disciples" (*le-hadded ha-talmidim*) is also said to have been practiced by Samuel;[3] by Rabbi Akiba;[4] and by Rabbi Akiba's teacher, Rabbi Joshua.[5] In another talmudic passage[6] the method is attributed to Rabbah's teacher, R. Huna. The fact that this practice of "alerting the disciples" is attributed to teachers of different periods seems to suggest that the method was widely pursued in talmudic times.

It is safe to assume that "sharpening the mind" was accepted as a high, scholarly virtue in the great post-Talmudic centres of learning, but the earliest collection of riddles compiled for this express purpose dates from the fifteenth century, when the German halakhist

Jacob Landau, author of *Sefer Ha-Agur*, wrote his *Sefer Hazon* (*Book of Vision*), as he states in the Introduction to the work, in the Italian city of Pavia on the River Ticino' in the year 1480.[7] Various editions of *Sefer Hazon* have been published. A scholarly edition was published as *Sefer Hazon Ha-Shalem*, edited by M. Herschler, together with Landau's *Sefer Ha-Agur*, in Jerusalem in 1960.[8]

In the flowery Introduction, in which the language of the vision of the prophet Ezekiel is adapted, Landau[9] describes his aim:

> The practical precepts are opaque so far as their full explanations are concerned, the measure of the Talmud being longer than the earth and wider than the sea and the hearts of men are too limited to grasp it in its entirety. Many profound matters are found in that work which, on a superficial reading, seem to be the opposite to the truth and the various theories [which remove the difficulties] are dispersed and scattered throughout the Talmud. Hence, I have shaken out my lap in order to gather sheaves after the reapers. These I collected at random without any preconceived plan, as I studied here and there. That it be preserved by me, I recorded a number of things which appear strange to those who first hear them, full of contradictions and opposed to the truth, but which, on deeper reflection, are seen by the discerning mind to be correct. I have called these riddles [*hidot*]. I have recorded these riddles in correct form engraved upon the tables so as to find relief from our toil and from the ground the Lord has cursed. This should not be thought of as an exercise in folly or vanity since my intention is for the sake of Heaven and the All-Merciful desires the heart. There is no vanity in such a work as this; it is only the perfection of the work that points to the perfection of the worker, covering all his errors with love. I have called this small collection: *Sefer Hazon* since when a seeker eventually manages to grasp things that had hitherto eluded him it is by a kind of vision and a manifestation of the prophetic faculty. For the prophet of whom the divine power takes hold comprehends spontaneously that which the sage can only grasp after much trouble and effort and after many prior postulates so that when a man suddenly hits upon the truth and with regard to difficult problems it seems to him as if it is due to the workings of the divine power.

Landau presumably means that a solution to a riddle comes in a flash of intuition comparable to the inspiration of the prophet.

Landau's little book contains 52 riddles, presented, one after the other, together with the solutions. The reader who wishes to cheat has no need to look at the back of the book for the correct solution. It is there immediately after the riddle itself. Only a few, typical examples can be given here.

(1) Two boys are about to celebrate their *Bar Mitzvah*. Boy A was born a day earlier than boy B and yet B will become *Bar Mitzvah* a month before A. How is this possible?

Solution: The boys were born in a leap year, which has two months of Adar. A was born on the 29th day of Adar I, B on the first day of Adar II. The year of the *Bar Mitzvah* is not a leap year and there is only one month of Adar in that year. B's thirteenth birthday will fall on the first of Adar while A's will fall on Adar 29. Landau adds that this is so because the Talmud, Nazir 7a and Meg. 5a, states that in these matters we count the year not in days but in months.

(7) How is it possible for a man to commit four separate transgressions by a single utterance?

Solution in the name of R. Moses of Coucy (13th century), the *Semag*: The man curses his father who is a judge and a prince. "Thou shall not curse the deaf" (Lev. 19:14) is interpreted by the rabbis to mean even a deaf man who cannot hear the curse but the offence is committed when anyone is cursed. Cursing a father is a separate offence (Ex. 21:17). Ex. 22:27 is understood by the rabbis to mean: "Thou shalt not curse a judge [*elohim*] and thou shalt not curse a prince," thus yielding two further separate offences. Consequently, the man who curses his father who is a judge and a prince commits with his single utterance four separate offences: that of cursing anyone, that of cursing a father, that of cursing a judge, and that of cursing a prince.

(9) How is it possible for a man who commits an offence in smaller measure to be punished by the Court and yet if he commits the same offence in greater measure to be exempt?

Solution: Three examples. (a) Where there is compensation to the victim of an attack, there is no separate punishment of a flogging for the attack. But if the damage suffered amounts to less than a *perutah*, this small amount is not treated as "money" so that the Court cannot order compensation. In the absence of compensation the Court can impose the penalty of flogging (Ket. 32b; San. 85a). (b) If a man passes his son through fire to Molech, he is to be put to death (Lev. 18:21 and 20:2). But if he passes all his sons through fire to Molech, he is exempt from the death penalty (San. 64b). (c) False witnesses who testify that an innocent man has committed a murder have to be put to death (Deut. 19:19). But this only applies where the execution of the man had not actually taken place. If the man had actually been executed by the Court on the testimony of the witnesses, the witnesses are not punished (Mak. 5b). Landau explains these examples in the name of the *Semag* that where the offence is in greater measure, the offender does not deserve to suffer the punishment by the Court that will cleanse him of his offence and God will punish him.

(10) How is it possible to give someone a single *zuz* and by that very act deprive him of 1,000 *zuzim*? Conversely, how is it possible to take away from someone a single *zuz* and by that very act enable him to gain 1,000 *zuzim*?

Solution: The *Mishnah* (Peah 8:8) defines a poor man entitled to receive poor relief as one who has less than 200 *zuzim*. Once a man qualifies as 'poor', he is entitled to receive from the charity chest whatever is available there, even to the extent of 1000 *zuzim*. The two cases, then, are: a) where a single *zuz* is given to a man who has 199; b) where a single *zuz* is taken from a man who has 200. For anyone familiar with the *Mishnah* this is an easy one.

(11) How is it possible for a Court to confiscate and legally destroy the property of a man innocent of any wrongdoing?

Solution: All the property in a city with idolatry has to be destroyed (Deut. 13:17). In tractate San. 111b, this is said to include the property of the minority of the inhabitants who have not committed any offence since the verse says that all the property in the city has to be destroyed.

(16) How is it possible for a man to eat three items of food,

each involving a different prohibition (e.g. He ate sacred food that had suffered contamination and had been left over and the priest had a wrongful intention [*tamei, notar, pigul*]) to suffer the penalty of *karet* where he ate them separately and yet suffer no penalty where he ate all three together.

Solution: (Zev. 78b) The three had been mixed together so that each cannot be identified. If he ate all three together each one is neutralized by the other two since the rule is that solids are neutralized in a proportion of two to one.

(21) How is it possible for a person's claim to be accepted by the Court if there are no witnesses to the claim and yet the same claim be rejected by the Court where there is a witness to support it?

Solution: Normally two witnesses are required to substantiate the claim of a woman, known to have been married, if she claims that her husband has divorced her but is unable to produce the *get*, the bill of divorce. However, if she makes the claim to the husband's face, she is believed without any witnesses since it is assumed that a woman will not be so brazen to declare to his face that her husband had divorced her if it were not true. But where she produces a single witness in support of her claim the claim, is rejected since, fortified with the support of a witness, she may be brazen enough to declare that she has been divorced even if she has not and two witnesses would be required as in normal cases. The source is Git. 64a.

(28) How is it possible for two witnesses to be believed more than three?

Solution: Shev. 42a. The rule is that two witnesses who have testified are of equal weight as a hundred witnesses. Thus A lends B some money and declares that he trusts B to claim that the debt has been repaid as if B had the weight of two witnesses. If later A claims that B has not repaid him, he is believed even if A produces a hundred witnesses that he had not repaid him. But if A states that he believes B as if he had the weight of three witnesses, by saying three and not two, A does not call into operation the usual laws of evidence but means three and not more than three. If A produces more than three witnesses that B has not repaid his debt, his claim is accepted.

(39) How is it possible for a man to commit a sexual offence with a woman and be punished for it if the woman is single, but get off scot-free if the woman is married to another?

Solution: Where a man is secluded with a woman forbidden to him because she is not his wife, he is to be punished with a flogging by rabbinic law. But if the woman is married to another, he is not punished since that might cause people to suspect that her children are not from her husband and are bastards. The source is Kid. 81a.

(40) A man greets his neighbor saying: "Peace to you, O my uncle," and the other replies: "To you peace, O my uncle." How can each be the uncle of the other without any incest having been involved?

Solution: A has a son B and a daughter C. C marries a man who has a daughter X from another woman. A then married X and they have a son Z. Z and C have the same father, A, so that Z is B's uncle, his mother's brother. But B, as A's son, is also Z's uncle from the same father.

(42) How is it possible for it to have been forbidden to handle an object on the Sabbath in the Talmud period and yet permitted to handle that same object on the Sabbath once the Talmud had been recorded in writing?

Solution: It was forbidden in the talmudic period to handle a *get* on the Sabbath because since a divorce cannot take place on the Sabbath, the *get* is a useless object, which must not be handled on the sacred day (Git. 60b). In talmudic times it was forbidden to study from a written text, only by heart. But once, as an emergency measure, it was permitted to have the Talmud in writing, it became permissible to use the *get* for study purposes, that is, to learn how it was to be written. Consequently, after the time of the Talmud, a *get* is no longer a useless object and may be handled on the Sabbath.

(50) How is it possible for a man who does more good than

evil to receive more evil than good, while another man who does more evil than good to receive more good than evil?

Solution: The man who has done more good than evil is punished in this life with more evil than good to purge him of his sins so that he will inherit eternal bliss in the Hereafter. The opposite is true with regard to the man who has done more evil than good. He receives his reward for the good he has done in this life.

Before going on to consider chronologically after Landau other works devoted specifically to riddles, it is worthwhile referring to a work, that, while not strictly of the same genre, does have strong similarities to it. This is the influential responsa collection entitled *Halakhot Ketanot* by R. Jacob Hagiz (1620-72), published in Venice in 1704.[10] Hagiz, a native of Italy, settled in Jerusalem where he presided over a yeshivah. From internal evidence it is clear that the questions he addresses in the book were, in the main, put to him by his students in the yeshivah. Both questions and replies are presented in abbreviated form so as to invite further investigation on the part of the student and reader. Azulai (*Shem Ha-Gedolim s.v. Halakhot Ketanot*) observes that the work is written in cryptic form in order to sharpen the minds of the disciples (*lehadded hatalmidim*). In part 1, no. 234, Hagiz, discussing whether it is permitted to present ideas in an ambivalent manner, frowns on this as trickery but permits it where the aim is to encourage disciples to be sharp (*le-hiddudei ha-talmudim*). In the final responsum in the book (part 2, no. 234) Hagiz says: "I have been asked why I am so laconic in several places." He replies in equally laconic fashion by simply quoting the verse, "A further word: Because Koheleth was a sage, he continued to instruct the people" Ecc. 12:9). In his note, the author's son, R. Moses Hagiz, explains that his father means that, like Koheleth, he was a sage who examined carefully all that he taught and was therefore able to put it all succinctly. But it is also possible that, in his reference to "continue to instruct the people," Hagiz suggests that the succinct form encourages others to examine the topic more thoroughly.

The following responsa are referred to in order to illustrate Hagiz's purely theoretical and academic approach, almost as if, in these responsa, he is dealing with matters in a playful manner. In part 2, no. 7 (p. 22b), to the obviously impractical question: "What is the punishment of one who scoffs at the words of the ages?" Hagiz replies that such a person belongs to the sectarians who have to be lowered into a pit to die there (A.Z. 22b) so that whoever gets in first to kill him is to be commended. It is a moot point, however, whether Hagiz is in reality preaching against the Shabbetians of his day of whom he was a fierce opponent. In part 2, no. 19, Hagiz raises the question of why Laban wished to destroy Jacob and his children, who were, after all, his own grandchildren. (Hagiz's remark regarding Laban's desire to see his grandchildren dead is obviously based, though he does not say so, on the passage in the *Haggadah* that Laban "wished to destroy all"). Hagiz replies that all Abraham's descendants had at least a trace of Abraham's loyalty to the One God and rather than having this element preserved permanently and thus be disloyal to his own gods, Laban would rather see his own offspring dead.

That Hagiz, occasionally at least, is writing with his tongue in his cheek or simply engaging in playful but ingenious pilpul can be seen from his responsa, part 1, no. 29 and part 2, no. 44 (the editors, in the table of contents, add to the note of no. 29: "The author only wrote this to sharpen the disciples" – *le-hadded ha-talmidim* – and add in brackets to responsum 44: "It is only for the sake of pilpul"). The question discussed is whether a man can have his marriage annulled by a sage just as a sage can nullify a vow. Hagiz presents arguments for and against, though he knows full well that the question of annulment by a sage only applies to vows, not to marriage. In no. 44 he says that a student (probably his own) was expelled for asking this question to which everyone knows the answer and yet, when apparently sound arguments were adduced for such an untenable view, the student was later readmitted. Hagiz can hardly be serious when he discusses part 2, no. 218) whether sugar can be used instead of salt for 'salting' the sacrifices in Temple times. In part 1, no. 113 Hagiz discusses the following case. According to the law a mourner must not cut his hair until his friends remonstrate at his unkempt appearance. But what is the law where a person has no friends? Hagiz replies that, according to the Talmud, one who has no friends is as one dead and the law is not concerned with dead people. If he has no friends he will simply have to let his hair grow. As if to say: "Ask a silly question and you will get a silly answer." For all the difficulties, it is great fun to read Hagiz. One can imagine him saying to his students from time to time: "Let's have a look at this question and see how you will deal with it."

Centuries later, a much larger collection of riddles was published by Solomon Hass of Dresnitz (d. 1847) under the title *Sheelot U-Teshuvot Kerem Shlomo*. The first edition of the work was published together with the author's *Kerem Shlomo* in Presburg in 1849 and on its own in Munkacs in 1900. The subtitle of the work is *Sheilat Rav le-Talmid le-Hiddudei* (*Question by Teacher to Pupil for Sharpening*). The title page follows with a description (evidently the author's) of the aim and contents: "Here are wondrous things, seemingly unreasonable at a superficial reading but impeccable after reflection").[11] Like Landau, Hass provides the solution after each riddle. Landau, writing before the time of the *Shulhan Arukh*, quotes the Talmud and the early codifiers as his sources, but Hass quotes chiefly the *Shulhan Arukh* and the commentaries to that work.

Hass's collection contains riddles on three parts of the *Shulhan Arukh*: 75 on *Orah Hayyim*; 96 on *Yoreh Deah* 95; and on *Even Ha-Ezer*. Some of these are too elaborate to qualify as simple riddles and are really actual responsa, albeit in abbreviated form. Some examples can be given here.

Orah Hayyim, no. 7. This is the same riddle as Landau's no. 1 about the two boys and their *Bar Mitzvah*. Hass refers to *Shulhan Arukh*, *Orah Hayyim* 55:10 the source for which is, in fact, Landau.

Orah Hayyim, no. 17. Where does one find that it is forbidden to reflect on the Torah even in a place that is perfectly clean?

Solution: On the Fast of the Ninth of Av it is forbidden to study the Torah (because this is "delightful") or even to reflect on the Torah. The source is given as *Shulhan Arukh, Orah Hayyim* 554 and commentaries. This is rather unfair since the place has nothing to do with the case as the reader is made to suppose. Hass, evidently, wishes to call attention to reflection on the Torah, and this expression is used for thinking on the Torah in unclean places (Ber. 24b), that is, everyone knows that it is forbidden to study the Torah and to reflect on the Torah in unclean places, but where is it stated that it is forbidden to reflect on the Torah even where the place is clean?

Orah Hayyim, no. 24. How is it possible for carrying from the private to the public domain to be forbidden on one Sabbath and yet be permitted on the next Sabbath?

Solution: Suk. 7a. For a private domain to be considered as such, it must be surrounded by at least three complete walls. A *sukkah* also has to have at least three walls, but the third wall need not be a complete wall. Even if it is only a handbreadth in width it qualifies as a wall for the law of *sukkah*. Now if a *sukkah* in the public domain, with only two complete walls and the third only a handbreadth in width, is placed against the door of a private domain, it is permitted to carry from the house into the *sukkah* on the Sabbath that falls during the festival of *Sukkot*. It is argued, in the talmudic passage, since the third wall qualifies as a "wall" for the purpose of the *sukkah* laws, it can serve as a "wall" for the Sabbath law, as well, so that the enclosed area becomes, for that Sabbath, a private domain. But this principle can only operate on the Sabbath of *Sukkot*. Thus the act of carrying from the private domain into such a *sukkah* is forbidden on all other Sabbaths of the year but permitted on the Sabbath of *Sukkot*.

Orah Hayyim no. 27. When is an ignoramus (*am ha-aretz*) allowed to adopt the role of a scholar (*talmid hakham*)?

Solution: *Shulhan Arukh, Orah Hayyim* 554. Although it is permitted, strictly speaking, for people to work on *Tisha Be-Av*, the

Fast of the Ninth of Av, scholars do not work on that day. Even an ignoramus is allowed to adopt the role of a scholar for this purpose.

Orah Hayyim, no. 31. When is it forbidden to eat in a *sukkah* even though the *sukkah* is perfectly *kasher*?

Solution: *Shulhan Arukh, Orah Hayyim* 628. The *sukkah* is on the back of a camel or on a tree. During the weekday portion of Tabernacles the *sukkah* is perfectly *kasher*, but it cannot be used on the first two days of *Yom Tov* since it is forbidden on *Yom Tov* to climb onto the back of a camel or up a tree.

Orah Hayyim, no. 32. When is it good to arrive late to prayers in the synagogue and to leave the synagogue as soon as possible?

Solution: On a festival the usual rules are relaxed in order to give people more time to enjoy the festive meals. Source: *Shulhan Arukh, Orah Hayyim* 529.

Orah Hayyim no. 57: On which day of the year are people accustomed to commit a number of offences?

Solution: *Shulhan Arukh, Orah Hayyim* 696. On Purim people wear masks, men wear women's garments and women men's garments, and they snatch things from one another (all otherwise questionable activities), but they do not do it to offend but only as a joke. Hass adds that, nonetheless, many authorities frown on this license to sin.

Yoreh Deah, no. 1. How is it possible for an animal to be *kasher* and its meat permitted to be eaten and yet its lung to be forbidden?

Solution: *Shulhan Arukh, Yoreh Deah*. 36. If the lung of an animal is found to be contracted, the procedure is for the lung to be left soaking in water for twenty-four hours. If, as a result, the lung becomes restored to its normal size the animal is seen to be *kasher*. But since the lung has been left soaking in water for twenty-four hours the law treats this as if the lung had been cooked with its blood still in it ('soaking is like cooking') and the lung would be forbidden because the blood had not been drained from it before 'cooking.' Thus the rest of the animal's meat is *kasher* but its lung is forbidden.

Yoreh Deah, no. 11. How is it possible for blood to be forbidden when it is on its own and yet permitted when something is mixed in it?

Solution: *Shulhan Arukh, Yoreh Deah* 66. Blood of fish is forbidden because people may imagine it to be the blood of an animal that is forbidden. But if there are fish scales in the blood, it is permitted since no false conclusion will be drawn.

Yoreh Deah, no. 4. How is it possible for an unclean fish (one without fins and scales, Lev. 11:9–10) to be permitted to be eaten?

Solution: A *kasher* fish swallowed the unclean fish and then spewed it out. The unclean fish is treated as if it had become part of the clean fish and is now permitted to be eaten. Source: the commentary *Siftei Kohen* to *Yoreh Deah* 83, note 31.

Yoreh Deah, no. 25. Where do we find that a son is forbidden to do something beneficial to his father?

Source: *Shulhan Arukh, Yoreh Deah* 241:2. If the father needs an operation it is forbidden for the son to perform it on the basis of Ex. 21:15 even though it is for the father's benefit.

Yoreh Deah, no. 49. How can an animal have all the signs of an unclean animal and is yet permitted to be eaten?

Solution: *Shulhan Arukh, Yoreh Deah* 79. A clean animal gave birth to offspring having all the signs of an unclean animal. But this only applies where people were present at the birth; otherwise the offspring may be that of an unclean animal.

Yoreh Deah, no. 82. When is it permitted to plow with two creatures that do not belong to the same species?

Solution: *Shulhan Arukh, Yoreh Deah* 297:16. An ox or an ass together with a human being.

Yoreh Deah, no. 83. When is it permitted to smash a precious "essel made of gold without offending against the prohibition of "wasting"?

Solution: *Shulhan Arukh, Yoreh Deah* 276:13. There is a

divine name engraved on the vessel. The vessel must be smashed and the section with the divine name taken away to be buried.

Yoreh Deah, no. 95. Reuben died many days before Simeon, and yet why do the sons of Simeon have to commemorate the *Yahrzeit* before the sons of Reuben?

Solution: *Shulhan Arukh, Yoreh Deah* 402. Reuben died on the 20th of Adar I and Simeon died on the 10th of Adar II in a leap year. When the *Yahrzeit* falls on an ordinary year, Simeon's is before Reuben's. This is Landau's and Hass's own problem in connection with *Bar Mitzvah*.

Even Ha-Ezer, no. 3. How is it possible for a woman to become pregnant and yet still be a virgin?

Solution: *Hag.* 14b. She became impregnated through bathing in a bath into which a man had deposited semen. Hass refers to the commentaries who discuss this passage at length, including the question of whether such a thing is scientifically possible.

Even Ha-Ezer, no. 4 This is Landau's No. 21 about the woman's claim supported by a single witness. Landau gives the talmudic source, Hass the law as recorded in the *Shulhan Arukh, Even Ha-Ezer* 17:2.

Even Ha-Ezer, no. 12. When is it a religious obligation to tell lies?

Solution: *Even Ha-Ezer* 64. When praising a bride. It is meritorious to praise her for qualities she does not possess, for example, saying she is beautiful and charming when she is neither. The commentators point out that this applies where the bride is praised in the presence of the groom so that it is not really lying since in the groom's eyes she is presumably both beautiful and charming, whatever others might think. These matters are relative in any event. Hass is not quite playing fair.

Even Ha-Ezer, no. 30. How is it possible for a man and woman to admit that their marriage took place and there was no legal impediment to it and yet the marriage is invalid?

Solution: *Even Ha-Ezer*, No. 42. There were no witnesses to the marriage and a "marriage" without witnesses is no marriage at all in Jewish law.

Even Ha-Ezer, no. 69. How is it possible for a legally married woman to be allowed to marry another man even though her husband had not died nor had he given her a *get*?

Solution: the commentary *Bet Shmuel* to *Even Ha-Ezer* 17, note 11. Like Elijah, the husband ascended to heaven and became an angel. This is purely academic, of course, but might be relevant to the case of a husband who undergoes a sex change operation.

Even Ha-Ezer, no.71. Polygamy was permitted to Jews in ancient times. Where do we find, nevertheless, that even in those times it was forbidden for a man to have more than one wife?

Solution: According to Maimonides (*Isurei Biah* 7:13) the High Priest was only allowed to have one wife.

Even Ha-Ezer, no. 74. In the *get* it is essential to record the name of the husband and the name of his father. How is it possible for the *get* to require the name not of the husband's father but of a man who is not his father?

Solution: *Even Ha-Ezer* 129:20. A proselyte is named "son of our father Abraham" and this is his name for the *get*, not the name of his gentile father. This is hardly fair. For the proselyte Abraham is his father as he is for all other purposes.

Even Ha-Ezer, no. 83. Where do we find that a man is punished when he commits a sexual offence with a single woman and yet not punished if the woman is married?

Solution: *Shulhan Arukh, Even Ha-Ezer* 22. If a man is secluded with a single woman he is flogged by the court but not if the woman is married, because to punish the man might lead to the conclusion that her children are bastards. This is the same as in Landau.

Even Ha-Ezer, no. 84. How can a *get* be *muktzah* in the time of the Talmud and yet not so nowadays?

Solution: *Shulhan Arukh, Even Ha-Ezer* 136:7. In the time of the Talmud the Torah was not studied from a written work, but nowadays it is permitted to study from a written work, so the *get* can be studied and is hence not *muktzah*. This is the same as Landau, but Hass gives the game away by actually referring to a *get*.

A third collection of riddles is *Divrei Hakhamim ve-Hiddutan* by Ephraim ben Samuel Zanwill Hechsher of Altona. The introduction states:

> This book I have compiled is small in quantity but great in quality. In it I have been aware of the prohibition: "Do not turn aside from that which they tell you to the right or to the left" (Deut. 17:11) upon which Rashi comments: even when they tell you that right is left and left right, all the more so when they tell you that right is right and left left. The meaning is that you erroneously conclude that the Sages are telling you that right is left and left right. I have cast my net wide to catch 213 riddles where, at first glance, the statement seems absurd and a perversion of the truth. Yet do not reject them for I shall explain each topic and adduce adequate proof. I have compiled this work to sharpen the minds of students [*le-hadded bahen et ha-talmidim*] as it is stated in tractate *Eruv.* 13a: "Rabbi Akiba only made the statement for the purpose of sharpening the minds of the disciples," on which Rashi comments: "that the disciples should put their hearts to the Torah." So I said, by means of the little book students will become enthusiastic in their studies of the Talmud and Codes. As the verse "teach them diligently" [Deut. 6:6] is understood by the rabbis to mean: "The words of the Torah should be fluent in your mouth. If someone asks you a question give him the answer without prevarication." For whoever has no expertise in the Talmud and the Codes is incapable of giving such a quick answer. May it be His will that my words produce fruit and this will accrue to my credit now and in the future.[12]

Hechsher's arrangement is different from that of Landau and Hass. The answers to the 213 riddles in the booklet are given at the back of the book. Here can be quoted a few examples from Hechsher.

(10) Where do we find a substance that is neither a food nor a drink yet when a man's intention is to eat it, it is treated as a food and when his intention is to drink it, it is treated as a drink?

Solution: Snow. Source: Nid. 17a.

(27) Where do we find that an item of food may be eaten if the

day is the Sabbath but not when the Sabbath is over?

Solution: If a person suspected of laxity in tithing his produce declares that his produce has been tithed, he is believed provided that he made the declaration on the Sabbath. His awe of the sanctity of the day will prevent him from declaring that the produce has been tithed if it has not been tithed. Source: *Demai*, chapter 4 and commentary of Bertinoro.

(73) How is it possible for a man to be released from a vow he had made without any official release but solely through something done by his fellow?

Solution: A said to B, who had taken a vow to be a Nazirite: "I, too, will be like you." B thus becomes a Nazirite because A is a Nazirite. If A then obtains an official release from his vow, his vow is rendered null and void from the beginning. A was never a Nazirite and it follows that B's vow was also ineffective.

(80) How is it possible for a man to contract a perfectly legal marriage and have children from his wife and yet the children are born out of wedlock?

Solution: In cases, a number of which are mentioned in the Talmud, where the sages used their power to nullify the marriage retrospectively.

(170) Who was the person living in this world who did not eat or drink for more than sixty years and then ate and drank as do other people and then died?

Solution: Honi the Circle Drawer, Taanit 23a, who fell asleep in a grotto for seventy years. This is far too easy since every schoolboy knows the story. Hechsher, evidently aware of this, tries to make it more difficult by speaking of "more than sixty years." The fact that Honi neither ate nor drank is not stated explicitly in the Talmud but can obviously be inferred, as Hechsher states, from the reference to Honi's enclosure in the grotto.

(208) When is it permitted to eat an unclean fish?

Solution: The same as in Hass, *Yoreh Deah*, no. 14. That some of the same problems occur in Landau, Hass, and Hechsher shows that some of the problems were not original, at least with the last two authors, but were known to scholars throughout the ages.

The most comprehensive collection of riddles is found in the work *Imrei Vinah* by R. Joseph Hayyim of Baghdad (1833–1909).[13] This work is in four parts, all dealing with puzzles of one sort or another. Part 1 for instance, deals with what surely is a unique feature of rabbinic works, a series of kabbalistic riddles. Part 2 (pp. 35–129), entitled: *Hiddud beDivrei Torah* ('Torah Riddles') is the section of the work relevant to our inquiry. The author's Introduction to this section (pp. 35-36) reads:

> I have called this section: *Hiddud beDidvrei Torah*. It consists of riddles and the logical solution to them and discoveries [*hamtzaot*] which I have collected and gathered from the Talmud, the words of the Tannaim and Amoraim, and the Commentaries thereon. With such things it has been my wont to sharpen the minds of the members of my household on festivals during the festive meals in the evening and during the day. Occasionally I would do so on weekdays as well. I thought it a good idea to record them in a book for a remembrance so as to make them available later on to teachers as a means of sharpening the minds of their charges or for colleagues in order to encourage them to invent new ideas and to make their own contribution. In this way, their minds will become more keen, their powers of discernment broadened and their wisdom illumined. For it is well-known that the mind becomes very keen when exercised in discovering new ideas.
>
> Now among the details that I have recorded and written down in this section, some can serve to sharpen the minds of even renowned scholars, others more suitable for men of average intelligence, and others, again, only really suitable for children. I have not arranged the problems in order of their difficulty but as they came to hand I used them to sharpen minds other than my own. The teacher will exercise his own discretion, adapting them to the proficiency in the oral Torah of those he teaches. Observe, dear reader, I have prepared for you a table laden with choice delicacies.

There are no less than 334 riddles in this section followed on later pages by the solutions. Most of these are questions and answers found explicitly in the Talmud with R. Joseph Hayyim simply paraphrasing the question and inviting the reader either to remember the relevant talmudic source or to invent the solution himself so as to be in accord with that given in the Talmud. A number of Hayyim's own riddles can here be quoted.

No. 7. A man said that a certain scribe wrote four hundred scrolls of the Torah in a single day and yet he did not lie. How is it possible to write four hundred scrolls of the Torah in a single day?

Solution: The meaning is that the scribe wrote the words "four hundred scrolls of the Torah." This is very school boyish but Hayyim may be referring to a version of the *Midrash* (*Devarim Rabbah* 9:9) that Moses wrote thirteen scrolls in a single day.

No. 73. A man had a scab, the result of a cut, on his skin and was told by the doctor to bathe the scab in hot water. But the day was the Sabbath and the local rabbi ruled that it was forbidden to instruct a gentile to warm up the water. A man filled a bowl with cold water and took it outside; when he returned later with it the water was hot. How was this possible without an offence being committed?

Solution: The man placed the bowl to be heated by the sun.

No. 82. It is reported that when the wife of Rabbi Eliezer Hazan died, they proposed to him that he should remarry. The sage replied: One, two, three: (1) I am afraid of her; (2) She is not suitable to me; (3) She is loathsome to me? What did he mean

Solution: He was referring to a widow, a young woman, and a divorcée. He was afraid to marry a widow because the spirit of her dead husband might harm him. A young woman would be unsuitable since he was an old man. A divorcée was loathsome because her husband was still alive.

No. 85. Twins were born, one a boy, the other a girl. The girl, at a later date, said to her brother that she was older than he, but when the boy asked their mother, she told him that they were twins. Moreover, the boy was the firstborn since he had emerged from the womb before his sister. The girl persisted in her claim that she was the older of the two and she was correct. How could she have been correct?

Solution: According to Jewish law a girl attains her majority (she becomes *Bat Mitzvah*) at the age of twelve, whereas a boy does not attain his majority (to become *Bar Mitzvah*) until he is thirteen. Once the twins have reached the age of twelve, although the boy is really the firstborn, the girl has attained her majority and the boy is still technically a minor, so she is fully entitled to be called the older of the two.

No. 6. The *Shulhan Arukh, Even Ha-Ezer* 48, rules that if a woman says to a man: "I am married to you," and he denies it, then he may marry her near relatives, but she may not marry his near relatives. Presumably the case is where the man did not divorce her since, if he did, that would be an admission that he had indeed married her and he would not be allowed to marry her relatives. But since there has been no divorce then according to her statement she is married to him. In that case, she cannot marry anyone else, so why state only that she cannot marry his relatives?

Solution: The ruling applies where the man has died. The woman is now free to remarry since even according to her admission her husband is no longer alive. But she may not marry his relatives, for example, his brother or father since these are forbidden even after the husband has died.

No. 89. Jews are fond of an item of food in the morning and yet reject utterly that item later on in the day without the food suffering any change. How is this possible?

Solution: The food is leaven and it is the eve of Passover.

No. 91. Where do we find that if a man wishes to open the door leading into a room he may do so, but he may not close that door?

Solution: A bird has flown into the room and it is the Sabbath day. To close the door and so prevent the bird flying away is technically to hunt or trap the bird, and hunting or trapping are forbidden on the Sabbath.

No. 167. The rule is that a physical defect by which a priest is disqualified from serving in the Temple is sufficiently serious to invalidate a marriage if it is discovered that a wife suffers from this kind of affliction, on the grounds that the man would not have married her if he had known of that defect. The ruling is that for a wife to have bad breath is considered a defect for this purpose. But a priest is not disqualified if he has bad breath. What is the difference between the priest and the wife?

Solution, source Ket.75a. The priest can take a breath sweetener so that his breath will not smell bad during the time he is actually serving in the Temple, whereas a man has to live with his wife all the time.

No. 194. If someone dated a letter, say, "The twenty-second day of the Omer,'"has he fulfilled his obligation to count the *Omer*? In other words, where a declaration is required by the law must it be a verbal declaration, or is writing counted for this purpose as speaking? The authorities discuss the question, and some seek to prove it from the ruling in the *Shulhan Arukh, Yoreh Deah* 221:10 that if a man takes a solemn oath not to speak to his neighbor he may, nonetheless, write him a letter. Does not this demonstrate conclusively that writing is not to be equated with speaking? Or can a distinction be made between the two cases?

Solution: Even if writing is treated as speaking, the oath was that the man would not speak to his neighbor. Even if the letter is treated as if he had spoken, he had not actually spoken to his neighbor but it is the letter that speaks to the neighbor.

Part 3 of the work is entitled *Hiddud be-Milei de-Alema* (*Riddles About World Topics*). Apologizing for publishing such frivolities, the author writes (pp. 129–130):

> I have called this booklet *Hiddud be-Milei de-Alema*. It consists of riddles and their solutions with the aim of sharpening the minds of old and young, each according to his ability. It was my wont to use these to sharpen the minds of members of my family. My intention was good to open the mind's eyes in secular topics so that they would become better intellectually equipped when they come to study the holy Torah. I used to set them puzzles, either such of my own invention or such I had heard in my boyhood. I have recorded them for a remembrance for I imagine they will be of help

to a man who wishes to test his children or his pupils in order to make their minds more keen. In this way, their minds will be opened to grasp, too, the words of the Torah.

Some of the riddles in this section are school boyish and fatuous. We need only refer to one of these (no. 4). A man instructed his son to bring him a certain food that, from its inception, consisted of two kinds joined together, each with its own separate flavour and colour. What did the son bring? Solution: He brought an egg. The white and yoke of the egg are together from the beginning yet are different in flavour and color. Part 4 of *Imrei Vinah* is also in the form of questions and answers but the items in this section are not riddles or puzzles so much as lengthy expositions of various biblical and Talmudic difficulties.

Rabbi S. J. Evin (1890–1978), renowned author and editor of the *Encyklopedia Talmudit,* ran a column of Torah riddles in the rabbinic journal *Shaarei Torah,* published in the first quarter of the twentieth century under the editorship of R. Isaac Feigenbaun.[14]

Rabbi Sevin introduces the readers of the journal [15] to this new feature as follows:

> We have decided to open from today a new section in *Shaarei Torah*, dealing with talmudic problems and riddles. . . . This feature will cater to a large readership, to all who are engaged in the study of the Torah, who will find much of interest and entertainment. They will help to promote skill in Torah learning among its students. . . . If we find in many places in the Talmud that the Talmudic sages used to make statements for the sole purpose of sharpening the minds of their disciples, that they might know how to give the correct answer, how much more so will the riddles we are pleased to present to our readers be of great advantage to sharpen and hone the minds of Torah scholars and also be an aid to the memory. We request our colleagues, rabbis and Torah scholars, to be good enough to send to the publishers sound and interesting talmudic problems and ingenious but sound examples of "where do we find?" We shall publish these under their name and all who delight in the Torah will be grateful to them. Please send the solutions together with the riddles. We also request rabbis and Torah scholars to try their hand at offering solutions to the problem we set and in subsequent issues we shall publish the names of those who sent us the correct answers.

The riddles, 125 in all, appear, a few at a time, in issues of the journal, though a little haphazardly.[16] Prizes are offered to those who hit on the correct solution to a particularly difficult problem. There are even one or two rudimentary crossword puzzles. All the riddles, addressed as they are to seasoned talmudists, are far from elementary. A few of these are now given.

No. 4. Maimonides rules that a penitent sinner is greater than the man who has always been righteous (a *tzaddik*). Give a talmudic source for Maimonides' ruling.

Solution: Kid. 49b. If a man betroths a woman on the understanding that he is a *tzaddik*, the betrothal is valid even if he is known to be a notorious sinner, because he may have repented one moment before his declaration. But even if this were the case, he would be a penitent sinner, whereas he had declared that he was a *tzaddik*, which shows that a penitent sinner is *a fortiori* a *tzaddik*.

No. 8. How is it possible for a man to marry a woman who then becomes forbidden to that man himself as a married woman?

Solution: Yev. 45b. The man is a half–slave and half–free man (a slave was owned by two men, one of whom freed the half belonging to him). The free half of the man changes the status of the woman into that of a married woman, but a slave may not marry a Jewess, and so far as the slave half of the man is concerned, she is a married woman.

No. 12. Where do we find that one who comes to testify has his testimony rejected precisely because the Court believes him?

Solution: Yev. 47a. A man comes to the Court and declares that he is a gentile. The Court believes him but, then, as a gentile he is disqualified from acting as a witness.

Similar to the above collections of riddles are collections of straightforward difficulties in which the problems are stated but the solutions left to the reader. The best known of these is that of R. Akiba Eger (1761–1837). The publishers of the Vilna Talmud, Romm, published these questions in the margins of the pages on which the problems are raised. The problem is usually stated very succinctly and concludes with the words: "This requires further thought." To a particularly difficult problem, R. Akiba Eger adds: "This requires thought." It became a favourite pastime for keen Talmudic students to try to solve the problems raised by R. Akiba Eger. Not so long ago the whole collection was published from R. Akiba Eger's autographed copy of his marginal notes to the Talmud (a far more comprehensive collection than in the Vilna Talmud) under the title *Kushyot Atzumot (Powerful Difficulties)* edited by I. S. Stern (Bnei Berak, 1982).

A similar collection was made by the famed Polish talmudist, R. Joab Joshua Weingarten (1847–1922) as an appendix to his responsa collection, entitled *Helkat Yoab*. Weingarten published: *Kaba de-Kushyata (A Kab of Difficulties)*, a list of 103 (the numerical value of *kaba*, a measure mentioned frequently in the Talmud) particularly difficult and seemingly insoluble problems.[17] Weingarten prefaces his difficulties with "*kashah li*" – "I find it difficult." Where the difficulty is particularly pronounced he uses the expression: "I find it astonishing."

A contemporary talmudist, Rabbi David Cohen, compiled a list of no fewer than 1,300 difficulties (most of these are culled from earlier authors but a few are original with him) arranged according to the months of the year so that for practically every day of the year there is a seasonal difficulty, that is, on the talmudic theme appropriate to the day or month. The book is entitled *Ve-Im Tomar* ("And if you say"), a formula often used by the Tosafists in their glosses to the talmudic text.[18] No solutions are given, the readers being invited to try their hand at finding these for themselves. In his preface Rabbi Cohen states that readers of earlier editions of the work found it very helpful for the purpose of sharpening the mind of students (*le-hadded et ha-talmidim*) and he himself, as a teacher of Talmud, found it of educational value to leave his class each day with a problem to which they should try to find a solution.

Finally, two works by the great Polish talmudist, R. Joseph Engel (1859–1920) should be mentioned, though they do not quite belong in the genre. R. Joseph Engel's *Gevurot Shemonim* (Pietrikow, 1905) consists of eighty different solutions to a particular talmudic problem, and his *Ayin Panim le-Torah* (Lemberg, 1889) contains seventy different solutions to another talmudic problem.

Notes

1. Louis Jacobs, *Teyku: The Unsolved Problem in the Babylonian Talmud* (London, New York: Cambridge University Press, 1981).

2. Ber. 33b; Hul. 43b; Niddah 4b.

3. Eruv. 13a.

4. Niddah 45a.

5. Nazir 59b.

6. Zev. 13a. The expression '"Oh sharpen the disciples" is also found in the Yerushalmi, Nedarim 11:10 (42d).

7. On Jacob Landau see *Encyclopedia Judaica*, Vol. 10, pp. 1393-4. Elijah of Smyra (d. 1729) refers to Landau's riddles and quotes a few of them in his *Midrash Talpiot* (Warsaw, 1874) *s.v. din*, pp. 152-53. It should be noted that even before Landau, there were "Halakhic Poetic Riddles" by Shalom Me'Oded' (Heb.), *Sefunot*, New Series, vol. 1, no. 16 (1980), pp. 273-86. Ratzaby examines eight poems, containing halakhic riddles by a 19th century Yemenite scholar, but most of the riddles are not so much puzzles as questions about unusual or seemingly strange laws. As Ratzaby points out, this kind of poem often served as an examination of pupils to see if they had learned their lessons properly.

8. The *Sefer Hazon* in the Herschler edition was later published without the *Sefer Ha-Agur*, but together with the totally different work, *Tzedah le-Derekh* (Brooklyn: Gross Bros., 1984).

9. *Sefer Ha-Agur* (1984 ed.), p. 236.

10. The edition consulted here was a facsimile edition (Jerusalem, 1981), a photo-copy of the Cracow ed., 1897.

11. On Hass see *Encyclopedia Judaica*, vol. 7, p. 1010.

12. Ephraim ben Samuel Zanwill Hechsher, "Introduction," *Divrei Hakhamim veHiddutan*, Lublin, 1909.

13. Louis Jacobs, "The Responsa of Rabbi Joseph Hayyim of Baghdad," *Perspectives on Jews and Judaism: Essays in Honor of Wolfe Kelman*, ed. Arthur A.. Chiel (New York: United Synagogue, 1978), pp., 189-214. The edition consulted was published in 1973.

14. A reprint of the *Shaarei Torah* was published in five volumes in 1964 and this is the edition I have used although it is very incomplete and a little confusing. Actually Rabbi Seven's presentation of the riddles appeared in the sections of the *Shaarei Torah* edited, after F. Feigenbaum's death, by the latter's sons.

15. In the New York edition, vol. 3, part 5, no. 12, pp. 17-18.

16. The run can be traced in the 1964 edition through the following parts: vol. 3, part 5, no. 12, pp. 17-18; no. 22, p. 34; no. 31, pp. 50-51; vol. 4, part 6, no. 14, pp. 32-33; no. 21, p. 50, no.32, p. 66; no. 47, p.98; no. 66, pp. 129-130; nos. 83-84, p. 162;nNo.96, p. 178; part 7, No. 15, pp. 29-30; no. 42, p. 62; no. 68, pp. 85-6.

17. The latest and best edition, in two volumes, of the *Helkat Yoab* is that of B'nei Berak, (1985). The *Kaba de-Kushyata* is printed in this edition at the end of vol. 1, pp. 349-370. The *Kaba de-Kushyata* was published on its own, together with the attempts by various scholars at solving the problems, edited by Weingarten's great-grandson, Amos Mar-Hain (Jerusalem: 1992). A less elaborate edition of the work was published with an attempt at answering the question entitled: *Loga de–Terutzah* (Jerusalem: M. Brandwein, 1991).

18. *Ve-Im Tomar* in all four parts was published in New York in 1982. Reference should also be made to *Even Ha-Bohen* by R. Yaakov ben Zevi. This is in two volumes, the first entitled *Hiddud Ha-Talmidim (Sharpening the Students)*, the second *Behinat Ha-Talmidim (Testing the Students)*. This work was evidently published in Warsaw in 1911. A reprint in two volumes appeared in Brooklyn in 1988. The riddles in this work are, however, of a slightly different order from the others considered in that they consist of elaborate questions regarding difficulties found in the Talmud and the commentaries, the aim being to encourage young students to delve more deeply into the niceties of talmudic casuistry.

CONTRIBUTORS

JACK COHEN has served on the faculty of the Jewish Theological Seminary, the Reconstructionist Rabbinic College, and the David Yellin College of Education as well as Rabbi of the Society for the Advancement of Judaism. He is the author of seven books, among them *A Case for Religious Naturalism* (1954), *Jewish Education in a Democratic Society* (1964), *Guides for an Age of Confusion* (1999), and *Major Philosophies of Jewish Prayer in the Twentieth Century* (2000). He and his wife reside in Israel.

JONATHAN COHEN is an Israeli–born scholar who directs the Center for the Study of Contemporary Moral Problems at the Hebrew Union College and as assistant professor of Talmud and Halakhic literature. He holds degrees from the University of Kent and the University of Liverpool. He has written on Jewish law and ethics.

DAVID ELLENSON is President of the Hebrew Union College–Jewish Institute of Religion and I. H. and Anna Grancell Professor of Jewish Religious Thought at the Hebrew Union College–Jewish Institute of Religion, Los Angeles, California, on whose faculty he has been since 1979. He is the author of several hundred essays on Jewish thought and has contributed to a multi–volume commentary on the prayer book. His books include *Tradition in Transition* (1989), *Rabbi Esriel Hildesheimer and the Creation of a Modern Jewish Orthodoxy* (1990), and *Between Tradition and Culture: The Dialectics of Modern Jewish Religion and Identity* (1994).

DAVID GOLINKIN is the President of the Schechter Institute of Jewish Studies in Jerusalem where he also served as professor of Jewish law. He is the long–time chair of the *Vaad Halakhah* of the Rabbinic Assembly of Israel. He is the author or editor of eighteen books, including *Responsa of the Va'ad Halakhah* (1990), *Halakhah for Our Time: A Conservative Approach* (1992), *The Responsa of Louis Ginzberg* (1996), *Rediscovering the Art of Jewish Prayer, The Status of Women in Jewish Law* (1998).

PETER HAAS holds the Abba Hillel Silver Chair of Religious Studies at Case Western Reserve University in Cleveland; previously he has held a professorship at Vanderbilt University. He is the author of *Morality After Auschwitz* (1988), *Recovering the Role of Women: Power and Authority in Rabbinic Jewish Society* (1992), and *Responsa: A Literary History of the Genre* (1996).

WALTER JACOB is Senior Scholar of Rodef Shalom Congregation, Pittsburgh, Pennsylvania. He is President and a professor at the Abraham Geiger College in Berlin/Potsdam, Past President of the Central Conference of American Rabbis, President of the Solomon B. Freehof Institute of Progressive *Halakhah*, and of the

President Associated American Jewish Museums. He is the author and editor of thirty-one books, including *Christianity through Jewish Eyes* (1974), *American Reform Responsa* (1983), *Liberal Judaism and Halakhah* (1988), *Questions and Reform Jewish Answers* (1991), *The Healing Past: Pharmaceuticals in the Biblical and Rabbinic World* (1993), *Not by Birth Alone: Conversion to Judaism* (1997), *Re-examining Progressive Halakhah* (2002), *Die Exegese hat das Erste Wort* (2002), *Th Environment in Jewish Law* (2003).

LOUIS JACOBS is a leading British rabbi and theologian and founder of the New West End Synagogue in London. He currently lectures at University College in London and at Lancaster University; he has taught at Jews' College. He is the author of numerous essays and more than twenty books, including *Studies in Talmudic Logic and Methodology* (1961), *Faith* (1968), *A Jewish Theology* (1973), *Teyku – The Unsolved Problem in the Babylonian Talmud* (1981), and *The Talmudic Argument* (1984).

PETER KNOBEL is rabbi of Beth Emet, Evanston, Illinois. He is chair of the Liturgy Committee of the Central Conference of American Rabbis and past president of the Chicago Board of Rabbis. He is the author of papers on assisted suicide, homosexuality, and spirituality among other subjects; he is editor of *Gates of the Season* (1983), *Duties of the Soul: The Role of Commandments in Liberal Judaism* (1999), and the new American Reform prayer book.

JOHN RAYNER is Distinguished Lecturer in Liturgy and Codes at the Leo Baeck College, London, and rabbi emeritus of the Liberal Synagogue in London. He is the author of *Understanding Judaism* (1996), *A Jewish Understanding of the World* (1997), *Jewish Religious Law: A Progressive Perspective* (1999), and many essays. He has been a major contributor to the creation of British and American liturgies.

DANIEL SCHIFF is the Community Scholar of the Jewish Education Institute in Pittsburgh. He is rabbi of Temple B'nai Israel in White Oak, Pennsylvania. Born in Australia, he was educated at the University of Melbourne and the Hebrew Union College–Jewish Institute of Religion from which he was ordained and received his doctorate. Daniel Schiff is the author of essays in halakhic books and journals and of *Abortion in Judaism* (2002), a study that deals with this question across denominational lines.

MARK WASHOFSKY is Associate Professor of Rabbinics, Hebrew Union College–Jewish Institute of Religion in Cincinnati, Ohio and chair of the Responsa Committee of the Central Conference of American Rabbis. He has published numerous studies in the field of Jewish law and legal theory. He is the editor of *Teshuvot for the Nineties* (1997), and author of *Jewish Living and Practice* (2000).